SCHOLAR WARRIOR

Other books by
Deng Ming-Dao

*THE
CHRONICLES
OF TAO*

*The Wandering
Taoist*

*Seven Bamboo
Tablets of the
Cloudy Satchel*

*Gateway to a
Vast World*

LU DONGBIN.
Anonymous. Yuan
dynasty. Nelson-
Atkins Gallery, Kan-
sas City, Missouri.

SCHOLAR WARRIOR

AN INTRODUCTION TO THE
TAO IN EVERYDAY LIFE

DENG MING-DAO

HarperSanFrancisco
A Division of HarperCollins *Publishers*

SCHOLAR WARRIOR: *An Introduction to the Tao in Everyday Life.*
Copyright © 1990 by Deng Ming-Dao. All rights reserved. Printed
in the United States of America. No part of this book may be used
or reproduced in any manner whatsoever without written permis-
sion except in the case of brief quotations embodied in critical arti-
cles and reviews. For information address HarperCollins Publishers, 10 East 53rd Street, New York, NY 10022.

FIRST HARPERCOLLINS PAPERBACK EDITION PUBLISHED IN 1990

Library of Congress Cataloging-in-Publication Data

Deng, Ming-Dao.
   Scholar warrior : an introduction to the Tao in everyday life /
Deng Ming-Dao.
     p.   cm.
     Includes bibliographical references and index.
     ISBN 0-06-250232-8
     1. Taoism.   2. Self-realization—Religious aspects—
Taoism.   3. Conduct of life.   I. Title.
BL1923.D45   1990
299'.514448—dc20   89-46453
                                        CIP

     98 99 RRD(H) 10 9

This edition is printed on acid-free paper that meets the American
National Standards Institute Z39.48 Standard.

CONTENTS

PREFACE

My teacher, Kwan Saihung, and I were traveling by car across Pennsylvania in 1988 when we first discussed writing this book. I'd been accompanying him as he taught individuals ranging from teenage members of a Vermont ski academy to adult professionals in New York City. We met young people who seemed so innocent and full of promise; all they needed was discipline and guidance to realize their talent. We met adults who had grappled with the difficulties of responsibilities and career, yet were still hopeful of cultivating a sound spiritual understanding in life. We met elderly people who had resolved the burdens of their earlier years, and now had the time and interest to fully pursue their deepest questions. We knew that Taoism could meet all their needs, and yet the views of Taoism we encountered focused on narrow aspects without knowing how it worked as a living and contemporary system. Although Mr. Kwan exposed his students to a curriculum that ranged from acrobatics, qigong, exercises with the staff, philosophy, and meditation, he nevertheless expressed some frustration that he could not make Taoism even more accessible.

Mr. Kwan's essential thesis is deceptively simple. Physical discipline and philosophical inquiry are preliminary to meditation; meditation is the essential way to spirituality. But the methods to accomplish these goals are diverse, and people have difficulty gaining a complete perspective.

This book is an attempt to lay out a systematic and comprehensive approach that takes a beginner from the first steps of health and ends by pointing the way toward the higher stages of spiritual understanding. This book will not substitute for learning directly from a teacher, but it will give a good background and act as a companion during many stages of your own progress. If you are practicing Taoist arts, then you should quickly benefit from the concepts and techniques. If you are practicing another system, such as Buddhism or yoga, then I believe that you will find a fresh perspective on your path without compromising your own practices. You might even enjoy borrowing some of the techniques, like the methods of restoring balance after meditation. Whatever your orientation, it is my sincere hope that sharing this information will be as beneficial for others as it has been for my master and me.

While writing this book, I have had to grapple with the difficulty of communicating Taoism through English. A proper understanding of at least some Chinese is important for understanding Taoism. Yet because Chinese and English are radically different languages, translation and clear communication of all the connotations of any particular word are not easy. In order to address these issues, this book has the following features:

A dual system of romanization. Although romanization is drifting increasingly toward the pinyin system established by the People's Republic of China, there are many words that are well known under the older Wade-Giles spellings. Among these terms are *Tao, Taoist, tai chi chuan,* and certain proper names. In order to prevent confusion, these words have been spelled as they are most widely known. All other words use the pinyin spellings. If a word is used in its Wade-Giles spelling, the pinyin equivalent is given in parentheses when it is defined in the margin notes.

Chinese words in the margin notes. Written Chinese is a series of pic-tures. Sometimes looking at these pictographs and understanding their symbolism makes the grasping of basic concepts simpler. Moreover, there are moments of interesting symmetry that appear in the Chinese. See, for example, the phrases on page 191 that mean "When the sun sets, the moon rises. When the moon sets, the sun rises." When viewed in its writ-ten form, the brevity and graphic symmetry of the Chinese words make the concept seem all the more direct. Such symmetry also extends to the frequent use of key terms. *Jing* and *qi*, for example, appear in a variety of contexts, and noting this will strengthen one's understanding of such pivotal words.

Definition of vocabulary. Words in every language have a variety of connotations, and these are problematic to convey in translation and im-possible to incorporate smoothly into prose. Yet learning its vocabulary is essential to knowing Taoism. Thus, notes in the margins will provide def-initions and will attempt to convey nuances relevant to the discussion. Most of the terms are widely used throughout Taoist literature, and study-ing their definitions will enable you to understand other books with greater depth.

The Chinese will not be accompanied by a romanization or a defini-tion if these do not directly contribute to the text. For example, romaniza-tion is not provided for the herbal recipes; etymological explanations for herb names would not be significant.

Compiling this book has been an enormous task. In particular, I would like to acknowledge my teacher, the primary source of the material. I am also grateful to the others who contributed. Betty Gee and Lance Ong posed for the drawings. May Tam and Joe Chan helped with translations. So Kam Ng helped supply the reproductions of art from the Asian Art Museum of San Francisco.

INTRODUCTION

Every generation seeks to define itself and to find a new way through life. Among people of each era, some have heard of the Tao and have sought to make it the basis for their path. The flexibility of Tao and the fact that it has served its adherents for centuries makes it an excellent precedent. Taoism provides a complete way of life that can be tailored to suit any individual. It incorporates an entire spectrum of techniques from the physical to the meditative. The Taoists want a comprehensive way of life that will help them survive, keep them vital and healthy, and provide an understanding of all the unknowns that haunt human existence.

The Taoists believe that it is humanity's refusal to regard itself as part of a greater order that causes confusion, ignorance, and sorrow. They feel that if human beings could balance themselves with this order, they would live a simple life of happiness and understanding. This divine order is regarded in mystical terms: it is so great, so profound, that it cannot be grasped by merely rational means. Declaring it to be the mystery beyond all mysteries, yet the doorway to all existence, the Taoists simply call this fundamental reality by a single name: Tao.

The word for Tao is an image of a person walking on a path. The rectangular part in the center of the word with the V shape on top represents the head of a person. The twisting stroke on the left that then extends across the bottom represents movement. The person is not specifically a man or a woman: no one is excluded from Tao. The implication is that each individual can know Tao directly. There is no need for organized religion, orthodoxy, scripture, or social conformity. There is only the need for direct experience.

But for most of us, such contact with Tao is rare. Modern civilization prevents undistracted involvement with Tao. Our lives are profoundly fractured. Our careers are frequently at odds with our personal desires, our family relationships are sometimes incompatible with our friendships, and our hobbies and avocations—perhaps even our dreams for some better life—are frequently at odds with our daily predicament. More significantly, the way we as modern people think, the way we take care of our bodies, and the philosophy of life we hold often have very little to do with one another. We are a people whose lives are a web of contradictions, compulsive categorization, and unconnected ends. Such a tangle cannot be called a life's path.

We need a way to organize and resolve all the disparate elements of ourselves, and then use our whole beings to know the Tao. For the Taoists, a complete way of life is deeply spiritual. But their definition of spiritual is unique. They define it as rooted in the body and rooted in life itself. The spirit is not separate from any other aspect of living. All aspects of daily existence are valid. They may be fit together into a cohesive approach, organized through the dualities of mental and physical, quiescent and active, refined and coarse. It is all a question of equilibrium. To be a Taoist, one need not engage in fanatical denial of any part of life, nor

TAO (DAO)
The word for Tao shows a person in the center, represented by only a head with two tufts of hair. The stroke on the left and the bottom is derived from the word for moving.

WEN WU XING
The first word applies
to all things cultural;
the second applies to
all things martial. The
third word means
way, or path.
Together, it means the
Way of the Scholar
Warrior.

does one need to leave family and career in order to gain a foothold on the path. One need only balance the various parts of one's personality and provide them with a strong focus.

This integration of all facets of life is the way of the Scholar Warrior. It uses specific practices involving the body, diet, breathing exercises, herbology, philosophical study, and meditation to open the way to Tao. Beginning with simple physical exercises and basic tenets of hygiene, it provides a methodical, thorough approach. Nothing is overlooked. All factors are equally important: what you eat, how you exercise, and how you treat your body are precisely as important as how you think and what you believe. With practice, balance will become second nature. You will live longer and be healthier, and you will develop insight into the deepest meanings of life. You need not give up anything that you do not want to give up, and you need not adopt strange customs or the trappings of religion. You need not be a particular age, race, or gender. All that counts is perception and accomplishment. Being a Scholar Warrior is not separate from being a Taoist. The two are synonymous.

You need go only as far on the path as you are comfortable, and you need accept things only after you understand them and prove them in your own life. It is experience, not book learning or scripture, that is the best teacher. That is why it is said that the path of the Scholar Warrior is one of self-cultivation. Concepts accepted through religion, books, hearsay, or from any other person will always be weak. But skill and wisdom gained through self-cultivation can never be shaken.

There was once a student, named the Realized One, who entered the mountains to study the Tao. He asked his master, the South Goose Beach Taoist, how long he had been living in the mountains. This was the polite way of asking about the master's path and philosophy. The master smiled and replied,

> Court gowns of red and purple are not attractive.
> Instead, I love white clouds embracing emerald mountaintops.
> So I sit in solitude, forgetting the year or month
> While in the mundane world below, lifetimes and generations pass.

Upon hearing this, another, more accomplished master, named Danger Evader, commented that though all things changed in the world, he himself changed with it. He was fully aware of all things, though he was aloof from them. His retort was,

> Like a raft adrift on the ocean
> It does not matter where I float or stop.
> Reaching the Tao is a matter of continuous motion.
> True nature is born from profound splendor.

In this book, we will be exploring various ways to harmonize with the Tao in everyday life. As the story and the poems illustrate, we will be going through three stages. The first stage is like that of the student who asked the question. Even to get to the point of entering the mountains, we need to become thoroughly familiar with the way of the Scholar Warrior. At the second stage, we may reach the level of the South Goose Beach Taoist, where he disdained imperial honors and the passage of time in society for the sake of contemplation. At the highest stage, however, we will be like the Danger Evader, who disdains nothing and floats without care on the enormous sea of Tao.

公石刼道人

明謝樗仙關山雪霽圖
乙卯四月八
日在永嘉石
趙亨

TRAVELERS IN A
MOUNTAIN PASS
AFTER HEAVY
SNOW. Attributed to
Hsieh Shih-ch'en.
Ming dynasty. Asian
Art Museum of San
Francisco, B67 D9.

開始

BOOK

I

The beginning
Is the essence
Of all that must be known,
And the place
Where all must return.

BEGINNINGS

The way of the Scholar Warrior
Unites wisdom with action.
The hero makes the era,
The era makes the hero.

SCHOLAR WARRIOR

MAXIMIZING VERSATILITY

SKILL IS THE ESSENCE of the Scholar Warrior. Such a person strives to develop a wide variety of talents to a degree greater than even a specialist in a particular field. Poet and boxer. Doctor and swordsman. Musician and knight. The Scholar Warrior uses each part of his or her overall ability to keep the whole in balance, and to attain the equilibrium for following the Tao. Uncertainty of the future inspires no fear: whatever happens, the Scholar Warrior has the confidence to face it.

It may seem strange, even paradoxical, to combine these two sides of human endeavor, yet the two have been related for hundreds of years. Difficult circumstances and a pragmatic attitude forged their links closer and closer. As in many other countries around the world, the successive empires in China were born from violent struggle, peasant uprising, and foreign invasion. Even learned persons had to defend themselves, and even warriors needed scholarly understanding.

Archaeological diggings reveal mural depictions of warriors as far back as the Shang dynasty (16th–11th centuries B.C.). In the Zhou dynasty (1111–222 B.C.), men like Lao Tzu and Confucius embodied the principles of the Scholar Warrior. Lao Tzu was a renowned swordsman, and Confucius held the title of Leader of Knights. Indeed, martial association may well have inspired Confucius' definition of the ideal scholar. At the heart of his *Analects*, he utilized the word *shi*, his designation for a scholar, which meant "warrior." A shi was a fighter of high rank—he went to battle in a war-chariot rather than on foot. Confucius' use of the word implied a person who would uphold the Tao (he used the word Tao to mean divine law) as valiantly as a warrior would. The term was eventually applied to all cultured people.

Soon, the entire Zhou court advocated the ideal of the Six Arts. In the book of Zhou rites, it is recorded that the imperial minister made this report to the emperor. He said that he was teaching the prince six different arts: rites, music, archery, horsemanship, literature (including reading, calligraphy, and divination), and mathematics. This establishes one of the earliest codifications of the scholar and warrior combined.

The mixing of things martial and cultural was part of Zhou state policy. The rulers believed that culture attracted emigres from neighboring states, thereby increasing the population and bringing fresh recruits for the army. Theatrical companies, painting exhibitions, and cultural envoys were regularly sent to non-aligned states. Confucius advised that if "the people of distant lands do not submit, then the ruler must attract them by enhancing the prestige of his culture." This mixture of culture and strategy was symbolized in the names of the first two emperors of Zhou: King Wen (the same word for culture), and King Wu (the word for martial). Both men were generals, and strongly believed that a cultural build-up of moral virtue was the prerequisite to triumph on the battlefields.

The Three Kingdoms (c. A.D. 220–260) was the era of clever military strategists. The classic book about that period, *Romance of the Three Kingdoms*, records the heroics of men like Guan Gong (later deified as the god of war); Liu Bei, a general and statesman; the Taoist Zhuge Liang, a

SAN GUO
Three Kingdoms

MU GUIYING. Contemporary picture book. Mu Guiying was among the most famous of women warriors. A member of the Yang clan, she joined the other women of her family under the guidance of the matriarch to fight in place of their brothers and husbands when they had all been defeated in battle. She is a symbol of loyalty, bravery, and patriotism.

brilliant strategist; and the surgeon Hua Tuo, who even today is recognized as one of the forefathers of herbal medicine, acupuncture, and therapeutic exercise.

By the Tang dynasty (A.D. 618–906), there was already a cult of the sword, and the literati adopted the romantic tradition of the knight errant. Among those who wandered the countryside championing the oppressed was the poet Li Po. Although better known as a man in love with wine, he was nevertheless well versed in swordsmanship and frequently defended the honor of the helpless. His contemporary, Tu Fu, wrote at length about a woman's sword performance in the poem "Viewing a Student of Madame Kung Sun," and the Song dynasty poet and government official Su Dongpo was a well-known master of the spear as well.

From the Tang dynasty onward, there was constant development of martial arts. Such a plethora of generals, secret societies, gangsters, monks, clan members, and imperial knights exchanged roles and knowledge that it is impossible to trace the history of martial arts in any linear fashion. Allegiances changed frequently; warriors hid their skills in obscurity until the time of some duel or uprising; and the religious orders of Taoism and Buddhism adopted martial arts for health and self-protection. It is important to note that throughout this time personal ability to do battle—as opposed to simple soldiers' techniques—became the standard for both women and men. Indeed, women appropriated entire sections of martial practice, bringing them to such high expression that

TWO WARRIORS.
Dish; carved red lac-
quer. Yuan/early Ming
dynasty. Asian Art
Museum of San Fran-
cisco, BL77 M15.

men could not compete with them in acrobatics, dart throwing, and use of poisons, whips, spears, and swords. Men continued to rely more on physical strength and larger cavalry weapons such as halberds and maces, but in actual combat, the faster and more clever women had their share of victories.

By the time of the Qing dynasty (A.D. 1644–1911), the Shaolin Temple, a Buddhist monastery that first gained fame as the host temple to the Zen patriarch Bodhidharma in the fifth century A.D., and Wudangshan, an alliance of Taoist monasteries grouped on seventy-two peaks, had become the two greatest centers for martial arts. The ways of the warriors and the ways of the monks became inextricably intertwined. Each school continued to gather new knowledge. Because of war, rebellion, and imperial edicts against them, scholars were killed and their books and other cul-

SHAO LIN SI

WU DANG SHAN

SCHOLAR WARRIOR

13

tural treasures were regularly destroyed. The monasteries, regarded as sacred and outside of society, were thus the only sanctuaries for precious things, and the holy people found martial arts as worthy of preservation as a piece of porcelain, a poem, or a scripture.

The Qing court, established by invading Manchus in 1644, was never fully accepted by the Han Chinese. The populace tried constantly to overthrow this foreign government, but the ferocity of the Qing warriors was formidable. The rebels needed sanctuaries to train their ranks. Because even the Qing government respected nonworldly temples, both Shaolin and Wudangshan became breeding grounds for anti-Qing revolutionaries. Men became monks solely to escape the Manchus and learn martial arts. The gun was nearly unknown, and people believed that the human body was the ultimate instrument of war. Men and women alike dedicated themselves with single-minded intensity to training.

The Qing dynasty soon found out about these rebels and directed its own forces against them. The emperors commanded not only vast armies but secret warriors as well. These knights had bodies of kinetic perfection. They had minds honed into instruments of perception and strategy. Their ability at hand-to-hand fighting far surpassed the puny talents of ordinary boxers, and their mental unity with their weapons made them the most fearsome champions of the throne. They worked the arts of war into the very fiber of their muscle and projected their will through glistening eyes. They fought dozens of opponents simultaneously. Whenever they fought, their prowess was so extraordinary that common people believed it to be sorcery or possession by spirits. The Qing warriors exploited this fear and dominated anyone who dared to oppose them.

These warriors were no mere killers. Whenever they were not on an imperial quest, they were members of the court and masters of their own fiefdoms. They had cultivated manners and were well educated. In their leisure time, they pursued literary and fine arts. They were gentlemen and gracious ladies who appreciated ephemeral beauty and fine scholarship. The blood they shed was always left to the cold of night or the privacy of lonely duels with worthy opponents. They saw no conflict between the ability to paint and the ability to wield a sword. For them, being a warrior was impossible without intelligence.

The emperors created a special title for the men and women who could demonstrate mastery in both academic and military arts. Painting, poetry, music, calligraphy, history, the classics, mathematics, sciences, medicine, and statecraft were among the skills one had to prove through written and oral examinations. Swordsmanship, horsemanship, archery, martial arts, and strategy were shown in both solo performance and combat against multiple attackers. In the Forbidden City, applicants strove to become members of this elite. Only after days of testing, supervised by the emperor himself, could the best qualified be awarded the cherished title Scholarly and Military Complete Talent. These Scholar Warriors of the Qing court fought numerous battles with the monk warriors, and their conflicts are known even to this day in books, films, and oral histories.

Perhaps one of the ultimate Scholar Warriors was the emperor Qianlong (1735–1795), who was trained at both Shaolin and Wudangshan, and who eventually engineered a plot to use the two schools to destroy each other. After learning all the techniques of the Buddhists at Shaolin, he intrigued to force the Wudangshan Taoists to attack the monastery. In the ensuing battle, his soldiers slaughtered hundreds of monks and burned the temple to the ground. Qianlong himself was a formidable fighter who honed his skills in personal duels with the best warriors of his time. He was the epitome of the Scholar Warrior. Not only was he the absolute ruler of a great nation and a mighty fighter, he was also a patron of the arts and an acknowledged calligrapher and poet.

A sample of Qianlong's calligraphy is illustrated, and the inscription on the cups reads as follows:

> Made to resemble chrysanthemum petals,
> Lifted in the hand, they are lighter than flowers.
> Let us sip tea, and compose verses
> To shroud them with dew and enhance their flowery nature.
> —Imperial brush of Qianlong, in the Bingshen year (1776)

During the nineteenth century, the gun began to eclipse the Scholar Warrior. When it was human skill that powered swords and spears, people were motivated to train their bodies and minds with the utmost fervor; twenty years was not considered too long to become a fighter. But technol-

WEN WU QUAN CAI
Scholarly and Military
Complete Talent

QIAN LONG
HUANG
Huang means emperor; Qianlong is his
name.

ogy wiped all that away. The gun and other modern weaponry, battle-ships, and motorized vehicles of war rendered extraordinary individual abilities superfluous. During the latter half of the nineteenth century, the Western nations forced China to open its ports. The clash between the Western powers and the warriors of China came to its most dramatic climax in 1900 during the Boxer Rebellion. In this, their last grand charge, the martial artists resorted to everything from their own skill to magic charms provided by shamans and priests. But the Chinese warriors were mowed down, and their defeat proved decisively the superiority of the gun in war.

Warfare continued in China for the entire first half of the twentieth century: civil war, wars between warlords, the Sino-Japanese War, and later, World War II. Personal combat became irrelevant, and the Scholar Warriors realized that they had to separate their way of life from constant warfare and rebellion. One such attempt was begun by the famous Huo

Yuanjia, one of the pivotal figures in a movement called the Zhengwu (Orthodox Martial) Athletic Association. This school tried to perpetuate the ideals of the Scholar Warrior that had first been established in the Zhou dynasty. The exact combination of martial and cultural skills had changed somewhat and varied from master to master, but a common saying was "Zither, chess, book, painting, and sword." These things symbolized versatility. The zither represented music as sacred and beyond entertainment. Chess (or actually, what is known as go) symbolized strategy. The book represented literature, and all academic arts from the sciences to poetry, as well as calligraphy. Painting symbolized all visual arts. Finally, the sword represented not just the ability to fight and defend oneself, but also indicated athletics, being a person of action and heroism.

But the schools themselves were overrun, first by the Japanese in the 1930s, and then by the Red Guard during the Cultural Revolution of the late 1960s. With the Cultural Revolution, the cultural context for the Scholar Warrior was effectively destroyed. Before its complete demise, Zhengwu tried to adapt by emphasizing martial arts as a way of discipline and health. Fighting became secondary, and the schools incorporated Western boxing, volleyball, football, and gymnastics as a means of expanding the athletic scope of martial arts. Though the events of the forties through the sixties eroded their efforts, they have left us with a good idea of how the warrior arts can be adapted for today: use them as the basis for health, discipline, and self-cultivation.

The Qing dynasty is long gone, and Zhengwu has also faded. The world has changed. Knights with superb skills seem quaint and impossible. Modern society, with its emphasis on equality and technology, does not support the cultivation of rarefied individuals. Yet the Scholar Warriors' compounding of human talent makes them perfect archetypes for contemporary culture. Humanity's inner struggles have not abated in the years since the Scholar Warriors were supreme. The soul continues to be a battleground, and everyone must confront the human dilemmas of life, self-identity, and death. We can learn much from the Scholar Warrior's sense of balance, discipline, and direction.

We all need balance between physical and mental, inner and outer, social and personal responsibilities. In an age of increasing specialization

HUO YUANJIA
One of the founders of Jingwu, he was poisoned early in the century.

ZHENG WU MEN
Zheng means orthodox or righteous. Wu, of course, means martial. The word *men* can mean something as simple as a doorway, but it also represents a system or association.

and acceptance of one's job and career as the primary element of life, we are in danger of becoming too narrow. We occupy ourselves with being materially and socially successful. We sacrifice personal priorities for the sake of business, career, spouse, or family. We think that as long as we do our job, raise our family, and accept a religion, then we will do reasonably well. But the problems in our society contradict this view. We face increasing health problems because of lack of exercise, careless diet, and urban stress. Our material desires never cease, and for many of us, our income cannot keep up with our ever increasing wants. We often fall into obsessive and excessive behavior, whether we are white-collar workers who work endless overtime hours or athletes who allow discipline to be swept away with celebrity status. We live in the most prosperous of civilizations, yet our personal problems belie our good fortune.

Perhaps most sadly, we find ourselves inadequate when tragedy strikes us. An unexpected death in the family fills us with fear and uncertainty, and we are unable to explain the event to our children. Sudden illness finds us too weak to fend it off. Our relationships swamp our hearts with confusing emotions. And when we try to face questions about who we are, what we are doing here in the world, what we are doing about our future, and how we can face our own death, we panic.

By balancing their personalities and engaging in daily self-cultivation, Scholar Warriors work to become capable of meeting such challenges. Those who have achieved this status would advise us to master a broad spectrum of disciplines, to balance the two sides of everything. If you are fighting in your career all the time, make the effort to also know compassion and philosophy. If you are cerebral, take the time to involve yourself in athletics. Eschewing sports because one is an intellectual is foolish. Not developing the patience to read or learn because one is committed to athletics is equally mistaken. The contemporary scholar who ignores his body is committing slow suicide. The modern-day athlete who does not pursue culture and letters is courting brain death. Use one side of a dichotomy to counter the excess of the other. Such equilibrium is not all that is needed to meet our problems, but it forms a strong base.

Self-cultivation requires discipline. If you want to be great, work hard and daily at what you want to do. It is only with discipline and perseverance that you will reach your goals. Discipline is freedom, and the companion to imagination. Discipline makes it possible for you to become whatever you want to be. If you want to give up a bad habit, it is discipline that will liberate you. If you want to become someone extraordinary, it is discipline that will show you the way. Look at the Scholar Warriors of the past. Without discipline, they would never have developed the nearly supernatural skills that they did.

We should each set goals for ourselves and strive to achieve them, bearing in mind that we must ultimately face all of life's most difficult questions. Most of our goals will be worldly: good health, better relationships, and a more satisfying career. But these should be played out against a backdrop of more spiritual goals. We are human beings first; workers, friends, parents, and any other identity second. It still behooves each of us to confront the deeper questions of our lives, inquire into our own nature, understand the universe, and face the question of death. By achieving our worldly goals, we become free to move on to more spiritual considerations.

Such spirituality is personal, and is quite apart from religious orthodoxy. Few of us are ready for monastery, convent, or hermit's hut. We all are involved with society and have varying degrees of ambition that must be discharged. The way of the Scholar Warrior is a method of achieving personal excellence while still in this world. If you want to seek the Tao, if you simply want to live a good life, you can follow the way of the Scholar Warrior and gain a balanced and healthy life. That doesn't mean that you will not need teachers or books or that you will not meet competition. What it does mean is that these are mere adjuncts to your essential quest. You are the solitary individual on a solitary path that is in the word *Tao*. By all means, learn and strive and reach for whatever you imagine. Your way will be easier if you have many arts and skills at your command.

三寶

2

Preserve the three treasures:
Body, breath, and mind.

THREE TREASURES

THE BASIS FOR PERSONAL HEALTH

IF YOU WANT to begin on a path, it is important to first assess your basic health and clear away any physical and mental health problems. For example, if you are in chronic pain—perhaps from an accident or an occupational injury—then it is best to resolve this at the beginning of your study. No one can be a successful Scholar Warrior, philosopher, or spiritual inquirer if plagued by constant backaches, high blood pressure, headaches, or arthritis.

There is nothing wrong with seeking out competent professionals for the sake of clearing away these difficulties. Being a Scholar Warrior is a lifetime investment, and injury or illness could compromise your efforts. Medicine and healing exist in this world, and we should seek out the proper professionals. As long as the expert is oriented toward constant progress, is willing to explain everything to your satisfaction, and is totally commited to making you independent of treatment as soon as possible, you should not hesitate to seek help.

If you need help for psychological difficulties, you should seek out this too. Why turn to the way of the Scholar Warrior when what you need is counseling, sound diet, or medical attention? It is not the function of the way of the Scholar Warrior to resolve these problems. In the past the world was more chaotic and knowledge more fragile because of constant warfare and social chaos, and the Scholar Warrior and the monks were perhaps the only ones who had preserved enough knowledge to help the people. Today, though there are still problems with malpractice, incompetence, and errors in thinking, the medical field has advanced far beyond what it was even fifty years ago. If you need help, find it, and try to become independent as soon as possible.

It is astounding that many people live with constant pain, discomfort, or ill health. They chalk it up to old age or mask their symptoms with liquor or drugs. The Scholar Warrior strips the individual down to the basics. Removing chronic health problems from your life is like clearing a field: if anything is to grow, there has to be sound and careful preparation first. For the Scholar Warrior, daily attention to health is the first step to knowing the Tao.

THE THREE TREASURES

After chronic health problems have been resolved, the beginning Scholar Warrior first concentrates on consolidating the health of body, breath, and mind. These are actually inseparable, for what one does on a physical level will reverberate to the other two. Cleansing the body yields immediate results and will have ramifications on the psychological level. In fact, the masters consider that physical training is the best way to discipline. Where the mind is fickle, vain, full of objections, the body is more responsive. It knows the difference between cleanliness and impurity. It will instinctively reject the bad, once it is grounded in stable health. Through the

SAN BAO
Three Treasures. The word for treasures shows three precious things under one roof: jade, pottery, and money.

JING QI SHEN

JING
Essence, sperm, hormones.

QI
Breath, vital energy, vitality.

cleansing of the body and control of breathing, the mind can gradually share in the body's wisdom, and well-being can become consistent. A person who knows and cultivates body, breath, and mind is said to possess the Three Treasures of *jing*, *qi*, and *shen*.

The first treasure is jing. The most widely known definition of jing refers to sperm in men and hormones in women. But this is only a small part of the total concept of jing. The term includes the entire endocrine system and the various chemical interactions involved in metabolism. Jing is the biochemical character of your body, from the secretions of your glands to the very genetic chemistry that created you. Jing determines your growth pattern and basic constitution and is responsible for how you develop and age. It does not, however, exist in unlimited supply. It can be exhausted by illness, overwork, nervousness, stress, poor nutrition, improper thinking, drugs, liquor, insufficient sleep, and excessive sexual indulgence. Dysfunction of jing is thought responsible for such problems as improper maturation, sexual difficulties, premature aging, lack of strength, and sometimes mental illness. Proper habits, by contrast, preserve jing. Calmness, a good diet, clear thinking, avoidance of intoxication, proper rest, and a regulated sexual life all help to preserve and even build jing. If you do the proper things, then you will not interfere with the basic function of jing—the development and functioning of the body—and you may even be able to slow the process of aging. When one succeeds in doing this, one is said to have stored one's jing, and it can then be used to compound qi.

Qi (chi) represents the aspects of movement in a human being. It is the life essence, what makes us live and breathe. Jing is our biochemical character; qi represents the energy of the body. It is related to the breath, but it cannot be confined to mere inhalation and exhalation. Qi is best understood as a description of *function* in the human body, not as a substance like blood or lymphatic fluid. It is a way of viewing energy circulation in the body. Qi is thought responsible for all muscular movements, involuntary acts such as breathing and heartbeat, and mental activity. Along with jing, it is involved in the processes of maturation and aging. Qi is also involved in circulation, oxygen in the blood, nerve impulses, and a variety of other functions that Western medicine attributes separately to the circulatory, endocrine, digestive, muscular, and nervous systems. What Western doctors categorize as separate, the Chinese group together in terms of their overall effect. It is both a poetic and empirical view. The traditional Eastern view is not an alternative to Western theories but can serve as a bridge between static concepts of separate physical systems.

Qi arises from four elements: the air you breathe, your jing, the essence from the food that you eat, and the qi inherited genetically from your parents. If any one of these four elements is diminished, then your life force will also be diminished. If you breathe polluted air, if you exhaust your jing through sexual excess, if you eat improperly, or if your parents were unhealthy, then your chances for having a strong and vigorous supply of qi are greatly reduced. One of the ways that the Scholar Warrior seeks to remedy deficiencies of qi and to store energy is through an art called *qigong*, which can gradually influence qi and bring it under conscious control. Any excess qi can be directed to parts of the body and nervous system that are normally dormant, and thus yield extraordinary power. If your qi is strong, your immune system will be strong; your stamina for sports will be great; and your longevity will increase. At the highest levels, qigong and related arts such as tai chi can have a positive impact on mind and spirit.

The Taoists believe that qi is naturally transformed into the more refined energy of the mind, called shen. One's mind is dependent on physical energy, and mental health is therefore dependent on physical health. Like qi, mental energy may be cultivated and further developed, primarily through academic study and meditation. But like qi, it can also be destroyed or wasted. Shen is vulnerable to distractions, lack of focus, inordinate attention to amusements, immorality, materialism, sensuality, egotism, and intellectuality. To preserve mental energy you must establish strong foundations of jing and qi and lead a balanced life.

SHEN
Spirit, mind.

Spiritual energy is a higher aspect of shen. Like qi and shen, it may be developed through self-cultivation. By implication, the difficulties are greater. Your mind must be capable of tremendous concentration. Naturally, this high level is not achieved swiftly. It takes intensive training of jing, qi, and shen, through exercise, diet, qigong, and meditation.

CULTIVATING JING

The two fundamental attitudes toward jing are preservation by nourishment and preservation by sexual conservation. Food provides the basic substances to build jing; the proper practice of sexuality helps to consolidate it.

Diet

The Taoists have some very simple observances for diet, but their ramifications are very great. The approach is to be fastidious about diet while avoiding fanaticism.

Balance your diet. Follow the middle path. Eat a little bit of many different foods at each meal. Select from meats, fish, poultry, vegetables, grains, fruits, juices, teas, milk, and herbs. It is senseless to deny the body a balanced diet. Don't be obsessive about your diet, and don't bore people with labels about what kind of eater you are.

Eat with your body, not with dietary trends. One of the most tragic mistakes people make is to eat according to bizarre theories. Learn to listen to your body, and indulge it within reason. If you have a craving for something, satisfy it in moderation—only make sure that the craving comes from the body. Too often, we develop dietary addictions as a result of psychological problems, habit, or social indoctrination. Sugar is a good example. Eating sweets once in a while is all right, but most people in our society today overindulge. With good practice, your body will be able to balance itself. It is a work of nature, and if you let it have its natural way, it can choose foods with wisdom.

There is no "standard" diet best for everyone. Our body types vary a great deal; our rates of metabolism differ; we each have different habits of exercise and work and live under different environmental conditions, so it is impossible to recommend one set of foods or amounts. Each of us has to determine what is proper for him- or herself. This requires self-observation and cautious experimentation, as well as an awareness of dietary studies being conducted. In general, one who has a high metabolism will need more protein and carbohydrate, while one with a slower metabolism will need much less meat.

How can you determine what metabolic type you are? The more you get a great lift out of high-protein foods, the more likely it is that you have a high metabolism. If eating a great amount of meat exhilarates you, then you have a high metabolism, and you must adjust your diet so that you get the protein you require. Some people, however, feel quite sluggish when they eat a great deal of protein. They have been instinctively drawn toward a low-protein or even a vegetarian diet because this is what suits their body best. Again, once you have determined the rate of your own metabolism, use this as a standard for your diet.

In addition to the two basic types of metabolism, there are six different states of the body: hot, cold, dry, damp, weak, and neutral. Often a person will be predominantly one or more of these states by nature, but this is not permanent. The states of the body can change with diet, illness, exercise, weather, and taking of herbal medicine. Because the six basic states can be affected in this way, Scholar Warriors use everyday diet to bring the state of their bodies into balance. A brief discussion of these six states will clarify the role they play in our daily well-being.

A hot person is one who is warm, even in cold weather, has a red complexion, and is generally active. Emotionally, such a person is often temperamental, explosive, and ambitious. Signs of excessive heat in such a person are dry mouth, cracked lips, canker sores, red eyes, headaches, or a burning sensation during urination and defecation. A heat condition will be aggravated by eating meat or fried, deep-fried, salty, and spicy foods; drinking alcohol; smoking; and even excessive exercise. A hot person should compensate by eating more vegetables and fruit, drinking liquids, and avoiding the foods that increase heat in the body. However, he or she must balance this carefully with body type; a person who is hot but of a high metabolism cannot give up meat entirely. A hot person is often vulnerable to dry conditions as well.

A cold person is one who cannot keep warm, whose hands and feet get cold easily, who is usually pale. Conditions such as anemia and malnutrition are common among cold people, and signs of excessive cold are chills and cold sweat on the palms and soles. Emotionally, such people are relaxed, calm, and not easily excited. A cold condition will be aggravated by eating too many vegetables, cold foods, sweets, iced drinks, salads, and fruit and living in a cold, damp environment. A cold person should compensate by eating more red meat (usually as stew, not as fried, deep-fried, or excessively spicy dishes), grains, beans, and warm foods. A cold constitution is often vulnerable to damp and weak states as well.

A dry person is one who has dry, flaking skin, a constant cough even when not ill, and a dry throat, eyes, nasal passages, and so on. Lung and skin problems are common signs. Usually, such a person is predominantly hot, so the emotional nature is similar. A dry condition will be aggravated by the same foods that aggravate a hot condition and will be further worsened if the person does not drink enough water or eat enough fruit, vegetables, and moistening foods. One can be hot and dry or one can be cold and dry, so it is important to balance this carefully. For a hot-dry person, the compensating foods are the same. But a cold-dry person has to carefully eat foods that moisten the system without cooling the body too much. Such a person would eat vegetable stews and meat stews, and drink warm soups to compensate for a cold-dry system.

A damp person is often fat, with excessive flows of mucus, a constant runny nose, water retention, and swelling of the joints. Rheumatism, arthritis, bloating, pains in the kidneys, and urinary problems are signs of a damp person. Salt, humid weather, spices, fatty foods, and dairy products aggravate a damp condition. Such a person can compensate for his or her condition by avoiding salt, living in a dry, warm climate, and avoiding dairy products. A damp-hot person must avoid foods like turkey, pheasant, mango, pineapple, wild game, and salted foods. A damp-cold person should avoid too much fish, bean cake, vegetables, cold foods and drink, dairy products, ice cream, and sweets.

A weak person is one who is sickly, tired, under deep stress, and has a poor immune system. Such people usually have an erratic diet; they are often undernourished; and they don't seem to respond to any kind of food. Emotionally, they are usually unstable, vulnerable to stress, hypersensitive, paranoid, or neurotic. A weak condition can be further complicated by being combined with other factors. For example, a common condition is cold-weak, in which all the signs of cold and weakness are combined. Or one can be cold-damp-weak, and this is, as you might imagine, an even more disastrous state. Such people need to eat a regular and well-balanced diet, and it is imperative that they seek competent medical attention to balance their bodies and regain a state of good health.

Finally, we come to the neutral person. Frankly, such a state is rare, for such a person would have to live in the perfect environment for his or her body, would have to have perfect mental, physical, and emotional health, and would either intuitively or consciously know how to eat in order to maintain this state on a daily basis. Such a person would eat a well-balanced diet, would know how to use herbal medicine to compensate for environment, stress, illness, or occasional lapses. We might all drift through this state at one time or another, but it is hard to maintain. However, the maintaining of a neutral state through diet is precisely our goal as Scholar Warriors.

One of the ironies of life is that we all tend to like the foods that are worst for our body type. Hot people tend to like hot, spicy, and deep-fried foods. Cold people tend to like salads, vegetables, and cold drinks. Dry people won't drink enough liquids, and damp people love fatty foods and sweets. But the way of the Scholar Warrior is to be conscious of one's body type and to compensate for one's state of health through the manipulation of diet. It is important to remember that these states are not permanent, but rather are descriptions of extremes that we can slip in and out of depending on diet, emotional health, and environment. Once you become more familiar with these states, you will be able to tell each time you sit down to eat what the state of your body is. By eating accordingly, you can build health and avoid illness. The recommendations that follow should form a sound basis for finding the best way to establish dietary balance.

Drink water. Be sure to drink enough water each day. Thirst is not a reliable indicator, nor does other consumed liquid count. Keep hydrated with at least six to eight glasses a day, and be sure to drink more when exercising or when ill. The water should be as clean and as pure as possible, and you should not drink it iced.

Even if you have determined that you are a damp person, you should drink enough water. You might think that you should drink less, but this is not the case. When you do not drink enough water, the body will perceive this as drought, and you will actually retain water. It is only when the body is sure that it will have sufficient water that it will release its reserves, with the wonderful by-product of flushing toxins out of the system.

Eat the proper amount. Do not fast without guidance and supervision; don't undereat, and don't overeat. You must remember that someone engaged in athletic activity will eat more food. Current studies and dietary theories focus on the needs of average people, who quite often are sedentary compared with a Scholar Warrior. As you exercise more, you will require more calories and better nutrition.

In general, the Scholar Warrior avoids fasting. There are two types of fasting. One is the abstention from all solid foods. This type of fasting requires the guidance of an experienced person. It is too easy to fall into fanaticism or to deplete your body unnecessarily. Such fasting is usually used in religious ceremonies or in cases of extreme illness. Otherwise, it is unnecessary.

The second type of fasting means the eating of a severely restricted diet for the sake of some goal that you want to achieve. For example, when eating ginseng, one should avoid all acidic foods, including citrus, and spicy foods, as they will neutralize the effects of the root. Sometimes fasting means avoiding foods incompatible with sports training. Carbohydrate loading is an example of what Taoists would classify as fasting. As with the first type of fasting, it is crucial to do this carefully and under proper guidance.

Eat foods fresh and in season. Grow your own, or buy direct from the growers if that is practical. Whenever possible, the meats and vegetables that you eat should be organic. Eat foods that are fresh and in season.

Vegetables. Vegetables should make up the bulk of one's diet, but you need not exclude meat and other foods. The complexity of modern society often precludes a life close to basic agricultural rhythms. But eating is more than devouring the food on the table in front of you. It is part of a whole process: planting, growing, cultivating, observing, and then finally absorbing. There is something much more integrated about a person who tends the harvest until it is ready to eat. The grower knows the soil, the weather, the sunlight, and the time that went into this food. By eating, he or she becomes a part of the natural cycle.

At each meal, eat at least three different types of vegetables. An easy way to combine vegetables is by colors: one red (carrots, beets, radishes, tomatoes, sweet peppers), one yellow (squash, yellow zucchini, corn), and one green (broccoli, cabbage, spinach, mustard greens, green beans, peas, and so on).

It is unnecessary to be a complete vegetarian. In monasteries such as those on Huashan in Shaanxi province, for example, the residents sometimes ate fish, frog, and game given by hunters. Vegetarianism was sometimes an economic necessity, or done for specific high meditations. The eating of meat was thought to make a student too active for the quiescent activities of a meditator. But temple living was a very specialized activity in a protected environment. The Scholar Warrior considers pure vegetarianism to be impractical in a competitive society.

Meats, fish, and poultry. Fish should be the primary source of animal protein, and it should be fresh and pollution free. Try to eat the fish steamed, poached, or broiled. Avoid deep-fried and breaded fish.

Chicken is a second alternative source of meat, and rabbit is also acceptable. However, both these meats should be avoided if you have a cold, fever, red eyes, or liver trouble. Avoid turkey and pheasant, as these are thought to create illness and irritation in the body.

Among red meats, it is best to eat lamb, veal, and lean cuts of beef like the shin and the tail. Red meats are thought to build blood and muscle. About twice a week is the right frequency. Eating more meat is permissible in the winter, when one needs to stay warm.

Organ meats may be eaten sparingly and are best combined with Chinese herbs to offset their bad qualities (chiefly high cholesterol) and enhance their nutritive qualities for one's own organs. The Taoists believe that animal organs combined with herbs supplement the corresponding organs within the human body. Chapter 5 has some recipes for these dishes.

Avoid the flesh of scavengers like pigs, ducks, and geese; filter-feeding shellfish like shrimp, clams, oysters, mussels, crabs, and lobsters; deep-fried, greasy, or heavily spiced foods; and heavily sugared foods.

Grains. Among the grains, rice and wheat are most favored, with oat, millet, and barley used sparingly, and only when cooked soft enough to digest. Noodles are acceptable. Bread is fine, especially whole grain breads (never white bread). You should eat some grain product at every meal, but the amount should be kept minimal.

Dairy products. Milk once a day is permissible as long as you are not lactose intolerant or damp in nature. Avoid cheese, ice cream, and other processed dairy products.

Fruit. Eat two fruits a day at a minimum. They should be fruits in season. Especially helpful are melons, berries, cherries, bananas, apples, oranges, tangerines, pears, snow pears, peaches, nectarines, plums, lichee, and longan. The only fruit to really avoid is papaya, and both mango and pineapple should be eaten sparingly as they can irritate some people's digestive systems.

Understand how diet affects you and your health. Through study and self-observation, you will quickly see how certain foods have an impact on your thinking, how you feel, and how your body functions. When you feel out of balance, you will know what foods to eat in order to put yourself back into balance. Do not wait to get sick until you take action; learn what foods to eat in order to avoid illness. Illness is not a normal part of life; it is a disorder. Proper health means using diet to prevent illness, and the proper use of foods is more powerful than medicine. The Taoist approach to diet requires sensitivity to what the body wants and understanding of how each specific food affects the body. With the voice of the body and the knowledge of what will help it, one may easily maintain balanced health on a daily basis.

Sexual Conservation

The second fundamental way to cultivate jing is through the control of sexuality. Many masters in the past interpreted this to mean complete abstinence—including avoiding even the mere thought of sexuality. Obviously, this would be quite difficult for most of us, and there are other masters who feel the same. Deciding what course of action to take on this fundamental subject is not easy, and the controversy surrounding the subject can be confusing.

The early Taoists identified jing solely as semen, and an entire cult sprang up that was centered around the notion that one should not lose any at all. Not only is this impractical for most people, but mere abstention from sex is not enough to ensure inner power. If that were truly the case, then people who could not find lovers would be very powerful indeed.

Other Taoists took a different approach and sought to exploit sexuality for the sake of what was called "sexual alchemy." This was a process of changing the basic substances of the human body and using them to gain longevity. They felt that a man and woman could exchange their jing and, in the process, gain energy that was not possible for the celibate to achieve. A man, they said, only had male energy, but needed female essence to be whole. A woman likewise needed male energy to complete her own. Therefore, the two could be combined during sexual intercourse, each lover giving the other what was needed. There are many Taoist sex manuals detailing various techniques to facilitate this exchange, including various methods of contraction and stimulation. Like the celibates, however, these Taoists still emphasized the preservation of jing. Because his sexual energy was considered so minuscule compared with that of a woman, a man was not to ejaculate during sex but was supposed to stimulate his partner to climax as many times as possible. In this way, she would release much of her own jing, which he would absorb. Obviously, she would get back very little. No one could accuse this school of Taoism of being fair to women.

The fundamental question for these approaches to sexuality is whether it is practical and healthy for a man to refrain from ejaculation for periods up to an entire year, as the sexual alchemists strive to do. If one understands that jing is not simply ejaculate, then the notion of holding back from climax is terribly primitive. Jing cannot be merely the physical sperm, because jing is the essence of the whole body, and there is no evidence that semen in its physical form can be used to compound qi. Physical and sexual energy may be tied to healthy sexual practices, but it does not follow that abstention from ejaculation, even during intercourse, is the best way to preserve one's energy. This so-called esoteric Taoist approach to sexuality—the refraining from ejaculation—is not a very convincing way to achieve greater health. Although this school of Taoism is a respected one, their masters age at the same rate as the rest of us, and their self-cultivation and enlightenment are dependent on having the proper partners.

The middle path accepts sexual conservation as an important component of self-cultivation but takes that to mean regulating the frequency and circumstances of sex. Sexual conservation must be combined with training and special techniques that transmute sexual energy into a more potent force. There is nothing mystical about this, for each person does this naturally; the progression from jing to qi to shen happens in each of us every day. What the Scholar Warrior seeks is to become aware of this process, cooperate with it, and enhance it. Cooperating with our own sexuality—obviously one of the most powerful forces within our bodies—yields a tremendous source of energy and vitality. In general, the Scholar Warrior observes the following principles.

Make sure your partner is healthy. Especially with the prevalence of sexually communicated diseases today, it is necessary to be careful about who you have sex with.

Control the frequency of sex. If you are under the age of twenty, and you are still not sexually experienced, there is no need to rush into it. Your energy is something much more valuable. Apply your energies to self-cultivation, and do not let them be swept away by the confusion of love. There is no need to listen to the sexual propaganda around you. It is far better to follow your own path as it unfolds. If the future has a lover for you, he or she will appear soon enough, and it only takes a moment to begin a sexual life.

If you are young and sexually involved, then you can do nothing but to follow that path too. At an early age, it is impossible and unhealthy to restrict sex to any set amount. Just do not exhaust yourself or become obsessed, and follow the other guidelines.

As one reaches the midtwenties, one should gradually endeavor to restrict sexuality to once a week or less. As one ages, the tendency is to restrict sex more and more, until by the sixties, frequency is no more than once a month. When elderly, past seventy-five or so, one should not have sex at all.

If you are single and without a lover, you must decide what you want to do with your life. First, you must know that it is unnecessary to have a mate in order to be a successful person. Second, you must decide whether you will remain single or seek a partner. Remaining single is fine and, for the Scholar Warrior, often more convenient. Masturbation should not be practiced. Releasing jing through nocturnal emissions is acceptable, however, because this is a natural part of the body's functioning.

Although some were married, there was still a strong tradition of sexual conservation among the Scholar Warriors of old. This was probably a result both of empirical knowledge and of Taoist theories. Controlled sexuality can still be very valuable to a couple. It strips away the emotional tangle that sexual involvement often causes and allows a couple to see their relationship more clearly. Being lovers is not a good enough reason to be together, and sex cannot be used to cement a relationship or bring it back together after conflict. Without sex, you are truly forced to find what is inherently good about your relationship rather than getting caught up in a whirlwind of emotions.

Restrict sex in the winter. At any age, sex should be restricted during the colder winter months because the body needs more energy to resist the weather. When young, this means reduction to once a month. People in their thirties and older should endeavor to abstain completely during winter.

Rebuild your energy. Sex does temporarily discharge one's sexual energy, so it should be built back through diet and herbs. Among the foods that build back jing are chicken, lamb, beef, and pork kidneys cooked with Chinese herbs. Study the recipes in Chapter 5 to find the ones best for your own body.

Avoid dead jing. Don't refrain from orgasm and ejaculation unless guided in this practice by a qualified master. This is a dangerous practice and is apt to be more frustrating than anything else. The Taoists accept what is natural. Sex is natural, and it is natural to climax. Holding back only results in what is called dead jing. Sexuality and the related processes in the body will stagnate. Some men who have tried to abstain completely have wound up with prostate trouble and testicle blockages.

Know the signs of sexual excess. For the Taoists, the signs of sexual excess are backache, weak legs, ringing in the ears, weakening eyesight,

SI JING
Dead jing.

premature graying or loss of hair, loss of memory, constant illness, inability to maintain weight, premature wrinkling, poor complexion, and insufficient stamina for physical exertion.

When abstaining, be complete. The Taoists believe that sexual energy resides at the acupuncture point called the Gate of Life (*mingmen*), along the spine roughly at the level of the adrenal glands and kidneys. Sexual stimulation causes this energy to descend to the genitals in preparation for intercourse. Upon sufficient sexual stimulation, the energy will stay in the area and will be discharged whether there is sexual release or not. Therefore, it is best to refrain from stimulation if you do not intend to complete the act. Looking at erotic literature, for example, will mean a loss of jing.

Understand sexuality and exercise. Ironically, athletics and the high cultivation of martial arts make one feel more sexual. It is important to understand what is happening to your body and to channel it properly. Only after the jing is constantly transformed into qi and one attains the fruits of high meditation does this exaggerated sexuality cease to become a problem.

It is because of the heightened sexuality that Scholar Warriors advocate the separation of sexes during training. They believe that there is a very strong magnetism between the sexes, and because self-cultivation and athletic training demand the utmost in attention, men and women should train apart from one another.

No matter how close a man and a woman are, the way of the Scholar Warrior looks at each one separately and declares that each one must still walk the path. A love relationship is not forever, and each person must still face life's problems. Each also has individual talents and special qualities that must be expressed. That has to be done by each person separately. Oftentimes the more each achieves, the happier will be their union.

Preserving your jing through proper diet and proper sexuality is the strongest way to establish your health. It may be difficult in the beginning, but once you settle on a proper way of life, you will find that your new habits take on a momentum of their own. If the essence of your body is full, then it is an easy thing to go on to the cultivation of the breath.

MING MEN
Literally, life gate. This point can be located by imagining a line going straight back from the navel to the spine.

CULTIVATING QI

The cultivation of qi first requires daily cleanliness on three levels: the outer level of the skin, the inner level of blood and body tissues, and the more subtle psychological and emotional levels. Impurity on any of these levels will block the cultivation of qi and reduce one's chances for good health.

Wash every day. This is one of the most important secrets of Taoism. How can you hear the whispering of the divine if you are sweaty, stinking, dirty? How are you going to sense the movement of the universe if not through the instrument of your entire being? And how is your entire being going to work unless it is in top working order and free of impurities? If you keep all nine openings of the body and the skin pores clean, your body will not be solely occupied with purging itself through sweating, discharge of phlegm, defecation, tearing, and so on. It will have more energy if you help it along by keeping clean.

Not only should you wash, but your home should be clean; you should be careful of how, where, and with whom you eat; and you should know the elements and use them to your advantage. Get into the sunlight if the weather has been damp; go into the shade if the weather is hot. Control your environment, and make sure that you do what is necessary to keep it free of disease.

It is essential to get enough rest. Unless you allow yourself enough sleep, how will you ever maintain yourself? Remember, the quest of a Scholar Warrior is lifelong, so your sense of pacing must also be for life. Proper sleep will allow the body to recover and will keep the mind fresh. Try to avoid a stressful life, and don't occupy yourself with trivialities.

Self-mutilation is forbidden. This may seem obvious, but the forms of self-abuse are many. Among them are tattooing; the piercing of ears, nose, or anything else; surgical modifications, even for the sake of athletic success (like the Amazons who removed a breast for easier archery); excessive exposure to physical danger for the sake of sports or money or academic success; the taking of drugs or steroids; and so on.

The Scholar Warrior includes emotions as part of hygienic practice.

BAO QI
Cultivating or protecting qi.

Sentiment, cruelty, love, vindictiveness, jealousy, greed, selfishness, insecurity, anger, envy, fear, grief, joy, and sympathy are just some of the feelings that beset us all. The Scholar Warriors say that emotions are natural, but that one cannot base one's actions on them. Rather, you must acknowledge them and keep them constantly circulating. One day you will feel one way; another day, you will feel another. These feelings are all valid at the proper times. The Taoists understand the emotions as being seated in the organs, and just as you need all your organs, you need all your emotions. If you allow yourself to dwell excessively in any one emotional sphere, you will become warped and will damage your health.

After establishing cleanliness, you can learn to circulate your qi. Qi circulates in two primary ways, in the blood and through the meridians. When the qi circulates through the bloodstream, blood is oxygenated in the lungs, and in turn carries that oxygen throughout the body. When qi circulates through body tissues, it follows specific pathways called meridians. These paths cannot be found through dissection, and some explanation of them may be useful. Chinese doctors in the past, many of whom were Taoists, knew anatomy. Though dissection was forbidden, it was conducted in secret, and the constant warfare, executions, and tortures that went on from dynasty to dynasty provided opportunities for doctors to observe the innards of human bodies in different states and at different ages in ways no medical student could today. Yet these doctors felt that the mechanical observation of anatomy was not enough. They viewed the human body as a fundamentally living thing, not some corpse butchered for well-meaning inspection. They turned to meditation as a technique of observation, for only through such introspection could the functions of the body be observed whole.

Through this self-examination, the early Taoists postulated that the body was a microcosm of the universe. Because the universe moves, they looked for movement within themselves. They were more interested in the functional aspects than the mechanical aspects, and they strove to understand this movement on the most minute levels. Meridians are, then, a summation of how all the various forms of energy flow through the body. They aren't tubes, like blood vessels, or fibers, like nerves, but patterns of energy flow. Differing energies may be conducted by different means and through different types of body tissues, but their effects will still be attributed to the flow of qi through the meridians.

These circuits may be blocked by illness, tension, poor diet, physical trauma, imbalance in the body, lack of movement, or improper thinking. Likewise, they may be "opened"—that is, the energy of the body may be induced to flow through these pathways by a wide variety of means. In medical treatment, for example, they may be manipulated through herbs, massage, and acupuncture. Doctors base their medical practice on stimulating the meridians, opening those that are blocked, regulating the energy in those that carry excessive flows. Herbalists, though they do not deal with the surface stimulation of meridians, formulate herbal mixtures in part through meridian theory. Through years of research, all properties of herbs have been documented, and manuals specify which meridians are affected by any particular medicinal herb. Whenever herbs are combined, the meridians that will be affected must be compatible. Other approaches to proper energy flow lie in good diet, hygiene, and exercise utilizing the same meridians that concern doctors.

These exercises are grouped together in series called sets. Especially in the past, when many people were illiterate, a set was a way to memorize movement that could not be described strictly through writing or any other means. Unfortunately, there were problems in such an oral tradition. The warriors, monks, and doctors who controlled these sets guarded them jealously. If they taught them to the public, they intentionally omitted key postures. They saved the entire set for themselves or for a few favorite disciples. This means that "traditional" sets are sometimes incomplete, or that they have been amended in an attempt to replace deletions made by earlier masters. Sometimes, a set is an amalgamation of fragments that are all we have after the more selfish masters died with their secrets. Masters must analyze sets very carefully and even adjust them to compensate for these problems. They may collect many different versions, compare notes with their colleagues, and practice a set themselves to observe its efficacy before passing it on to their students.

In actuality, no set "belongs" to a master. Seeing them that way only compounds the problem once again. The naming of styles (like Chen style or Wudang style) should be regarded only as an indication of origin, not

QIGONG
Breath training.

of proprietary rights. When you study with someone, don't make the mistake of thinking that this master teaches the same set as another one so one of them is not original. Professors may use the same textbook, and mathematicians certainly use the same formulas, but the final advantage is in learning from a skillful practitioner.

Qigong—the art of cultivating the qi—is breath control through the performance of sets. Strictly speaking, anything that trains the breath and builds stamina can be considered qigong. Two sports can serve as examples of the effects of classical qigong. The first is swimming. The meridians are affected by gentle movement and are opened through stretching and contracting. Breathing is regulated as a matter of course, and many swimmers report increased lung capacity, better circulation, improved muscle tone, and relief from stress. The second example is hiking, which demands working against the resistance of the land, variation of effort with changes in terrain, breathing clean air directly from the trees and the mountains, and maintaining the heart and lungs at a constantly elevated pace. The uplifting contemplation of nature is a wonderful by-product. Both swimming and hiking are beneficial for qi, but qigong's effects are greater still. Several chapters will be devoted to this important art, but a brief overview will give some sense of its immense scope.

Qigong has a long history in China and has evolved into a vast body of knowledge. During the time of China's first emperor, Qinshi Huang, there were various Taoists who advocated the cultivation of physical immortality by means of herbs and all sorts of metallic compounds. Not only were they unsuccessful, but many of them died because they were experimenting with such substances as mercury, cinnabar, and lead. Other Taoists speculated that the cultivation of the vital force itself was enough to bring longevity. Instead of taking elixirs, they felt that qi should be the primary means of self-cultivation. The basic premise of qigong has remained central since that time: if one preserves and stores qi, one will have the energy for extraordinary feats and for longevity.

Early methods were primitive, consisting of different ways of holding the breath or regulating inhalation and exhalation. Postulating that an individual had only a certain number of breaths allotted by fate, they naively reasoned that taking fewer of them and slowing the rate of respiration would extend life. Other techniques involved swallowing saliva, called the Jade Nectar, while engaging in different techniques of holding the breath.

By the second century A.D., Taoists were experimenting with movements mimicking the behavior of animals. Hua Tuo, of the Three Kingdoms period, created the Five Animal Frolics, based on the movements of cranes, bears, deer, monkeys, and tigers. He declared, "A used threshold never rots, and flowing water never becomes stagnant." Thus, he reasoned, movement would extend life. Like other Taoists, he saw that animals had many qualities that humans lacked: long life, strength, flexibility, leaping skills, immunity to illness, virility, and so on. The Taoists ascribed many of the qualities to "exercises" or movements that the animals did, and sought to gain such powers by imitating these actions. For example, they noticed that a tortoise lived for a long time, so they copied its method of extending and withdrawing its neck. They noticed that a deer was light in running and had great virility, so they copied its prancing movements. They noticed that a tiger was unusually strong, but that its strength was relaxed, flexible, and effortless, and they copied its powerful actions.

These observations of animals included noticing their still postures. The Taoists copied these too. They concluded that animals meditated, and that this also contributed to long life. They saw cranes stand for long periods on one leg. They saw turtles sit unmoving with their heads stretched toward the sun. They saw frogs sitting while puffing and contracting their throats. Standing and sitting meditation thus became part of qigong. Tai chi chuan eventually took its form in this way as well. Originally consisting of thirteen static postures, it was only later that movements were added. You can still see part of this legacy in tai chi, as it is essentially a series of still postures strung together. Names like White Crane Spreads Wings and Snake Creeps Down indicate postures that were once held for long periods.

Incessant wanderers, the Taoists also appropriated breathing methods from other cultures. By the time of the Tang dynasty, they had incorporated the Indian arts of *pranayama*, mantra, *kundalini* yoga, and tantra wholesale into the art of qigong. They appropriated methods of Buddhist breathing and exercise such as Bodhidharma's Muscle Change and Mar-

QINSHI HUANG
This emperor was responsible for the building of the Great Wall. Determined that China's history should start with him, he ordered all books burned except those dealing with divination. Because he was opposed by scholars, he ordered them burned or buried alive. Obsessed with immortality, he supported numerous efforts to find the elixir of immortality, and it is popularly believed that he died from ingesting an unsuccessful elixir.

row Washing Classics and the Vase Breathing methods from Tibet. Nor did these eclectic collectors stop there. They raided the whole of Chinese martial arts methodology and took the working habits of farmers, fishermen, craftsmen, and even drunks as templates for their exercises. In return, of course, they gave the art of qigong, and Taoist theories of qi have been applied to everything from painting (Does the stroke show qi?), to music (Does the flautist have qi?), to even cooking (Does the cook's qi burst up from the skillet?).

Qigong was traditionally the art of master practitioners. These extraordinary men and women cured people when necessary, but in a context much different from today's qigong clinic. These masters lived away from society, many of them in anonymity. They did not publish their findings; they did not seek publicity; yet they became famous because of their marvelous powers of healing. They developed their skills through hard work, decades of apprenticeship with their own masters, and daily practice to develop their qi. Each of the old masters came from a lineage, like a line of family descent, and this was the assurance that what they learned was authentic and tested.

When they were called upon to demonstrate their prowess, almost always in private and before other masters, they could do remarkable things. A legend regarding one such demonstration is memorable. The master, a thin man in his sixties with close-cropped hair, had been invited by other masters to prove his achievements. He complied. The first test was to resist the attacks of warriors. He stood calmly and allowed them to hit him everywhere, including the eyes and the groin, all to no effect. But this apparent invulnerability to strikes and kicks wasn't enough. He had to prove that he could also issue qi. To do this, he stood above an urn of plain water. A deep gurgling sound came as a response to the palm that he held motionless above the water. The audience set seven candles in a straight line, each one foot away from the next, and with a simple pointing of his finger, the master put out all of them. Only then was this man acknowledged as close to divine. After his demonstration, and after receiving this rare approval, the master was never seen again. Humility demanded that he sink back into obscurity.

This story is admittedly unbelievable to many people, but the principles that it symbolizes are quite important. First, qigong establishes a strong immunity, at least to disease if not to strikes and kicks. Second, qi can be issued forth, as in the sound that came from the water and the force that extinguished the candles. Third, a master maintains great humility. The master neither advertised nor displayed himself to common people, nor did he attempt to capitalize on his achievements. He sank back into obscurity like a jewel into a bog. Though the story may well be apocryphal, the essence of qigong—immunity, projection, and humility—is real and important.

As recently as the 1930s, traditional qigong doctors used their own qi in conjunction with herbs, acupuncture, massage, herbal baths, and sometimes relocation of the patient to another part of the country. They usually began with herbal broths and acupuncture and did not use their own qi until they felt that the patient's own body could adequately respond to the doctor's qi.

There were two options for the doctors working with qi. In the first, they attracted the patient's own qi to the surface. This would usually stimulate blood circulation and strengthen the patient's ability to ward off illness. The patient's skin will turn red where the doctor touches. In the second, the doctors actually projected their own qi into the body to disperse hemorrhaging or kill infections. Whichever option was exercised, projecting qi was only one of several therapeutic methods and was always used in conjunction with other forms of treatment. For example, if the qigong practitioner destroyed the bacteria that was causing an illness, the dead bacteria still had to be flushed out with purgative medicine. Or if qi was used in an emergency, such as a sprain or a broken bone, follow-up care included conventional therapies such as splints, herb poultices, and internal medicine. After the patient recovered, he or she was taught qigong for health maintenance.

Qigong has proved effective against cases of high or low blood pressure and digestive trouble, and it even helps reduce mild psychological problems. The practice of qigong has not, however, proven to be effective against most cases of cancer, AIDS, tuberculosis, polio, leprosy, meningitis, paralysis, and a host of other diseases. As the masters have tartly noted, if qigong cured everything, there would be no cancer in China.

A great deal of attention has been recently focused on qigong, both in China and the West. Audiences in both China and the United States have been given demonstrations of its seemingly miraculous powers. Some of these performances show stones being broken over the head of an expert; others show a man successfully resisting a spear thrust against his throat. To the incredulous questions of the audience, the mysterious explanation is qi. Little more is said, and this only serves to compound the misconceptions about qigong.

A near carnival showcase for qigong has extended into the medical community. In the hospitals of Beijing, Shanghai, and other cities of China, there are now "qigong clinics" with doctors who claim that they can issue qi from their own palms into the bodies of patients, and where the patients in turn learn qigong to recover their health. Visiting doctors from the West have claimed to have seen a man move an object from a distance, and another light up a fluorescent bulb by simply holding it. The interaction between these qigong practitioners and the Western medical community has evolved toward exchange programs and full-blown scientific studies. There has been ongoing research in the West to determine what qi is, and whether it, or anything else, can be projected from one person to another for therapeutic purposes, but the results have been inconclusive.

A few qigong healers have begun to treat patients in the West. In the claims that have been made about the miraculous healing powers of qi, qigong has been applied to everything from cancer to psychological illnesses. Volumes have been written and scientific papers published, and many people have gone to qigong healers in the hope that they would be cured of their illnesses. Today's qigong practitioners say that the qi they project into their patients bolsters the immune system in a way that no other medical treatment can yet duplicate. They cloak their treatment in a pseudoscientific air, wearing white lab coats and seeing their patients in modern clinics. People are hoping that qigong will be the new wonder treatment. What is not understood is that qigong is a vast body of traditional knowledge quite different from what has come to be marketed as qigong in today's world.

This clash between the authority of the old tradition and the assertions of modern, science-based approaches is a microcosm of the greater struggle of all the Scholar Warrior traditions to survive in the contemporary world. The old ways are cloaked in secrecy, held tightly by a few, and place an enormous emphasis on ethics and high standards. Healing is not seen as a profession or a job but an extension of the total person. Learning how to heal is not just mastering techniques but cultivating every part of the personality. Skill, for the traditionalist, cannot be divorced from the person practicing it. Creating a person who can heal as an extension of the total self demands a lengthy apprenticeship system that both imparts knowledge and constantly tests the ethical and perceptual components of the student's character. There aren't many willing masters, or many willing students, for this arduous process today.

The qigong of today came in the aftermath of China's 1949 revolution. Determined to use the best of the past, the government gathered all known qigong masters and demanded that they divulge their secrets. Those who resisted were either forced to comply or were killed. The masters were required to show all that they knew for researchers to analyze. The information was then edited. Supposedly "superstitious" and "nonscientific" practices were eliminated; practices were simplified; and different sets of movements were combined. A careful reading of the literature will disclose frequent references to simplification, combined forms, modern forms, and revised forms. It is not difficult to see that the old masters, resentful of their treatment by the government, did not reveal everything, or even taught techniques that would cause dangerous side effects. Much of today's "scientific qigong" is a product of this sad legacy. In the new scientific qigong that is coming to the fore, practitioners are not particularly well trained, have not had long years of ethical testing, and have not been closely supervised. Above all, it is quite possible that they do not have a strong enough foundation in their chosen field. Who can be sure that the heart of qigong was not thrown out in their scientific analysis?

THE TRUE RANGE OF QIGONG

When practiced for a long period and with great dedication and discipline, qigong can reach spiritual levels. When one practices the proper proce-

刑意拳 八卦掌

太極拳 六合八法拳

XING YI, BA GUA,
TAI CHI (TAI JI),
LIU HE BA FA

查拳

CHA QUAN

dures, the meridians are kept constantly open, the body is maintained in balance, and the mind is supplied with a steady amount of energy. One's whole personality becomes a sensitive instrument, and the qigong practitioners believe that a person who is more sensitive will naturally be drawn to higher levels of existence.

But attaining either a strong constitution or spiritual insight through qigong involves more than casual contact with it. It requires daily training, a diverse program, and mastery in ten almost distinct art forms: martial arts, weapons or implements practice, calisthenic movements, concentration exercises, visualization, use of sounds, meditation, use of colors and mandalas, use of stones, and use of weather and location.

Martial arts. Martial arts in China consists of very demanding athletic training in gymnastics along with stretching, acrobatics, and strength training. The fighting aspects are reduced almost to a by-product of overall physical and mental excellence. In qigong, people use basic martial arts training as a foundation for their own practices. Among the exercises qigong has incorporated are push-ups, rope climbing, weight lifting—all to build endurance, stamina, and muscular strength. There is an enormous range to choose from. There are hundreds of styles, from the very easy to the extremely demanding, and there are styles suitable for everyone. The range of Chinese martial arts can be divided into two classifications. One, the internal school, includes predominantly Taoist-inspired styles. Among these are *xingyi, bagua,* tai chi, *liuhebafa,* and so on. The other is the external school, which emphasizes a more physical, athletic approach to movement. This group is divided according to religious affiliation. Shaolin is Buddhist, *Chaquan* is Islamic, and Wudang is Taoist. All these classifications are merely for the sake of description, of course; no style is better than the others. All that matters is whether it is suitable to the practitioner.

It is from this broad spectrum that the qigong masters take fist sets, a choreographed series of movements of a mock fight, and use them to increase the student's grace, coordination, and concentration. The student shadowboxes by reenacting a battle. Some of these sets are a mere dozen moves long; some take as long as fifteen minutes to perform in their entirety. Tai chi is an example of a fist set, but the majority of sets are done at

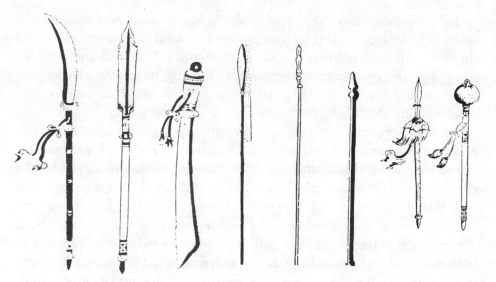

fighting speed and with an exertion of strength comparable to that of an actual fight. Many of the postures involve low stances, vigorous jumping, high, spinning kicks, rolling on the floor, and acrobatics. It is easy to see how a solid training in martial arts could lay a firm groundwork for any athletic endeavor.

Weapons. Just as martial arts is not primarily concerned with actual fighting, neither is weapons practice focused solely on their use as killing tools. Weapons are manipulated in sets—a commonly seen example is tai chi sword—and the attention is mainly on the effects that such exercise has on the body. A weapon teaches you to extend the qi outside yourself. If you are using a staff, for example, you need to take into account angle, leverage, extension, balance, and so on. Each time you thrust the weapon outward, your qi will naturally flow forth as well. Each time you bring it back toward you, the qi will contract. Since a weapons set of fifteen minutes or so involves a tremendous amount of back and forth movement, as well as a great variety of twisting movements, qi flows vigorously and will permeate every part of your body.

There are over 108 different weapons in the conventional Chinese arsenal, each of which yields some unique health benefit. Use of the staff, for example, shapes and balances the muscles on both sides of the body, and the twisting movements help to define the muscles and massage the lungs. The straight sword teaches pinpoint accuracy, concentration, and the control necessary for very small movements. All the twisting involved stimulates the qi (which is regarded as flowing in spirals). Using two weapons, like maces, is usually to develop the body bilaterally, almost like manipulating dumbbells or Indian clubs. In some schools, instruments other than weapons are used, for example, the famous tai chi ruler (a twelve-inch length of wood with knobs carved at each end and held between the palms) that is often used for recovery from illness, and the tai chi sphere, which stimulates the meridians of the body as the practitioner rolls it back and forth on a table with different parts of the hands and arm.

Also popular are *baoding* balls, two spheres of metal or stone about 1.5 inches in diameter that one rolls around one's palms. Use of baoding balls is considered especially good for lowering blood pressure and soothing the nerves. Whether weapon or instrument, the use of certain tools further extends the development of qi.

Calisthenics. Only after practitioners reach proficiency in martial arts and weaponry do they go on to the calisthenic practice of qigong, sets of movements dedicated not to mimicking battle but to stimulating the flow of qi directly. Although these sets might sometimes be based on the movements of animals, most of them were constructed to directly guide the qi through the body. Qi conforms to the postures of the body, and so both movement and static postures are valuable.

In this book, three examples of this type of calisthenic qigong are given: the Marrow Washing exercise, Northern Star qigong, and *daoyin*. Each of the postures has specific purposes related to guiding the qi into certain meridians and specific organs.

By moving the arms and limbs, the meridians are stimulated, and energy is made to flow through them into the very core of the body. The organs and the circulatory, lymphatic, nervous, and skeletal systems are especially emphasized; and in this way seemingly simple movements with the body stimulate the internal life systems.

Concentration. The transition to more meditative forms of qigong is made through the practice of concentration. In these methods, the student concentrates on certain points in the body, or specific pathways. These types of concentration sometimes accompany movements and sometimes are done while standing or sitting still. Examples may be found in the daoyin exercises in Chapter 9.

It is in the practice of concentration that one begins to work more fully with the interface between qi and shen. According to ancient classics, "Where the mind leads, the qi will follow." Even for a novice, there must be a melding of the mental with the physical aspects of breathing. Whether it is the simple procedure of holding one's breath while thinking of a certain part of the body, or mentally tracing entire meridians, concentration opens the gateway to the more profound aspects of qigong.

Visualization. From concentration, the next step is visualization of spheres of light, colors, or sometimes the figures of gods or flowers or patterns within one's body. These heighten the effect of concentration on specific body points. Such concentration is known not only in Taoism, but in kundalini yoga, Tibetan tantric practices, and in other sects of Buddhism as well. When coupled with controlled breathing, prolonged concentration on these points through visualization is said to cause a variety of unusual effects in the body. A qigong example of this practice is the set known as the Six Sounds, in which the chanting of each sound is followed by a visualization of a specific color around a particular organ. The effect is a stimulation of blood and qi circulation to the organ, as well as greater mental awareness of that part of the body.

Use of sounds. Controlling the rhythm, volume, and frequency of breathing is inherent in all qigong, and one of the ways to do this is through the repetition of sounds coupled with listening and feeling in the body the resultant vibration. This is not mere hypnotic chanting or prayer. It is stimulation through harmonics, the controlling of breath, and the soothing of the mind through listening to the sound. Examples of this are the Six Sounds qigong and the meditative repetition of mantras prevalent in nearly all Asian health and religious practices.

Meditation. Meditation is the combination of breath control, concentration, visualization, and use of sounds. There are four types of meditation used in qigong: standing, moving, sitting, and lying. In the first case, the practitioner stands unmovingly, with the hands in a specific posture and the legs usually slightly bent to facilitate the flow of qi into the interior of the body. The duration ranges from one to twenty minutes, with some practitioners going beyond that. It is believed that the qi will conform to the posture, and flow automatically into the proper channels. Examples of this can be found in Northern Star qigong and daoyin.

In moving meditation, one stimulates the qi by walking from posture to posture. Here we see the Taoist premise that because all things in the universe move, and because all things in the body move, so too should qigong make qi move as well. Naturally, movement stimulates the circulatory system, provides resistance for training the limbs, and massages the internal organs through twisting and stretching. Examples can be found in the second half of the Marrow Washing exercise.

The third type of meditation, sitting, is used when the main aim is to cause the qi to flow upward in the body. The practitioner locks off the legs by sitting cross-legged and usually concentrates on different parts of the torso or head. Examples may be found in the chapters on daoyin and meditation.

The fourth type of meditation is done while lying down. This is normally used by people in weak condition or those recovering from illness. Many of the visualizations are similar to those used in other forms of qigong. There is even a little-known form of "sleeping qigong," in which the practitioner tries to prolong his or her life by sleeping for days and days at a time.

Use of colors and mandalas. Whatever the form of meditation, some schools enhance its effect by having the student gaze at certain colors (green, for example, to calm the mind) or even patterns of colors, such as those used in mandalas. Persons using such patterns will often use prescribed breathing as their gaze pauses upon a particular spot.

A procedure like this is often used to empty the mind of extraneous thoughts. Beginning at the outer edge of a mandala, one gradually directs one's gaze around the perimeter and slowly toward the center. Different colors will have different effects upon the psyche, and each part of the mandala will symbolize some insight or even an entire lesson for the student to absorb. When one finally reaches the center of the mandala, meditation should have attained a transcendental level, and one is propelled into extraordinary altered states of consciousness.

Use of stones. Holding gemstones and crystals is another way to supplement meditative practices. These stones are not regarded as imparting anything to the body. Instead, they focus, amplify, or suppress certain types of energy. Qigong practitioners approach stones like crystal, diamond, coral, jade, lapis lazuli, aquamarine, ruby, turquoise, and others with great care. The effects of each stone are known and are taught to the student as part of an oral tradition. There is no such thing as picking a stone arbitrarily, or simply because one likes it. Stones are specific instruments and are used to produce known effects.

In practice, the stone may be held in the hand during meditation, held against specific points on the body, or worn constantly as an amulet, ring, or bracelet. Though this may all seem silly in today's scientific world, qigong practitioners assert that these practices work, and they note all the ways in which stones have been used since ancient times. They say that the jewels in breastplates, scepters, and crowns and in alchemists' laboratories are not there merely as decoration or symbols of wealth but because they impart certain powers to the user.

Weather and location. Finding the proper place to practice qigong is also considered essential. Recovering patients will sometimes be advised to move to a different location until they are well. A tuberculosis patient may move to a warm, dry climate, for example. Qigong practitioners may go to the high mountains to practice certain procedures. There, where the air is both thinner and cleaner, the student will be able to drive the qi deeper into the tissues of the body. Breathing is slower and deeper, and a feeling of elation is common.

The Taoist art of geomancy, or *feng shui*, is strongly related to qigong. Although it has degenerated to a level of folk superstition for most people, geomancy in its purer forms is extensively used by qigong practitioners. Just as the body has meridians and points where energy is strong, qigong practitioners declare that there are similar pathways and points in the earth. Just as the body breathes, there is a breath of the earth, which they call the dragon's breath, or the divine qi. By aligning themselves with these spots on the earth, or by traveling to where they feel the air is vital and pure, qigong practitioners enhance the quality of qi that they take into their own bodies. It is not hard to imagine that it is better to breathe clear

FENG SHUI
The Taoist art of geomancy, literally, wind and water. Masters of this art are concerned with following and channeling the qi of the earth. Rural geomancers are primarily concerned with the formations of mountains and watercourses and help establish or improve farms as well as wander and live in the mountains, following the qi as it moves. Urban geomancers select propitious sites for businesses, homes, and graves. They will tell you how to decorate, what position your building should face, and how to arrange the furniture.

SHEN QI
Divine qi.

air in a tranquil location with scenery that inspires you than it is to be stuck in some polluted and cramped inner city. Locale is an essential part of qigong.

The art of feng shui is an entire study in and of itself and involves complex theories of magnetic lines, geography, water courses both above and below ground, meteorology, and astronomy. Students will usually be apprenticed to a master and will follow the master on long trips to study the effects of landforms, climate, and constellations. They will note how people living in certain places fare and will study how their own qigong practice varies from locale to locale. Sometimes, they will find very odd places to practice, like a sea cave or atop a tree. All that matters to them is to feel the flow of both the earth's qi and their own qi with the utmost power. As in all other forms of the Scholar Warrior's path, students endeavor to reach a level where knowledge of feng shui is deeply intuitive. At that time, they will come and go, "chasing the Tao," and will know precisely what to do to have location meld perfectly with their own qi.

In summation, the true practice of qigong goes far beyond a few routines of inhalation and exhalation, and the application of qigong is not limited to treating patients in a clinic. It is a deeply profound art. It is unfortunate that today's qigong has degenerated to such a shallow level, and that it has had the heart stripped out of it by bureaucrats, ideologues, and charlatans. But if you would learn qigong, learn the full range of qigong. Do not mistake superstition for tradition. Find the forms of qigong that the master can prove to you to be efficacious and, more importantly, that you can prove to yourself to be worthy of practice. Only then will you be able to follow the flow of breath into the very Tao itself.

CULTIVATING THE MIND

Although Scholar Warriors place ultimate importance upon the mind, they approach it gradually when training beginners. A young student has much to experience, and youth must be allowed certain follies and times for experimentation. Direct interference only leads to resistance and rebellion. The masters exert their influence subtly through diet, exercise, and

BAO SHEN
Cultivating or protecting the spirit.

simple example. Initially, they teach a mental hygiene of ethics that parallels physical hygiene. Ethics provide provisional guidelines until deeper philosophical understanding and experience emerge.

"The ends justify the means" is a common saying, although it is often used ironically. For our archetypal warriors, value lay solely in the fulfillment of an assigned quest, and so one might assume that they had no ethics. But that wasn't the case. The Scholar Warriors believed in chivalry and justice. Today, we may have our own quests—in our careers, our learning, our spiritual life. But we will not achieve our goals unless we uphold our ethical values.

Compassion without possessiveness is the heart of ethics. Compassion signals the consideration of others before yourself. Only with a wisdom to see into the future and a willingness to calculate the outcome of a particular action is compassion possible. When you can arrange to maximize the benefits for all concerned and minimize any negative ramifications, then you will be acting according to Taoist ethics.

An act of compassion is often an act that restores balance. Taoists conceive of the universe as being in constant flux, and there are times when human beings or nature become out of balance. The compassionate person tries to resolve problems by rebalancing. Sometimes the action required is gentle. Sometimes it must be violent. Those who are skillful at doing the right thing at the right time and in the right proportion are said to be superior among people: their actions are flawless and seamless.

To accept the importance of balance is to acknowledge consequences. Retribution follows wrongdoing. This does not happen because there is some karmic police agency ready to mete out punishment for the slightest infraction. Nor will gods and devils pursue you for all your misdeeds. There is retribution because when you do bad things, you create misery that remains attached to you in some way or another. Perhaps someone will come back to take out their resentment on you, or perhaps you will make some future mistake because of your shortsighted behavior. Selfishness isolates you from others because you cease to care about even simple communication. Gradually your thinking will change, to the point that you cannot even conceive of what you are doing wrong, and so you will fall by your own folly. No one—except your own mind—is recording

REN DAO
Compassion, humanism. *Ren* is the word for person. The words together imply that compassion is the very way to be human.

anything. But that is devastating enough. "Divine justice" is the web of flaws that we wrap our lives in. There is no heaven, and there is no hell. There doesn't need to be. Our hubris is the quintessential form of retribution. We create our own suffering.

The qualifier "without possessiveness" is very important. Compassionate action is fine, but too often people think too highly of themselves for their charitable acts. They try to take credit. They do good deeds because they think that earns them merit in heaven. At other times, we may do good deeds to try to bind the recipient of our good intentions to ourselves. Perhaps it is a mother who tries to increase the ties with her child. Perhaps it is a master who wishes to maintain the loyalty of a student. Maybe it is a younger person who flatters an older one in hope of advantage, or a lover who wants to seem more attractive. These are all selfish actions. Do good things, but don't think about reward or have ulterior motives. Then compassion is a great thing. If you are going to do good things, do them without thinking that you should receive any significant reward.

There is nothing in the Taoist attitude toward compassion that encourages self-sacrifice or martyrdom. Selflessness doesn't mean the negation of your own value as a human being. Everyone is on the path as an individual. It is wonderful to help, but it isn't necessary to destroy your own path for the sake of another. All too often, good people forget to be compassionate toward themselves. A Taoist does not exploit others, and does not suffer him- or herself to be exploited.

There is little to waste in life. Our own lives get shorter every day. Our energy is finite. The earth's natural resources are limited, our perceptions even more so. In this world, ugliness predominates all too often, and beauty is ephemeral and fragile. Try to make conservation of all things part of your priorities. Respect life. That doesn't mean you will never kill, for killing in some form or another is inevitable. But don't engage in wanton killing, or killing for pleasure, or killing that pleases some deep, unnameable lust.

A sense of ethics helps to turn one away from base instincts toward the spiritual. Certainly, the world is a better place for compassionate behavior, and most assuredly, we are all happier when we follow some form of ethical behavior. It takes a strong person to be ethical, for ethics are standards that you may decide to follow even where others do not agree. Unless you are completely in control of your life and have a great deal of discipline, you cannot be ethical. You'll be mowed down along with all your sentimental little do's and don'ts.

CULTIVATING THE INTELLECT

Higher education is a boon for most people. Anyone who has some intellectual ability, nurtured perhaps from childhood curiosity by a caring adult, can benefit from the broader perspective learning brings. In fact, there are few people one meets who haven't learned some subjects well. Even so-called dumb people are interested in some body of knowledge, whether it be the ball scores of their favorite teams, or how to play cards well. For the levels of intellectual accomplishment that the Scholar Warrior demands, however, it is clear that a wide variety of subjects should be mastered. The arts, sciences, history, literature, and applied technology are all necessary components. One should understand chemistry, physics, astronomy, geology, and biology—especially one's own body—and have proficiency in at least art and music. Obviously, you have to go to school for these things. If you're in school, stay until you've learned what you want and need to know. If you have already left school, but sense that your education is incomplete, then continuing education is a wonderful resource. Although a great deal can be learned from books and experimentation, the fastest and most reliable method is still to study with teachers. There is always something intangible that a teacher communicates—maybe it's only the confidence of having someone tell you something, or maybe it's only that you're able to ask the questions that most concern you, but the experience of learning person to person is really the best.

Any one intellectual discipline is infinite within its own particular parameters. Any single subject has become something no one individual can grasp in its entirety because it has been formed by generations of thinkers. But that only increases the rich field of knowledge for us to cultivate, and it allows us to find our own special areas of interest. Learning makes life vital, stimulating. With knowledge and the cultivation of intellectual abilities, you need not be buffeted by great forces or victimized by the limits of your own minuscule pool of thoughts. You can think through your problems and realize your aspirations.

The diversity of knowledge teaches the learning of learning. Through the constant acquisition of knowledge and the mental exercise of learning, one can master the skills of investigation, exploration, experimentation, and application. Throughout life, one's questions will never cease; new frontiers and mental challenges will arise; and one needs to be able to apply the utmost in one's intellect to conquer them.

The crux of the matter is that you should minimize your limitations. If you don't understand why a war is going on in a particular land, or if you don't comprehend the socioeconomic forces that define society, or if you fail to see the likely outcomes of governmental policy, you will gradually be hampered more and more by your lack of understanding. If you can neither read nor write well, nor add and subtract, if you cannot even grasp how your own health is meaningful, you are quite limited. It is important to gain freedom of thought by knowing these things. Knowledge need not be acquired merely for furtherance of career, or for prestige, or to become a pompous know-it-all. Knowledge dispels the basic ignorance that is so rampant today.

Yet it is important to take scholarliness a step further toward creativity. Even learning a myriad of subjects, even developing the skill to learn more, will amount to mere accumulation of facts. We are not receptacles or machines to be programmed. We must interact with knowledge. One of the greatest limitations of Chinese scholarship was its lopsided insistence on pure memorization and its exclusive veneration of past classics. Creativity was not always emphasized. Although memorization and respect for the great achievements of the past are fundamental, scholarly pursuits shouldn't lead to dead thought. Composing words or music, drawing, designing, experimenting, rearranging patterns—if only your furniture or surroundings—are wonderful ways to express our creativity.

Establishing ethics builds character. Academic involvement builds intelligence. With these two assets, the third treasure, shen, is safeguarded.

Once the mind is disciplined, it becomes like a skillful general who can command the troops of jing and qi. In this chapter, we have tried to define the basic areas that a beginning student in Taoism must cultivate. Jing can be preserved by sexual conservation and augmented by diet. Qi is cultivated by assiduous cleanliness on all levels of life and by circulating the qi. When all three levels are brought into harmony and are made secure, one can truly be said to have the Three Treasures. In the remaining chapters of this section, we will examine actual methods for achieving these goals.

洗髓經

3

Stretching,
And the heat of exercise,
Temper the steel of your body.

THE MARROW
WASHING CLASSIC

A COMPLETE APPROACH TO
STRETCHING AND EXERCISE

AN IMPORTANT FIRST STEP in self-cultivation is exercise. Nearly everyone stretches. It feels good. If we have been sitting a long time, it is natural to stand up, raise our arms over our heads, and reach very high. We may also stand on tiptoe, or we might twist slightly to the left and right. When we go to the beach or to the mountains and get that first breath of clean, fresh air, we may throw our arms out to our sides and tilt our heads upward—all instinctive ways to straighten the throat, stretch the arms and chest, and expand the rib cage to take in more air. If we think about it, we do many stretches during the day, and this natural movement is what the Taoists seek to exploit.

56

However, we all have habitual movements as well. We like to do certain kinds of things with our bodies, no matter how hilarious or eccentric. We may avoid certain movements too, because of habit, laziness, structural imbalances in our bodies (such as skeletal defects or unbalanced muscle development), or simple ignorance of proper exercise. The Scholar Warrior learns basic stretches and exercises to compensate for these problems. Initially some of the techniques may seem quite odd or foreign, but this is because they are taking you beyond habitual movement.

An exercise like the Marrow Washing Classic is a comprehensive system of stretching and breathing for the entire body. It involves all the muscles, tendons, and skeletal joints and also addresses the organs and the breath. (Remember how you bend over when you've got a stomachache? Body posture affects the organs. We also bend over when winded or throw our arms back to take in more air.) Marrow Washing provides all these basic movements and therefore is an excellent way to maintain flexibility, relaxation, vitality, and immunity to disease. Stretching will help your joints and your muscles and will physically stimulate the meridians along which qi flows. Twisting movements will stimulate your metabolism and the production of jing. Breathing movements will increase the flow of qi. Exercising will restore balance in your psychological health as well.

We have all experienced the muscle aches that signal the approach of illness. We have all felt the muscular tension in the head, shoulders, back, and stomach that accompanies stress, fatigue, and trauma. By exercising every day, we can not only counter these symptoms but take a progressive approach to health improvement as well.

According to legend, the Marrow Washing Classic was passed down by the Twenty-eighth Zen Patriarch, Bodhidharma. It is important to note that there is a bewildering array of sets called Marrow Washing Classic. Some are meditative, some are even more vigorous, and some are advertised under totally different names. Given the secrecy of masters in the past, the tendency to change sets or give them names of famous exercises in order to bolster their acceptibility, and the geographical isolation of different parts of China, it is not surprising that we are still saddled with this confusion. There is no way to say that this set is the "original" set, only that it is a good group of effective exercise, and a variant of this set has

XI SUI JING
Marrow Washing Classic. *Xisui* means to wash the marrow, or to change the body fundamentally. *Jing* is the word for a classic or scripture. The word symbolizes the warp of silk weaving and signifies dealing with the very fabric of things.

recently been popularized in China by a master named Chang Weizhen.

We know from writings that the original set had only eighteen simple movements. This current set has twenty-four, so it is clear that other masters have added exercises that they considered necessary supplements to the original eighteen. Though we are unable to determine which were the original movements, this set is still very useful for doing what Bodhidharma intended: purifying and building the body.

Each exercise is given here with sketches and instructions. Because learning exercises from a book may be daunting at first, it is helpful to have a friend read the instructions out loud. When examining the drawings, it is helpful to hold the book upside down; you can avoid confusion between left and right in this way. Note that the arrows show the movements that lead to the position shown.

It is important to pay special attention to breathing. Note that breathing is always coordinated with movement, and that it has differing durations. Inhalations should be through the nose, exhalations should be through the mouth.

BEGINNING MOVEMENT

預
備
式

1. Begin with your feet together, hands at your sides. Let your mind become calm.

2. Take a wide step to the side, so that your feet are farther apart than the width of your shoulders.

3. Raise both arms over your head as you inhale deeply.

4. Bring them sharply down, slapping the backs of your palms on your thighs as you exhale forcefully and drop swiftly into a squat. Your back should remain straight; eyes look forward.

5. Raise your hands, palms up, to waist height, keeping forearms parallel, and inhale deeply.

6. Thrust your palms out sharply to the front, straightening your elbows, and exhale forcefully.

7. Inhale in this position.

8. Push palms backward slowly as you exhale steadily. Imagine that you are pushing against a heavy object. Only your arms should move.

9. Stop when your arms will go no further. Your exhalation should end at the same time. Pause in this position to inhale deeply.

10. Bring your arms back to your sides as you exhale. Your wrists should be bent as if you are trying to point inward with your palms. Your exhalation should end at the same time. Pause in this position, then inhale deeply.

11. Bring your palms in front of you and push upward and outward as if lifting a very heavy object. Push until your elbows are straight. Keeping palms up, rotate hands so that your fingers point backward. You should exhale for the duration of this lifting, and the lift should be at a medium speed (about five seconds to reach the top of your push).

12. Pause in this position briefly, and inhale deeply. Note that your legs are still in their squatting position.

13. Exhale, and place your hands in front of you as if you are "holding a ball," that is, elbows bent, fingers pointing in opposite directions, one hand above the other, palm down, the lower hand palm up.

CARESSING THE BALL IN HORSE STANCE

梨馬滾球

1. From the "holding the ball" position, left hand on top, take a half step (about the length of your foot) wider with your left leg into a deeper squat.

2. Gradually shift your weight to the left, and twist your waist so that your torso turns to the left as well. Note that your right leg will stretch straight and that the quadriceps will roll forward.

3. At the apex of your shift, steadily turn your hands over, so that your right hand is now shifting toward the top. All the time, imagine that your hands are on a ball, so they must remain equidistant. Shift back to the center.

4. Gradually shift to the right and twist your waist so that your torso turns to the right as well. Reverse the position of your hands as you did in

step 3. Note that your left leg will stretch straight and that the quadriceps will roll forward.

5. Your breathing pattern should be as follows: inhale when you are passing to the center, exhale as you shift to either side. If you know tai chi you will recognize this exercise as a derivative of Cloud Hands.

6. Do four repetitions on each side.

7. To end, inhale deeply, raise both hands out to the sides, palms up, and then over your head, palms down, fingers inward. Lower your hands as if pressing something down in front of you and exhale. Your fingertips remain facing one another. Your exhalation should last until your hands press all the way down and your elbows straighten briefly.

FISHERMAN ROWING THE BOAT

漁翁搖船

1. Take a big step to the side and repeat the opening sequence of posture 1 (Beginning Movement), steps 1 through 4.

2. Inhale, and lift your hands in front of you, elbows bent and palms up. It is important that you expand your rib cage to the maximum (but do not lift your shoulders). Lift your diaphragm, and your floating ribs should lift up and protrude outward. Throw your shoulders back, as if you could make your shoulder blades touch. This lift and inhale should take about two seconds.

3. Turn your torso to the left, and immediately push your left hand outward in front of your torso, palm out, while your right arm straightens at your side. Your right hand should form a hook shape with all the fingers and thumb touching and palm facing back. Your exhalation should last for the duration of the push, about two seconds. Push steadily. Note that your legs are in a "bow stance"; the left leg is bent as if still squatting, while the right leg straightens and stretches.

4. Shift back to the center; bring your hands together; and repeat step 2. This time, push to the right. Alternate sides until you have performed four on each side.

5. To end, repeat step 7 of exercise 2 (Caressing the Ball in Horse Stance).

FISHERMAN ROWING THE BOAT, WRIST TWIST

1. This exercise is similar to the previous posture in this set, with the addition of a wrist twist to stimulate and build your forearms.

2. Take a big step to the side, and repeat the opening sequence of posture 1, steps 1 through 4.

3. Cross your fists in front of your body. Begin with your left arm over your right. Inhale.

4. Roll your arms inward and then turn your torso to the left and immediately push your left hand straight out while your right hand straightens. Your right hand forms a hook shape with all the fingers and thumb touching. Your exhalation should last for the duration of the push, about two seconds. Push steadily. Note that your legs are in a "bow stance"; the left leg is bent as if still squatting while the right leg straightens and stretches.

5. Shift back to the center; bring your hands together; and repeat step 3. This time, your right hand must be on the outside, and you push to the right. Alternate sides until you have performed four on each side.

6. To end, repeat step 7 of exercise 2.

CLOUD HANDS

1. Take a big step to the side, and repeat the opening sequence of posture 1, steps 1 through 4.

2. Inhale and raise your hands up as if holding a ball, the fingers of both hands pointing forward. Your left hand should be above your right. Now exhale in this position.

3. Inhale and twist to your left, keeping your arms horizontal.

4. Make two big circles with your arms, twisting your waist to follow the movement of your arms. When your arms dip below horizontal, lean forward and exhale. When they circle above the horizontal, lean back and inhale. The circles should be smooth, constant stretches.

5. As you come out of the second circle, twist to the right, continuing your exhalation. Pause for a moment to stretch.

6. Twist to the left and inhale.

7. Twist to the right, and exhale into the stretch. Try to touch your head to your right knee and stretch your right arm upward. Your palm should be turned forward, and your elbow must be straight. Try to make your arm perpendicular. Your left hand holds your waist on your right side.

8. Hold this position for about five seconds. Then relax, inhale, and carefully straighten up from your bent over position. Inhale and raise your hands up as if holding a ball, the fingers of both hands pointing forward. This time, your right hand should be on top and you should twist to the right in order to do the sequence in its mirror image.

9. Do four repetitions on each side. You should do this stretch cautiously if you have lower back problems, although the stretch should ultimately help your condition.

10. To end, repeat step 7 of exercise 2.

HIT THE TREE IN HORSE STANCE

1. Take a big step to the side, and repeat the opening sequence of posture 1, steps 1 through 4.

2. Inhale, and raise your hands up as if holding a ball, the fingers of both hands pointing forward. Now exhale in this position.

3. Without changing the position of your body, vigorously thrust out each hand alternately, palm down. Note that the hand not thrusting pulls back to your waist and twists palm up. When you thrust your hand out, it twists quickly palm down.

4. Think only of exhaling with each thrust, and let your lungs inhale lightly and spontaneously between the rapid thrusts. Perform nine thrusts on each side.

5. To end, repeat step 7 of exercise 2.

SQUATTING AND LIFTING

曲膝蹲馬

1. Begin by simply standing straight with your feet facing heel to heel, toes apart.

2. Inhale, and raise your hands to the sides and over your head. Your inhalation should last until your hands are overhead, about four seconds.

3. When your hands reach the highest points and are coming together, place them back to back fingers pointing downward.

4. Begin to exhale, lower your hands, and squat. Your exhalation should last for the duration of your squat, about five seconds.

5. Bring your hands out to the sides and close them into fists as if holding two heavy buckets. Your thumbs should be inside your fists. Do not breathe as you move your hands to this position. This should take about one second.

6. Stand up steadily and inhale, about five seconds. At the apex of your inhalation, lift your diaphragm, and inflate your chest to the maximum.

7. Then exhale, like a sigh; drop your diaphragm; and let your hands open at the same time. Your palms should push slightly forward.

8. Repeat four times.

9. To end, repeat step 7 of exercise 2.

DOG WAGGING TAIL

1. Stand upright, with your heels touching.

2. Raise your hands overhead as you inhale. Palms should face inward.

3. Close your hands into fists, the thumbs inside your fingers.

4. Exhale and push down to your feet. Keep your knees and back straight. First push to one foot, then the other, then push to touch the ground. Each push should be done with an exhale, and there are no inhalations in between these three exhalations. Always keep your face lifted and look straight ahead so that blood will not rush into your head.

5. Resting your fists on your shins, inhale and then twist to the left, with an exhale. Return to the center. Inhale. Then exhale as you twist to the right.

6. Slowly inhale as you stand up and repeat from step 2. Do four repetitions.

7. To end, repeat step 7 of exercise 2.

SCHOLAR OPENING THE SCROLL

1. Stand upright, with your heels touching.

2. Inhale and raise your arms up in front of you, hands touching. Your hands are in fists with the thumb on the inside.

3. Turn to your left side, and push your left fist upward while you push your right fist downward. Exhale for the duration of this stretch, about four seconds.

4. Turn back to your original direction, and repeat from step 2 by turning to the opposite side and doing the movements mirror-image.

5. Do four repetitions on each side.

6. To end, repeat step 7 of exercise 2.

文人開書卷

THE MARROW WASHING CLASSIC

SWIMMING SNAKE

1. Stand straight with your heels touching and your fists at your waist.

2. Inhale and bring your left hand up to head height, palm turned inward.

3. Twist your forearm so that the palm is outward, and exhale as you close it into a fist with the thumb on the inside.

4. Inhale and fully extend your arm above you.

5. Exhale as you open your hand and sweep it down and across the front of your body all the way to your right. Twist your waist to the right as well, and bend your knees slightly.

6. Inhale as your left hand returns to your left side and you bring your right arm out, palm inward. Your right hand sweeps past your knees and you twist all the way to the left. Your knees must still be slightly bent.

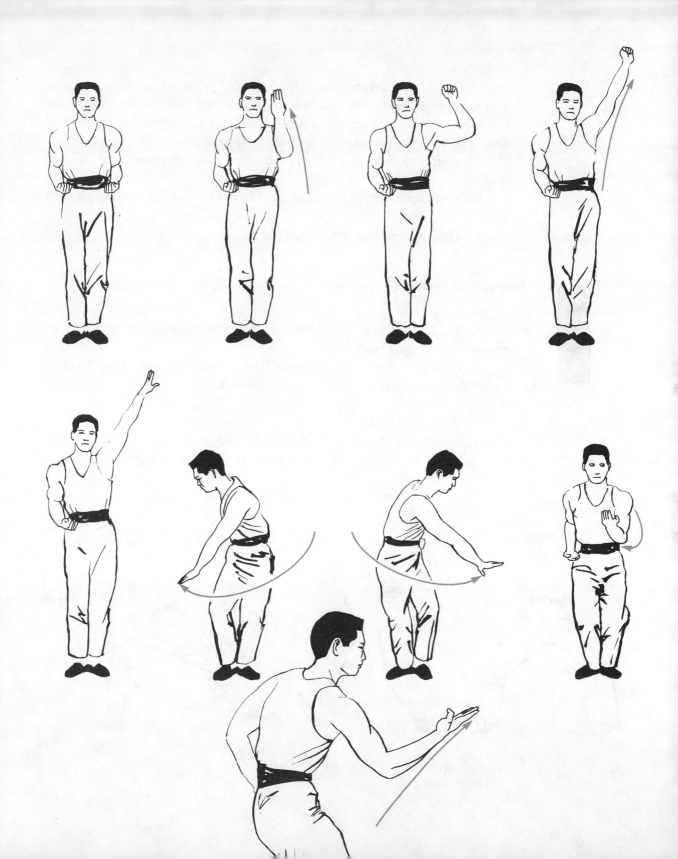

7. Exhale and thrust your left hand out, palm up, at the same time you bring your right hand swiftly back to your right side. Be sure that your left elbow is well in front of your body (about six inches), and that you pull it toward the center. If you do this properly, you will feel a contraction in your abdomen on your left side. This massages your liver, spleen, and intestines.

8. Stand up and repeat on the right side. Do four repetitions on each side.

9. To end, repeat step 7 of exercise 2.

THE BUTTERFLY

1. Take a big step to the side, and repeat the opening sequence of posture 1, steps 1 through 4.

2. Inhale, and pull your elbows back, palms up and at the level of your lower pectoral muscles. Inflate your chest and pull your shoulders back.

3. Turn to the left.

4. Step forward with your right foot, and extend your arms as if you are about to dive into a pool. The important point is to twist your elbows

to the sides, turning your palms back to back, and compress your chest while rounding your upper back to stimulate your lungs.

5. Inhale, and pull your palms back to their original position. Inflate your chest and pull your shoulders back. Turn to the opposite side, and repeat the sequence by stepping forward with your left foot.

6. Do four repetitions on each side.

7. To end, repeat step 7 of exercise 2.

CLUTCHING EAGLE

1. Take a big step to the side, and repeat the opening sequence of posture 1, steps 1 through 4.

2. Inhale, and raise your fists to your waist.

3. Exhale as you rapidly punch with your left hand to the side in a short strike.

4. Immediately strike all the way to the side, continuing the same exhale.

鷹爪橋手

5. Bring your fist back to your waist and inhale.

6. Exhale and thrust out to the front with your finger in the shape of an eagle's talons. Immediately extend your arm to the side and rapidly contract and release your fingers in rapid alternation. Do eight contractions, using your abdominal muscles to do rapid exhalations with each clawing motion.

7. Repeat on the opposite side. Do four repetitions on each side.

8. To end, repeat step 7 of exercise 2.

YOUNG LAD WORSHIPING BUDDHA

童子拜佛

1. Stand in place for this exercise, arms at your sides, heels touching.

2. Inhale as you raise your arms out to each side.

3. Exhale as you push outward with your palms by flexing your wrists. Pause for a moment in this position and inhale.

4. Exhale, and bring your fingertips together in front of you, back of hands together, elbows rolled upward, chest hollowed, shoulders rounded. Pause for a moment in this position and inhale.

5. Exhale and open your hands and bring them into a palms-up offering position. Elbows will straighten somewhat.

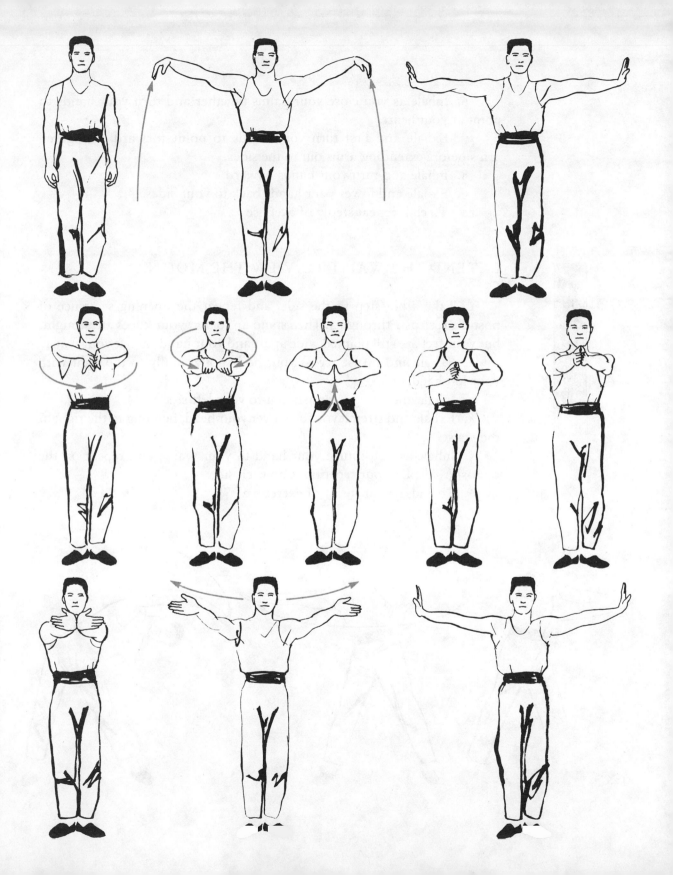

6. Inhale as you close your palms together and turn your hands to point at your heart.

7. Exhale and first turn your hands to point forward. Straighten arms before extending arms out to the sides.

8. Inhale and turn your hands upward.

9. Exhale and lower your hands back to your sides.

10. To end, repeat step 7 of exercise 2.

EXTEND THE WAIST TO VIEW THE MOON

伸腰望月

1. Take a big step to the side, and repeat the opening sequence of posture 1, steps 1 through 4. Then stand up so that your knees are straight, but your feet are still planted wide apart and your hands are at your waist.

2. Exhale and thrust across your body horizontally to the right with your left hand.

3. Inhale and bring your arm out to your left side.

4. Exhale and stretch your arm over your head, bending to the right at the waist.

5. Inhale as you return your hand to your waist, and repeat on the opposite side. Do four repetitions on each side.

6. To end, repeat step 7 of exercise 2.

SWALLOW RETURNING TO NEST

1. Take a big step to the side, and repeat the opening sequence of posture 1, steps 1 through 4.

2. Exhale and thrust across your body horizontally to the right with your left hand, bending your right leg.

3. Inhale and bring your arm out to your left side, bending your left leg.

4. Exhale and stretch your arm over your head, bending to the right at the waist, but then continue the circle by bringing your left hand down on your right side and down and back to your left hip.

THE MARROW WASHING CLASSIC

77

5. Immediately follow with a sweeping motion with your right arm as you inhale. Bring your right arm down across your body in a big circle up over your head until it too returns to your hip. Lean back slightly and hold this position for a moment.

6. To repeat, exhale, and thrust across your body horizontally with your right hand and repeat from step 2.

7. Do four repetitions on each side. If you do this properly, your two hands will look like two swallows circling each other as they return to their nest.

8. To end, repeat step 7 of exercise 2.

CAT LOOKING AT THE MOON

貓望月

1. This is a powerful stretch that will loosen your body in many ways. However, if you have knee or lower back problems, you should do this exercise cautiously. If there is any sign of pain, you should stop. As you become more limber, you should gradually add movements as your body permits.

2. Take a big step to the side and repeat the opening sequence of posture 1, steps 1 through 4.

3. Exhale, and thrust your left hand directly across your body and upward as your torso twists to the right.

4. Twist to the left as your hands form a cradling gesture. Pause for about four seconds and inhale deeply.

5. Slowly bend your right leg and lower your body down. Make sure that your left leg remains straight, both heels on the ground, and your back as straight and plumb erect as possible. Exhale constantly but slowly as your complete this partial squat in about four seconds.

6. Continue to exhale as you stretch your palms toward your straightened left knee. Hold this position for about another four seconds. Then inhale deeply without changing your position.

7. Glide forward and lay your body down on your left thigh. Both

your upper thigh and your torso must be horizontal. Hold this position for about four seconds.

8. Raise your body up without changing your stance and inhale.

9. Hold your right palm with your left, and exhale as you place your right elbow on your left knee. Twist as far as is comfortable, turning your head to look at your left elbow. Exhale slowly as you hold this pose for about four seconds.

10. Relax and slowly untwist. Repeat step 7 of exercise 2.

11. Begin again, this time thrusting upward with your right hand to reverse the procedure. Do four repetitions on each side.

From this point on in the set, the postures are performed in moving lines of repetition. Stand at one end of your exercise area and move toward the other side while performing these movements.

RAISING THE FLAG IN GOOSE STANCE

鴨子步抬旗

1. Stand at one end of your workout area. Inhale as you briefly cross your fists in front of your body.

2. Take a step forward with your left leg into a goose stance (front leg bent with the toe pointing outward, knee bent, rear leg straight). Twist to the left, and raise your left arm behind you and upward into the stretch. Exhale for the entire time it takes to raise your arm, about two seconds. Be sure to twist your fist so that you can only see the back of it as you twist your face to the left. Your right fist is touching your sternum.

3. To repeat on the other side, turn back to the front, and inhale as you cross your fists briefly and step forward with your right foot. Raise your right arm.

4. Repeat until you reach the other end of your training area.

5. To end, turn to face the center of the room, and repeat step 7 of exercise 2.

ELBOW PUSHING IN GOOSE STANCE

鴨子步搖肘

1. Stand at one end of your workout area. Place one palm over the other, both palms facing downward, and step into a goose stance with your left foot in front.

2. Leaning slightly forward, twist your waist fully to the left, pushing your elbow up as far as it will go. Do four quick twists, exhaling each time, and letting the inhalation come by itself.

3. To repeat on the other side, pull your fists to your waist and inhale as you step forward. Immediately put your palms together and twist to the right side.

4. Repeat until you reach the other end of your training area.

5. To end, turn to face the center of the room and repeat step 7 of exercise 2.

GENERAL TAKING OFF HIS BOOTS

將軍脫鞋

1. Stand at one end of your workout area with your left foot in front of your right, both knees straight.

2. Inhale, then exhale as you push palms down, fingertips facing, to the level of your left knee.

3. Pausing only a moment, exhale again as you push down to your foot.

4. Inhale as you rise up slightly and swing to push down to your right foot.

5. Inhale, step up with your right foot. Exhale while moving your arms out and in to an embracing position. Both palms must face down, and your left hand should be forward of your right hand. Compress your chest and round your shoulders, expelling all air from your lungs.

6. Inhale briefly but deeply, then twist your right foot outward to form a goose stance, and exhale as you twist to the right.

7. To repeat, untwist and repeat from step 2 by pushing down toward your right knee.

8. Repeat until you reach the other end of your training area.

9. To end, turn to face the center of the room, and repeat step 7 of exercise 2.

MONKEY LIFTS THE CAULDRON

Part One: Waist Bending

1. Stand at one end of your workout area. Your hands are clasped with the back of one hand in the palm of the other. One foot should be in front of the other. The rear foot should be slightly bent.

2. Exhale and slap forward with the backs of both hands.

3. Circle them inward toward you; inhale; and push outward with both palms.

4. Extend arms overhead, and stretch backward, keeping your head forward. Exhale for the duration of the stretch, about five seconds. Lift the heel of your forward foot to enhance your stretch.

5. Reverse your motion as you inhale and return to an upright position with your hands still clasped before you and step forward with your rear foot. Repeat from step 2 until you have moved the length of the room.

猴子托鼎

6. To end, turn to face the center of the room, and repeat step 7 of exercise 2.

Part Two: Jumping

1. Stand at one end of your workout area. Your hands are in fists, with the thumbs inside your fingers, and your hands are in front of your shoulders, elbows bent. Your feet are parallel and about shoulder width apart.

2. Stretch up onto the tips of your toes while you stretch your arms up over your head. Grasp the thumb of one hand in the fist of the other. Inhale for the duration of the stretch, about four seconds, and return to your starting position.

3. Without moving your hands, broad jump forward. When you are in midair, your heels should touch your buttocks. Inhale as you leap up; exhale as you land.

4. Repeat until you reach the other end of your training area.

5. To end, turn to face the center of the room, and repeat step 7 of exercise 2.

APE DESCENDING THE MOUNTAIN

大猿下山

    1. Stand at one end of your workout area with your feet apart and your arms hanging down, as apes do.

    2. Inhale, then exhale as you jump into a side stretch. Reach for your outstretched foot.

    3. To repeat, leap up onto the leg that was just stretched and stretch to the opposite side.

    4. Repeat until you reach the other end of your training area.

    5. To end, turn to face the center of the room, and repeat step 7 of exercise 2.

MONKEY KING WALKING ON CLOUDS

悟空行雲

1. Stand at one end of your workout area. Clasp your hands palm to palm in front of your waist. Your weight should rest predominantly on one foot, while the other is out to the front with just the toe touching the ground.

2. Inhale, and lift the knee of the forward leg.

3. Exhale, and bend at the waist, straightening the leg to the rear and arms to the front, parallel to the ground. Your arms, torso, and out-stretched leg should be on a horizontal line. Look forward, to keep your balance, and straighten and stretch every joint in your body.

4. Bring the outstretched leg back, and return your hands to their position in front of you. Take one step forward and repeat. You have the option of extending the same leg each time until you reach the other side of the room and then returning using the other, or alternating legs as you travel.

5. To end, turn to face the center of the room, and repeat step 7 of exercise 2.

CRANE STANDING ON ONE LEG

1. Stand at one end of your workout area.

2. Inhale, and pull one knee to your chest with your hands.

3. Holding your foot with the opposite hand, exhale and extend your leg straight forward. The other hand should be on your hip. Both legs must be straight, and your back should also be straight. Hold this position for a moment.

4. Inhale, and twist your head to look behind you.

5. Exhale as you turn your head back and lower your leg to take a step forward.

6. Repeat on the opposite side until you reach the other end of your training area.

7. To end, turn to face the center of the room, and repeat step 7 of exercise 2.

BREATH REGULATION

    1. Stand upright, heels touching. Make your hands into fists, thumbs inside the fingers. Place the backs of your hands against the small of your back.

    2. Inhale and rub upward over the erector spinae muscles as far as the base of the rib cage. Simultaneously rise onto the balls of your feet.

    3. Exhale, and rub back down to the top of your pelvis. Simultaneously lower your heels with a slight impact.

    4. Repeat nine times.

    5. To end, repeat step 7 of exercise 2.

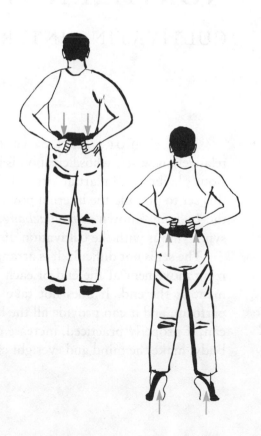

擦腰踏腳

89

天罡氣功

4

Breath is the gateway
Between body and mind.

NORTHERN STAR QIGONG

CULTIVATING INTERNAL ENERGY

董海川

DONG HAICHUAN
This martial artist re-
portedly learned his
bagua from two
Taoists.

NORTHERN STAR QIGONG, or Tiangang qigong, is a
relatively new set, whose creation is ascribed to Dong Haichuan, the notorious playboy and martial artist of the eighteenth century. He formulated
this set to provide the internal power for the martial arts style inspired by
the *I Ching*. Known as *baguazhang*, or Eight Trigrams Palm, this style is
synonymous with the cultivation of the internal energy and the qi.

The set is not difficult. It is arranged in twelve postures, with a neutral-
izing movement at the end of each posture and a final grounding movement at the end. It does not take more than about twenty minutes to
perform, and it can provide all the health benefits attributed to qigong. It
can, if properly practiced, increase circulation, stretch the muscles of the
body, make the mind and eyesight clearer, stimulate the appetite, increase

the overall health of the internal organs, build resistance to illness, help recovery from illness, and train the breath for higher applications.

According to qigong theories, qi will move either in response to body postures or at the direction of the mind alone. Those of us who wish to direct the qi need to use posture, or body form, to move it. When one exercises through stretching, muscle contraction, balance, and effort, qi will respond by moving along specific pathways and concentrating within different centers. The centers and pathways that are most predominantly affected by the Northern Star qigong are called the Three Dantians and the Eight Meridians. A brief discussion of these points and pathways will be helpful for understanding this set of qigong in particular, and all qigong in general.

BA GUA ZHANG
Eight Trigrams Palm.

THE THREE FIELDS OF CULTIVATION

Jing, qi, and shen, as mentioned in Chapter 2, each have a focal point called a dantian. *Dantian* literally means a field of cultivation. The word *dan* means pill or elixir, and is probably a reference to the days when Taoists still tried to formulate a pill for physical immortality. *Tian* is a field. Through this agrarian imagery, the Taoists indicate three points of concentration that will stimulate and build the Three Treasures. The three dantians are simply labeled lower, corresponding to jing; middle, corresponding to qi; and upper, corresponding to shen.

SAN DAN TIAN
Three fields of cultivation.

The lower dantian is in the middle core of the body at a level halfway between the top of the pubic bone and the navel. It is the center for physical strength and the health of our lower organs. Connected to the kidneys, the lower dantian is regarded as the source of power in the human body. Thus you will notice that many qigong postures begin with a mental focus on the lower dantian and end with a channeling of energy back to this point for storage.

The middle dantian is in the core of the body at the level of the solar plexus. The Taoists graphically represent transformation of jing to qi with pictures showing jing rising to the middle dantian, breath descending from the lungs, and the essence of food migrating laterally from the spleen to

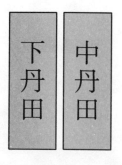

combine with the original qi (inherited genetically) in this field. One who has a great deal of physical vitality is said to possess great qi, and more specifically, *zhong* (central or middle) qi, meaning the qi from the middle dantian.

The upper dantian corresponds to the location of the pineal gland. If you can imagine a line through your head from points above each ear, and another horizontal line beginning at the point midway between your eyebrows and extending straight to the back of your head, you will find the upper dantian exactly where the two lines meet. The upper field of cultivation represents the center of mental and spiritual energy, and meditation upon this center enhances intellectual abilities and the full exploration of consciousness.

In the exercises that follow in this book (and in other systems of meditation, yoga, and movement), you will notice that these centers are brought into play. Sometimes one draws energy from them; sometimes one seeks to store energy in them; and at other times they function as transformers or junction points for the flow of energy. Our previous discussions of the Three Treasures have dealt only with how they might be safeguarded through proper conduct. But the Three Treasures each have tangible places for cultivation in the body and are definite fields of focus in all levels of Scholar Warrior training. In the practices that follow, emphasis on these centers will increase.

THE EIGHT MERIDIANS

THE THREE
DANTIANS

Although acupuncturists use a complex system of twelve major and eight extra meridians, the Taoists favor another system called the Eight Meridians. Qigong exercises stimulate this system of energy flow, and certain exercises may call for a mental tracing of these meridians in concert with inhalation and exhalation, so it is necessary to acquaint ourselves with this system. Reference will be made to these meridians in the course of detailing sets.

Reconciling the Eight Meridians with available documentation in Chinese and English is difficult. Quite frankly, accounts disagree on the location of all the meridians. As was the case with the Marrow Washing Classic, the discrepancies are undoubtedly the result of individual masters' research, experience, learning, sectarian beliefs, and geographical isolation. Those who wish to look into the literature will find that very few writings give a lucid explanation of how the meridians fit together or how they can be used for qigong. However, this should not deter the interested student; the diversity of descriptions, if all regarded as having some validity, should add to one's understanding.

The pathways given here are based on oral teachings, the writings of Northern Star Qigong and daoyin, as well as on personal experience.

These are the Eight Meridians with notes on how to find them:

1. Dumei: Beginning at the perineum and rising up the back along the center line of the body, this channel rises over the scalp and down the forehead, and ends at the upper palate of the mouth (just behind the teeth).

2. Renmei: From the tip of the tongue, this channel descends along the center line of the front of the body back to the perineum.

3. Chongmei: This channel rises vertically from the perineum to the top of the head. This meridian is heavily utilized in qigong and meditation; however, accounts of the exact location are complex and sometimes contradictory. Anatomically, the chongmei is regarded as rising from the perineum through the center of the spine (where the spinal cord is) and through the pineal gland to the top of the head. It is thus in concordance with the yogic *sushumna.* Functionally, however, qigong practitioners and meditators concentrate on chongmei as a vertical line through the center of the body connecting the Three Dantians in a straight line. In a pragmatic sense, this latter method works better. It is easier to imagine, and it makes the basic geometry of meditation simpler. Perhaps such concentration not only stimulates the energy in the meridian itself, but also affects the nerve plexuses, the aorta, and the inferior vena cava as well.

4. Daimei: This meridian encircles the waist like a belt. It begins at the navel and runs around the torso to reconnect at the navel.

5. Yangyumei: From a point on the dumei these channels travel bilaterally along the back of each arm, around the tip of the middle fingers, along the inside of the middle fingers to the point *laogong.*

BA MEI
Eight Meridians. The word *mei* is appended to mean channel. Thus, du*mei* means the du channel, and so on.

6. *Yinyumei:* From the laogong point of the palm, these meridians travel along the inside of each arm, curve across the pectoral muscles, descend through the nipples, and connect with the renmei via a brief trip along the daimei.

7. *Yangqiaomei:* These meridians begin at the perineum and emerge

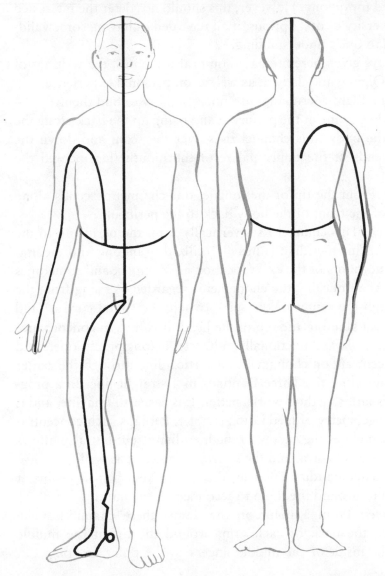

onto the front of each leg. They each descend the front of a leg to the instep and pierce through to the sole of each foot to the point known as *yongquan*.

8. *Yinqiaomei:* From the soles of the feet, these two meridians rise up the inside surface of each foot, loop around the ankles, and ascend the inner thighs back to the perineum.

Junction Points Along the Eight Meridians

You may have already noticed that the meridians intersect in various places or have their beginnings and endings along other meridians. This binds them all together into a closed system. These junction points all have names and are also important places used in the channeling of qi.

1. Huiyin: This point between the legs and halfway between the genitals and the anus is the junction for the dumei, renmei, chongmei, yangqiaomei, and yinqiaomei.

2. Mingmen: This point is along the dumei, at a point directly behind the navel. It is where the daimei intersects the dumei.

3. Gaohuang: This point is along the dumei between the shoulder blades, directly behind the heart. It affects the heart and lungs.

Acupuncture charts do not list this point along the dumei, but rather along the bladder meridian, which is closely parallel to dumei. However, several authorities agree that dumei has additional supplementary pathways on either side of it that coincide with the bladder meridian. This is why gaohuang is considered the link between dumei and yangyumei.

4. Niyuan: This point is on the top of the head in the very middle. It is the upper junction point for the chongmei with the dumei.

5. Laogong: This point is on each palm. To find it, curl your hand into a fist; laogong is located exactly where the middle finger touches the palm. This point connects yangyumei and yinyumei.

6. Shenque: This point is the navel and is the junction for the renmei and daimei.

7. Yongquan: This point is on the sole of each foot. It is along a line between the middle toe and the heel, and is about two-thirds of the way forward from the heel.

In addition to these seven points, the Three Dantians connect to the system of Eight Meridians in two ways. First, they all lie on the chongmei, the center channel. Second, they have lateral connections to the renmei and the dumei at these points:

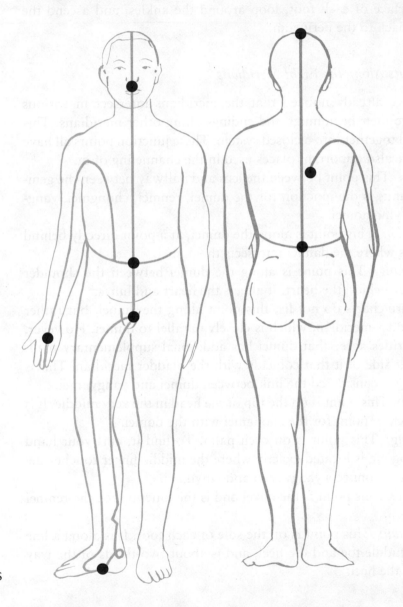

1. The lower dantian connects to the renmei at the qihai point.
2. The middle dantian connects to the renmei at the zhongwan point.
3. The upper dantian connects to The dumei at the yintang point.

Altogether, the entire system of points used in qigong comprises the Eight Meridians, nine points of intersection (five in the torso and one in each hand and foot), Three Dantians, and three points where the dantians have lateral connections to the Eight Meridians. In the set that follows, there will be references to various meridians and points. Concentrating on them as directed will be the first step toward gaining awareness of qi.

THE PRACTICE OF THE NORTHERN STAR QIGONG

The Northern Star Qigong should be performed once a day in its entirety. One should be alone in a clean place free from drafts and dust. One should not stand in the sun, which will cause overheating, nor should one practice in fog, rain, or wind, which will chill the body. The ideal place is in a forest by running water where it is tranquil and quiet. Otherwise, simply practice indoors where it is clean and comfortable and where you will not be disturbed. The restrictions of qigong are discussed in greater detail at the end of this chapter.

Be sure to learn the dispersing and harmonizing movement and perform it at the end of each posture. Though the qi will take the pattern encouraged by the body's posture, it will tend to accumulate at the various junction points of the meridians. The dispersing movements will distribute the qi throughout the body. Qigong done without dispersals is very dangerous, for you are dealing with the life force itself. Signs of improper practice are headaches, dizziness, internal bleeding, sharp but elusive pains in the abdomen, and at the very worst, insanity.

Throughout this set, one should utilize what has been termed reverse breathing. Despite this rather exotic name, all that reverse breathing entails is contracting the abdomen and pulling the diaphragm upward whenever one inhales, and relaxing the abdomen and expanding only the portion of the abdomen below the navel when exhaling. (The natural pattern is for us to expand our abdomens when we inhale; thus the name

氣海　中脘

印堂

天罡氣功

TIAN GANG QI GONG
Tiangang is an esoteric name for the Northern Star.

reverse breathing, because it pulls the stomach in on inhalation.) Reverse breathing concentrates on chongmei. On inhalation, one should visualize energy rising up this channel. On exhalation, one should visualize it descending back to the perineum. This is critical; a great deal of proper qigong lies in the isolation and control of the muscles. Be sure that you exercise this reverse breathing unless there are instructions to do otherwise.

調息功

HARMONIZING THE QI

After each of the postures of the set, perform the movements called Harmonizing the Qi. The function of each posture is to move the qi; the harmonizing movement returns all qi to a neutral mode again. If this is not done, the qi can stagnate, flow uncontrolled, or injure the body, causing hemorrhaging and pain.

1. Stand with the feet pointing outward at a slight angle. The heels should be touching, the body relaxed, the knees slightly bent. The hands should be in front of you with the fingertips touching and the palms up.

2. Inhale and raise your arms to the side, gradually turning the palms until the fingers nearly touch above the head in a palms-up position. Your inhalation, using reverse breathing, should have reached its fullest by this point.

At the same time that you do these cycles of inhalation and exhalation,

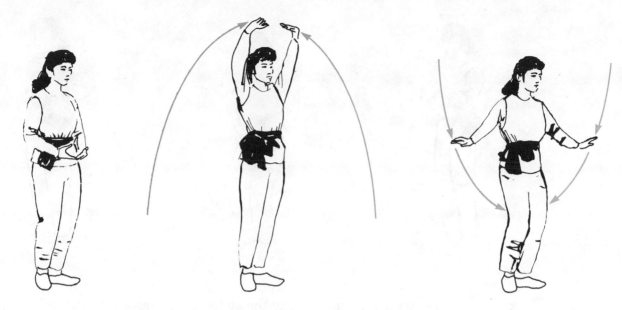

you should mentally direct the qi to flow through the meridians as follows: on inhalation, the qi ascends from the dantian up the dumei to the gaohuang point. There, it branches into three tracks, one out each arm along the yangyumei, to the laogong points, and a third continuing up the dumei to a point called baihui, located slightly behind the niyuan point. The qi should reach the laogong and baihui points simultaneously at the end of your inhalation and movement.

3. Exhale and slowly return to the starting position. The qi, which has come to the crown of the head and to the hands, reverses its path and returns to the dantian as you complete your exhalation. This forms one round. Do six rounds after performing each of the following postures of the Northern Star Qigong.

ACCUMULATING TREASURES INTO THE VASE

The set begins by stimulating the qi in the dantian so that it may be used in the rest of the set.

1. Warm the hands by rubbing the palms briskly together.

聚寶於瓶內

2. Place them on the front of the abdomen, preferably on bare skin. Allow a few seconds to feel the warmth sink in.

3. Exhale and rub slowly downward toward the pubic bone. Bend the knees at the same time.

4. Inhale and rub slowly upward as high as the lower edge of the rib cage. Use enough pressure so that you feel that you are gently massaging your intestines. As the hands rise up, the legs straighten. Begin the second round by sinking again, rubbing downward, and bending the knees. Do six rounds.

5. Harmonize.

EAGLE FLYING IN THE HIGH HEAVENS

鵬展高空功

As we have seen, the laogong points in the hands are two of the most important junction points for the Eight Meridians. The purpose of this posture is to raise the energy toward the palms.

1. Stand relaxed with the feet wide apart in a horse stance (so called because the legs are as if astride a horse), hands with the fists closed around the thumb, and the arms crossed at the wrists. Notice that the

thumbs will naturally press on the laogong points in a form of self-acupressure.

2. Inhale, and raise the arms to the sides and over the head until the fists are close to each other. Squeeze the fists to press the thumb into the laogong points. The legs should straighten simultaneously.

3. Exhale, relax your grip, and return to the starting position. This comprises one round. Do six rounds.

4. Slide the feet back together. Harmonize.

DRAW IN THE RAINBOW AND RADIATE ITS COLORS

1. Stand in a horse stance. Hands are in front of the dantian, fingers touching, palms up.

2. Without changing from a squatting position, raise the hands slowly, palms up, in a straight line close to and in front of the body to the lower end of the sternum. Simultaneously inhale, using reverse breathing, and mentally concentrate on the qi rising up the chongmei to the level of the

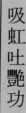

吸虹吐艷功

throat. By the time the hands reach the sternum, the throat should be vibrating with energy.

3. Turn the palms over and slowly press them down. Exhale back down the chongmei to the dantian.

4. Continue to exhale from the dantian down to the genitals. Press the hands all the way down and straighten the elbows and wrists. Men should imagine that the qi completely fills their testicles. Women should imagine that the qi enters into their ovaries.

5. Bring the feet together. Harmonize.

HOLD THE BREATH AND WARM THE BODY

閉氣暖身功

1. Inhale and bring the hands upward to the sternum, palms up and close to the body. Exhale, and press the hands downward, bending over and placing the hands flat on the ground in front of you. Knees should be straight.

2. Hold this position for a count of six. Hold your breath, and concentrate on the mingmen point.

3. Inhale, and reverse the procedure. Do six rounds.

4. Stand up. Harmonize.

ENTER THE CROWN AND WASH THE MARROW

1. Stand with feet shoulder width apart. Inhale while lifting both arms to the sides.

2. Raise the arms over the head and interlace the fingers, palms up. Keep your head level, but roll your eyes upward as if they could see through the top of your head by looking through the baihui to the laogong points. Hold your position and hold your breath for a count of six.

3. Exhale and reverse. Do six rounds.

4. Harmonize.

入頂洗髓功

TRAVEL TEN THOUSAND MILES TO HOLD UP THE SKY

This is an introduction to standing meditation.

1. Stand in a horse stance. Inhale and raise your palms.

2. Exhale and push your palms downward, bending at your waist until your hands touch the floor. Hold this position for one second.

3. Inhale, and raise your arms to shoulder level in front of you as you straighten your legs and trunk.

4. Squat slightly and lower your elbows. Your fingertips should point upward, and your palms face away from you. Keep your back straight. Relax and hold this position for up to one minute.

5. Lower your arms, and begin again. Do six rounds, and then harmonize.

DRAW THE BOW TO SHOOT THE EAGLE

1. Stand again in a horse stance. Bring your fists to chest level and keep the thumbs inside your fingers.

萬里擎天功

彎弓射鵰功

2. Look to one side and extend the arm on that side. At the same time, pull back with your other arm, as if drawing a bow. Extend your chest, and imagine that you are trying to make your shoulder blades touch in the back. Inhale as fully as possible throughout.

3. Exhale and bring your hands back to the starting position. When you do so, push your chest inward and round your back, flexing the shoulder blades as far apart as possible.

4. Harmonize.

TURNING HEAVEN AND EARTH

1. Stand in a horse stance, with your palms at waist level.

2. Step to one side and stretch the opposite leg. Bring your palm out, arm extended, fingers pointing down.

3. Make a big circle all the way over your head. Keep your arm straight while rotating your shoulder. Keep circling until your hand is at face level. Throughout this segment, let all the joints in your body move naturally. Inhale from beginning of the circle to the end.

4. Bring your other hand up.

5. Extend both arms, looking at your rear hand and exhale throughout. Both palms face downward.

旋乾轉坤功

6. Return to your beginning position and repeat on the other side. Once on each side forms one round. Do six rounds.

7. Harmonize.

IT'S WISE TO LOOK BACK

1. Stand in a horse stance with your arms crossed before you and your hands in fists. Inhale up the chongmei, and exhale back down to the dantian.

2. Inhale again, and twist to one side and bring the back of one hand up to your forehead while the other straightens at your side.

3. Release your fists, and straighten both arms and your fingers as you exhale.

4. Return to the beginning position with an inhalation. Exhaling to the dantian begins the sequence on the opposite side. Once on each side forms one round. Do six rounds.

5. Harmonize.

滄
州
定
馬
功

A STABLE STANCE AT THE WATER'S EDGE

1. Stand in a horse stance with your fists, palms inward, resting on your bladder.

2. Inhale and straighten your legs; exhale and squat down.

3. Each time you squat, imagine that all your energy is sinking to the soles of your feet.

4. Repeat for six rounds. Harmonize.

搖
頭
擺
尾
功

SWAYING THE HEAD AND WAGGING THE TAIL

1. Bend at the waist as you exhale. Keep your legs straight and hold your ankles.

2. Inhale. Slowly twist to each side, exhaling as you twist, and inhaling each time you return to the center. One twist to each side is one round. Do six rounds.

3. Inhale and stand up slowly. Harmonize.

WHITE CRANE SPREADS WINGS

1. Take a big step to the side and squat into a very low horse stance, your palms resting on your thighs.

2. Bring one foot over to your other foot and then lift it upward while the arms rise to shoulder level, palms outward. Note how the fingers are spread like the feathers of a crane. Hold this position for up to one minute.

3. Without putting your foot down, grasp your ankles and extend your foot straight out in front of you. Hold this position. Inhale as you extend your ankle, exhale as you pull your foot back. Mentally concentrate on yongquan points during this step.

4. Return to the posture in number 3. Hold for five seconds, and return to a standing position.

5. Repeat on the other side. Harmonize.

白鶴亮翅功

CLEAR ALL THE MERIDIANS

1. Stand still. Inhale. Exhale while slowly thrusting both fists outward and sinking into a horse stance.

2. All at once, inhale, push your elbows back and take three hops backward. Inhale with each hop.

3. When you come down for the third hop, punch forward strongly with your fists while landing with a significant stomp.

4. Harmonize.

GENERAL GUIDELINES FOR QIGONG

The quality of your qigong is directly affected by the circumstances in which you practice. The air that you breathe, the food that you eat, your state of mind, even the weather, are all factors. To have the greatest success, it's important that you observe the following principles.

Qigong should be practiced in a clean area. If you practice outdoors, you should be in open shade, and the temperature should be comfortable. You should not practice outdoors in the rain or snow or during storms. The air that you breathe must be as fresh and pure as possible, and it is quite beneficial to practice facing dense shrubbery or trees, both to absorb the oxygen that they give off, and to provide a soothing view. You should be undistracted by other people or any commotion.

If you practice indoors, your room should be clean and dust-free and of comfortable temperature. If you have pets like a dog or a cat, they should be kept away, so that you do not inhale their fur and dander. Let a window be open, so that you get fresh air flowing gently into the room, and have as few electrical objects functioning as possible. Electricity disrupts the qi (it is for this same reason that you should not practice during lightning storms).

Your body should be clean, and your clothing should not be restrictive. You should not wear a belt for your pants (cuts off circulation), and you should not wear any metal (including glasses) or anything electrical like a watch, because these disrupt the qi.

Your state of mind is important. You should be calm and optimistic about practice. If you are tired, angry, or frustrated, you shouldn't practice until you resolve your problems. Qigong doesn't make you invulnerable, and it is no substitute for everyday problem solving. If you are already upset, qigong will only excite your temper and send an off-balanced personality further off-balance. Nor is qigong a substitute for sleep. You should make regular rest a part of your daily schedule.

If you are ill, you should refrain from practice until you are convalescing. Although it is true that qigong can be effective for certain illnesses, you must go to a competent instructor and doctor for this; no book can guide you in this type of practice.

Women should not practice qigong during menstruation. Although there are some styles of qigong that are safe for a woman to practice during her period, most are not. Qigong and concentration in the lower dantian increase the pressure in the uterus and can adversely affect the flow of blood. Women should thus wait until their bleeding stops, and they should refer to the herb section for herbs to replenish themselves after their periods.

Wait twenty-four hours after sexual relations before practicing qigong again. When you have sex, you temporarily exhaust your jing, and because qigong draws upon this raw power, you will only tax your body by demanding it supply something it cannot. Be circumspect and regulate your sexual life.

Don't expect mystical things of qigong. Instead look for real and tangible results. Unless these happen, you cannot be sure that you are practicing successfully. If you were to take up running, for example, you would naturally expect your stamina to increase, and if it did not, you could be sure that something was wrong. In the same way, qigong is a simple exercise, not some esoteric activity that you must do on faith. If you are practicing qigong properly, you can expect clearer skin and eyes, a stronger immune system, increased stamina, better appetite (but not so that you become fat), improved circulation, and a clearer mind.

As qigong purifies you, you must go along with it. If you persist in bad habits like eating poorly, smoking, and drinking, your body will rebel against you. When the body gets a taste of purity, it craves more. Once begun and practiced, qigong leads you onto a narrow path of good health; you will feel physically uncomfortable if you try to indulge in things that your now-cleansed body does not like.

藥材

5

Herbs purify, strengthen, heal.
Their true use is in daily diet.

HERBS

THE SECRET OF DIETARY TRANSFORMATION

IN SPITE OF OUR BEST EFFORTS at exercise, diet, and qigong, there may be times when our bodies are still exhausted or some imbalance develops. Herbal supplements counter these problems. Herbs to be used in this way should be thought of as medicinal plants and substances, not cooking seasonings. The traditional pharmacopoeia contains over ten thousand herbs. Most herbalists use six hundred to eight hundred favorites, including such exotica as wild ginseng and tiger bone. Each herb is well understood. In hundreds of years of research, herbalists and doctors have documented the medicinal properties of each one, and the volumes written about them would fill an entire library.

Herbs are used whenever people become ill, but the more important emphasis in Chinese medicine is to keep the body balanced day to day. Traditional medical philosophy declares that medicine exists to keep people well, not simply to cure the sick. Doctors believe that curing the sick rather than preventing disease is a case of applying medicine too late; they compare this to "marching after the enemy has arrived." Thus, most herbs are used to build intrinsic health. They buffer the effect of environmental factors like dust or wind or smoke. They counter weather by cooling the body in summer, drying it when damp, bringing moisture during arid times, and warming it in winter. Herbs balance the effects of one's occupation: scholars take herbs to build their brains and soothe their nerves; workers use herbs to relieve fatigue in their legs.

This preventive maintenance is largely responsible for some of the legends of healthy and long-lived Taoists: they knew how to use herbs, gathered them wild during mountain wanderings, and supplemented their meals with them. Although we may not be able to wander in the mountains for our herbs, we can still use herbs today. Admittedly, learning about them is a slow process, and the actual preparation can be vexing to people accustomed to eating only what is convenient and quick to cook. They don't want to take the trouble to find the herbs and take them home to brew. But the proper and timely application of herbs will regulate your body and mind, keep you integrated with your environment, and provide you with many of the nutrients that you need. As a Scholar Warrior, your nutritional needs will not be like those of ordinary people, so you must be ready to supplement your diet. The intense thinking of a scholar depletes the qi and the mind. Great amounts of physical exercise and qigong deplete the body as quickly as sex or any other activity, and you must build back your jing. If you want to follow the way of the Scholar Warrior, you cannot leave herbs out of your development and your practice. If you do, you will decline, not advance.

JUAN HSIU IN A LANDSCAPE. Ch'en Hung-shou (1599–1652). Ming, early Qing. Asian Art Museum of San Francisco, B79 D8.

The herbs in this section are arranged according to the role that they play. The bulk of the herbs given here deal with tonification as a part of daily diet. This is a gentle and constant way to build health. If you want to treat a specific illness with herbs, then obviously you must find a competent doctor.

For each recipe, there will be a brief introduction and instructions on preparation, followed by a detailed account of how each ingredient affects your body. There are notations about the flavor of the herb, its effects, and which meridian it enters. This last feature is something that may require a little explanation. If you refer to any good acupuncture book, you will see that there are twelve meridians in the body. Each one is associated with a particular organ, such as the heart, the liver, or the kidneys. Acupuncturists use needles, massage, moxibustion, or cupping to stimulate these pathways, thereby rebalancing energy flow and regulating the function of selected organs. In the same way, herbalists use medicine to stimulate the same meridians, and this is why the accounts that follow will sometimes discuss this. Each herbal formula is then listed in Chinese, with weights and measures, and the botanical name for each component is also shown. A photograph of each herbal preparation is also provided, to make the formula more familiar and for you to verify that you have found the right herbs. When you get your herbs, you can compare them to the picture and confirm that you have not been given substitutes.

Going into a Chinese herb store is bound to be somewhat intimidating. It may be best that you photocopy a formula that you want to try and pick a large, well-stocked store. If you are in a city with a Chinatown, walk around, and you will soon see that some stores have a large amount of merchandise, whereas others seem to be rather shabby. Naturally, you should look for a clean place with people who seem friendly.

Go in and give the paper to the herbalist, asking the price before the formula is put together. Be wary of people who might want to take advantage of you, and try out several stores before you settle on one as your regular supplier. Don't allow substitution for any ingredient until you are quite familiar with the herbs. Then, if the herbalist you know wants to add to or change the formula, you can learn from this by having him or her write down the name for you to look up. Almost all formulas can be augmented, and learning from your herbalist in this way will gradually expand your understanding.

What if you are in a city that doesn't have Chinese herb stores? This need not be a hindrance to your exploration of herbology. Simply select a formula that you wish to try, and photocopy its Chinese version.

Write to an herb store and ask for a price, and you can then order by mail. In some ways, this might be an even better approach because you can patronize the best herb stores rather than be restricted by geography.

Making contact at an herb store is important. If you can go to a metropolitan area like New York or San Francisco, try to find one that will respond to you. Get their card and arrange for mail order. Many have fax machines, catalogs, and established mail order procedures. The larger companies will be happy to help you, and many of them have younger English speaking employees. If you are not going to be traveling, then you can write to the herb store listed in the margin. Like doing business in any other context, be sure to ascertain the price and build a sound working relationship with a company that you feel is fair and helpful.

At the beginning of your herb use, you might notice some rather dramatic improvements in your stamina or some other aspect of your health. Later, as you become stronger and more used to the herbs, it may seem that nothing is happening. This is natural. When someone is weak and receives good nutrition and medicine, the effects are bound to be noticeable. But when one is already in good health and the herbs are functioning more as a food than as a supplement, the effects will be less dramatic.

Finally, a caution against excess is in order. Herbs are meant to support your health, and they should not be abused by excessive ingestion, increased dosages, and so on. Too many people in today's society have a cavalier attitude about what they put into their bodies. Follow instructions. Don't start thinking that if one is good, two must be better.

There is a mania nowadays for isolating one type of food and then having it predominate in one's diet. Carrots are good, but there is no reason to eat pounds of them a day. In the same way, herbs should be used in the proper amounts, and you should always strive to maintain a sense of proportion in whatever you ingest. If you gradually and sensibly explore the world of herbs, you will soon find yourself with better health and a clearer mind. When you combine those assets with the breathing practices, you will attain a state of health and well-being far beyond the average.

The best herb stores in North America are in San Francisco, New York, Vancouver, and Toronto. There are others wherever there are Chinatowns, including Seattle, Portland, Oakland, Los Angeles, Chicago, Montreal, Boston, and Washington, D.C. For mail orders, write to China Herbs and Native Produce Company, 622 Broadway, San Francisco, CA 94133.

PREPARING HERBS

There are very definite guidelines to follow when preparing herbs. Never buy more than you can use within a three-month period. Although some herbs age well, others do not, and many of them require special storage techniques. It is best to get them fresh from the herbalist.

When you are ready to begin, wash your herbs by rinsing them in clear water (unless they are powder or seeds or in some other small form that will slip away too easily). If you have ever been to Asia and seen how herbs are sold—in open roadside marketplaces subject to dust, insects, animal excrement, and car exhaust—you will understand the need to be fastidious about the cleanliness of your herbs.

Whenever the recipe calls for meat or other fresh ingredients, use the freshest and highest quality available. The formula will only be as good as what you put into it.

There are three primary ways of cooking herbs, and they depend on the type of vessel that you use. The first way is in a special herb pot that has a spout. This style is primarily used for herbs that are cooked without meat and that are usually taken for illness. The second is an earthenware pot with a cover. The herbs are simmered inside the pot, and the liquid often is reduced dramatically during the cooking. This style of preparing herbs is relatively quick—it takes about one to two hours—and is used when the liquid must be concentrated. The third method is to use a double boiler. A covered porcelain container is filled with liquid and the herbs and is in turn placed in another pot of water. Heat is thus never directly applied to the herbs, and nothing is lost by evaporation. The liquid is not reduced very much in this case (any loss of liquid is usually due to absorption by the herbs), but the resulting broth is rich in all the available nutrients. This is also the longest method: herbs in a double boiler usually cook for two to eight hours.

Each recipe given here will specify the cooking method, but you can see that they all use earthenware containers. Metal is usually taboo in the preparation of herbs. Glass, stainless steel, and enameled steel are reluctant substitutes. Clay vessels are preferred for all herb cooking.

All the recipes are for a single person. If they specify meat, you should

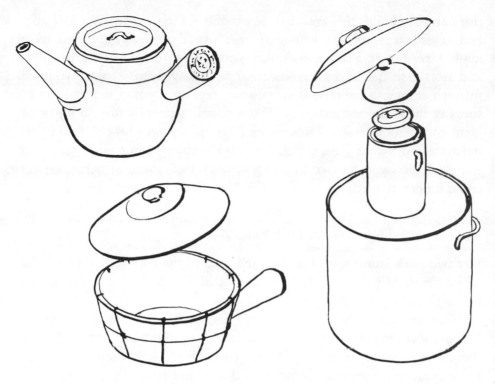

THE THREE TYPES OF VESSELS FOR PREPARING HERBS. The pot on the upper left is an herb pot. Handle is nearly parallel to the spout so you can easily pour toward yourself. The lower-left drawing is an earthenware pot for stews and large soups. The right-hand drawing shows a schematic arrangement of a double boiler. Herbs are put in the smaller container and covered with two lids. The vessel is placed into a larger pot with boiling water reaching up to three quarters of the height of the porcelain. The larger pot should also be covered, adding water only when necessary.

use about a quarter to a half pound if no amount is specified. Should you want to prepare these herbal broths and foods for more than one person, simply tell the herbalist how many people you are cooking for, and he or she will increase the amount for you.

BUILDING KIDNEYS AND JING

One of the first areas that the Scholar Warrior considers building are the kidneys. This doesn't simply mean the kidneys as they are defined in Western anatomy, for the "kidneys" to Chinese doctors comprise a single system along with the organs of urination and reproduction. Traditional references to the kidneys thus include the genitals and jing as part of the whole.

Since jing is the basis for qi and eventually for shen, the Scholar War-

保腎保精

rior naturally builds this area first. Sex is one of the ways that we lose jing, and so it makes sense to take one of these formulas the day after you have made love. But you can also deplete your jing through qigong practice, and it is essential to understand that you may even weaken yourself through strenuous exercise if you do not replace the jing that is used to support the body and make qi. Those people who practice tai chi with great constancy also stand to weaken their kidneys, for tai chi is an internal art that demands great supplies of jing in compounding and circulating energy. Unless you replace that jing through the taking of herbs, tai chi could hinder, not help, you.

Du Zhong and Niu Xi with Pork Kidneys

杜仲牛膝

Buy two pork kidneys, and cut out and discard the core sections with the white veins. Salt the remaining pieces of kidney, cover, and refrigerate overnight.

The next day, when you are ready to prepare the formula, rinse the kidneys well, for the salt will have leached out many impurities. Blanch the kidneys quickly in boiling water. You will see scum and a brownish foam come to the surface. Drain the kidneys, and rinse them again.

Boil the herbs in a clay pot for a minimum of one hour. Keep the lid on the pot, and keep the water simmering, not at a rolling boil.

Add the kidneys, and cook for half an hour more. Drink the liquid, and eat the kidneys if you like. This recipe may be eaten up to twice a month.

This is what each herb does for you.

Du Zhong (Eucommiae Cortex): According to legend, this tonic is named after Du Zhong, who became enlightened after taking it. It is the dried bark of a tree, *Eucommia ulmoides*, and is usually partly sliced to allow easy dispersion during boiling. You will see characteristic elastic fibers between each cut.

Du zhong is sweet, mild, and somewhat pungent in flavor. It warms the body and enters into the liver and kidney meridians. It lowers blood pressure, decreases the absorption of cholesterol (thereby balancing the cholesterol in the pork kidneys), and has an analgesic action.

Bottom: *du zhong*
Upper right: *niu xi*

牛膝，三錢　杜仲，三錢

Niu Xi (Achyranthis Radix): The name literally means "cattle knees," because of the shape of this root's nodes. This blood-regulating substance is both bitter and sour, and of a neutral property. Niu xi enters the liver and the kidney meridians, and it has a wide variety of effects upon the body: it removes stagnant blood, disperses swelling, strengthens tendons and bones, is beneficial for back pain, and enhances the function of the kidneys.

Pork Kidneys: The herbalists believed that eating the organs of an animal would strengthen the corresponding organ in a human body. They felt that both the kidneys and one's supply of jing were enhanced by eating kidneys.

Sea Horse and Sea Dragon

海馬海龍瘦肉湯

Here is an example of two "herbs" that aren't plants. Both the sea horse and the sea dragon are aquatic animals, but they have very beneficial properties. To make this soup, rinse and salt about a quarter to a half pound of meat, and wash it again. Slice it into one-inch cubes. Combine all the ingredients in an earthenware pot, and simmer for two to three hours, adding water as needed. Drink the broth and eat the meat. You may prepare this as often as every two weeks. The herbs have the following properties.

Hai Ma (Hippocampus): As did Westerners, the Chinese imagined this animal as a sea horse. They found its flavor to be sweet, salty, and mild, and that it warmed the body. It has been used to build the kidneys, strengthen the yang, promote blood circulation, and remove stagnant blood; it is also effective against impotence.

Hai Long (Syngnathus): This pipe fish is sweet and mild in flavor and warming to the body. It nourishes the yin, supplements the kidneys, and disperses stagnant blood.

Chen Pi (Citri Leiocarpae Exocarpium): This is a dried and aged citrus peel that is pungent, bitter, and warming. It enters the lung and spleen meridians, thereby regulating the qi, strengthening the spleen, and expelling excess moisture.

Mi Zao (Zizyphi Fructus): Literally translated as "honey jujube," this

Center: *hai ma*
Right: *hai long*
Left: *chen pi*
Top: *mi zao*

海馬，五錢

海龍，五錢

陳皮，五錢

蜜棗，五錢

small fruit has been considered superior for supplementing and tonifying the spleen and stomach, moistening the heart and lungs, nourishing and pacifying the spirit, and harmonizing any herbal formula to which it is added. It originated in North Africa and Western Europe and has been used since ancient times. It is very sweet, warms the body, and enters the spleen meridian.

Beef or Lamb: The amount of meat that should be used in this formula may vary according to your own taste. Lean beef builds blood; lamb builds the qi. Whether you use beef or lamb, be sure that they are as free of fat as possible. Many people prefer to blanch their meat as a means of removing fat, toxins, and blood. Beef and lamb are both good for cold and weak people.

Chinese Cornbind Oxtail Soup

This formula is especially good for men, although women can take it as well. It builds the kidneys, liver, and lower back, strengthens tendons and bones, and builds muscle. Backaches, weak legs, and general debility are signs that you need this soup. It is a very warming recipe, however, so one should be careful not to take it if the weather is hot or if one suffers from an overheated system. You can take the formula up to twice a month, but don't take it in the same week as either of the preceding herbs and generally avoid this formula when the weather is very hot.

Buy an oxtail and have the butcher cut it up. The very best way is to divide the tail section by section by cutting with a knife. Clean the meat; salt it; and wash it again. Blanching is optional. Put the tail into an earthenware pot with the herbs, and simmer for three to four hours, adding water as needed. You can eat some of the *he shou wu* and *qi zi*, if you like, but you cannot eat the du zhong.

Here are the backgrounds of the herbs in this formula:

He Shou Wu (Polygoni Multiflori Radix): It is said that he shou wu was named for a man who, at the age of 58, had still not been able to father a child. A monk recommended this herb to him. Not only did he father several children as a result, but his gray hair turned black, and he

Left: he shou wu
Upper right: qi zi
Lower right: du zhong

杜仲，三錢

杞子，五錢

首烏，五錢

lived to be 160 years of age. This is an indication of the powers attributed to this herb and its ability to strengthen the body and nourish jing.

It is bitter, sweet, and astringent and has warming properties. It enters the liver and kidney meridians. Nourishing the yin, replenishing jing and blood, tonifying the liver and kidneys, and controlling involuntary emissions, he shou wu is a very effective tonic.

Qi Zi (Lycii Fructus): Qi zi, wolfberry, is a small, red fruit that is sweet and neutral in property. It enters the liver and kidney meridians, supplements both those organs, promotes both sperm and blood, and clears the vision.

Du Zhong (Eucommiae Cortex): This is the herb used in the earlier pork kidney recipe; its primary role in this formula is as a builder of the kidneys and a nourisher of jing.

BUILDING QI

保氣

Building qi is largely a matter of tonifying the body. In general, deficient qi manifests itself as either spleen weakness or pulmonary weakness. A problem in spleen qi appears as general lassitude, insufficient stamina, weak limbs, loss of appetite, abdominal aches and distension, dizziness, and lax muscle tone. These are all problems of the *zhong qi*, or central qi. Pulmonary qi weakness is usually indicated as shortness of breath, pale skin, and excessive perspiration.

You will notice that the following qi tonics generally enter into the spleen and the lungs to attack these specific deficiencies. In addition, they often include herbs that help the blood as well. The herbalists believe that qi and blood are closely related and that blood is generated and moved by qi. It is in this way that the tonics enhance the physiological functioning of the organs and improve physical strength and stamina.

How often should you take qi tonics? The normal advice is to take them "when one feels weak." Thus, you need to be sensitive to the needs of your body. When you notice that your stamina is poor or when you are unusually fatigued, you should add one of these recipes to your dinner. However, you should not take them any more frequently than once a week, for you will build up a resistance and a dependency upon them, and you should never take them when ill, for the herbs will hold your illness in and make you more sick.

Foxnut with Beef Shin

Combine dates, citrus peel, and foxnut with cubed beef shin to suit your taste. Put the mixture in a ceramic pot, and simmer for three hours. Drink the broth, and eat the herbs.

The foxnut is an excellent way to build vitality, jing, and qi and to purge your body of excessive heat. Here is more about the individual herbs.

Qian Shi (Euryalis Semen): These dried seeds, called foxnut, are sweet, astringent, and bland in flavor. Their essence enters the spleen and kidney meridians. One of foxnut's unique properties is to consolidate the qi of the kidneys and expel dampness from the body. It is often used for cases of nocturnal emission or leukorrhea.

Chen Pi (Citri Leiocarpae Exocarpium): In addition to what has already been said about chen pi, it is important to note that the age of the peel is part of its value. The older the better, and you will find many grades of it. The common variety is enough for this formula, but if you someday investigate the more expensive ones, you will find them fragrant and full of a wonderful citrus taste.

The peel can also be held in the mouth alone and allowed to melt, and it is useful for dry mouth and coughs.

Apricot Seed and Foxnut Cooked with Fish

This formula calls for equal parts of apricot seed and *qian shi*. Use a mortar and pestle to grind them into a fine powder, or place them inside a plastic bag and pulverize them with a hammer or the butt of a cleaver. You can buy more, pound it, and save it for another occasion.

The fish can be carp, catfish, rock cod, or any freshwater lake fish, but the usual preference is to have the fish whole. "Have both the head and the tail," is the common saying, symbolizing thoroughness as well as a good

芡實湯

杏仁芡實保鯉魚

*Below and outside of
dish: qian shi*

Above: chen pi

陳皮，五錢

芡實，五錢

Below mortar, left:
xing ren

Below mortar, right:
qian shi

Inside mortar: both
seeds crushed together

芡實，一両

杏仁，一両

beginning coupled with a good ending. Scale, clean, and gut the fish. Marinate it in a little wine, soy sauce, and sliced ginger. Place the fish in a deep dish large enough to hold it, and sprinkle the powdered herb on the fish. There should be a fine, thin layer.

In a pot big enough to fit the fish, put a metal stand tall enough to hold the dish above an inch of water. When the water comes to a full boil, put the dish on the stand and cover the pot. Steam for about twenty minutes for a whole fish, less if you are using steaks. Generally, a fish is done when a chopstick poked into it will go easily into the back.

This formula will build your kidneys and spleen, build your qi, and purge your body of excessive heat, dryness, swelling, and toxins. It will also regulate the flow of urine. You can use this as a regular dinner dish, and each individual herb will have the following effects on your body.

Xing Ren (Armeniacae Semen): These seeds are bitter in flavor and warm in property. They enter the lung and the large intestine meridians, thereby moistening the lungs and intestines and promoting bowel movement (the fatty content of the seeds lubricates the intestines).

Qian Shi (Euryalis Semen): In addition to what has already been said about qian shi, it is also useful in case of diarrhea and enuresis.

Astragalus and Jujubes with Chicken

This formula will clear water retention and build vitality. To make it, simply combine the two herbs with chicken in a double boiler, and cook for two to four hours. You can eat the chicken and the jujubes (jujubes have a pit, so be careful), but you cannot eat astragalus. For variation, you can substitute beef shin for the chicken. This formula should be taken no more than once a week.

Bei Qi (Astragali Radix): Another name for this herb is *huang qi,* which means "yellow leader." In Imperial China, yellow was the royal color; no one besides the emperor was allowed to use it. "Yellow," combined with the name "leader," indicates the high regard that existed for this tonic herb. It is sweet, mild, and warming. It enters the spleen and lung meridians, thereby building qi, increasing yang, and dispersing swelling.

北芪紅棗

北芪，三錢

紅棗，三錢

Hong Zao (Zizyphi Fructus): This is a different variety from the honey jujube that we saw earlier. This dried fruit is smaller and is a deep cinnabar color. It is sweet and neutral, is tonic to the spleen and stomach, and builds the blood.

Rice and Dang Shen Soup

Stir fry about a bowlful of cooked rice with a small quantity of oil until golden brown. Put aside. Fill a double boiler with water; add the rice and *dang shen,* and cook for three hours. Drink the liquid as a beverage gradually over the course of a day. This soup will build your qi, your vitality, and it will strengthen your stomach.

Although rice is listed in the formula, you need not buy it in an herb store, of course. Just buy the dang shen, and combine it with an equal amount of rice by weight.

Dang Shen (Codonopsitis Radix): This commonly used root is often regarded as an economical but effective alternative to ginseng. The dried root is sweet in flavor and mildly warm. It enters the lung and the spleen meridians, thereby invigorating those organs, replenishing the qi, harmonizing the spleen and stomach, and increasing the secretion of fluids.

Mi (Oryzae Semen): Rice is sweet in flavor and warming. It enters the spleen, stomach, and lung meridians and replenishes qi. It also provides starch and protein.

Rabbit to Build Vitality

This formula not only builds vitality, but also strengthens the immune system. It is, however, a very tonic formula and warms the body dramatically, so it is best to take this during colder weather, not during hot summer months.

Cut up the rabbit and marinate with wine, soy, and ginger. It should be braised first, then simmered together with the herbs in an earthenware pot. Cook for one to two hours. The amount of water used depends on the style of the dish you want to prepare. Use more water if you want to emphasize the medicinal qualities by drinking the broth. Use less liquid if

米，一両

黨參，一両

you want to prepare it as a stew. Each herb will help you in the following ways.

Huai Shan (Batatatis Rhizoma): This is a dried and peeled rhizome that appears chalk white when finally processed. It is sweet, mild, and warm, entering the spleen and lung meridians. It supplements the spleen and stomach, tonifies the lungs and kidneys, and is helpful in cases of cough from debility, with diabetes, with nocturnal emissions, and with leukorrhea. It is a delicious herb to eat, and has the texture of a potato.

Qi Zi (Lycii Fructus): Qi zi was discussed earlier under the oxtail recipe. Because of its neutral nature, it is an often used herb. Wolfberry is a good supplement for both the liver and the eyes.

Dang Shen (Codonopsitis Radix): Here we have dang shen used again, underscoring its usefulness in food and herbal preparations. It is the qi builder in this formula, and harmonizes especially with the huai shan in building the spleen and the lungs. The spleen is regarded as the organ most associated with the zhong qi (central qi), which forms adjacent to it in the solar plexus and is the source of our physical vitality.

Da Zao (Zizyphi Fructus): This is a third type of jujube, and the one generally regarded as the most potent of them all. It enters into the same meridians and has the same properties as the others, but it is usually used when the blood must be especially fortified. Recent studies have also indicated some antiulcer properties to this herb.

保肺

LUNGS

Qi depends partially on the lungs for its source, so it is good to be able to nourish them specifically.

燕窩湯

Bird's Nest Soup

One of the best recipes for nourishing the lungs is bird's nest soup. The herbalists observed how mother birds would gather food, digest it, and then feed it to their young. Bits of this mixture would fall around the nest, and herbalists, their young assistants, or trained monkeys would gather it.

Left: *huai shan*

Right: *qi zi*

Middle: *dang shen*

Upper left, in lid: *da zao*

淮山，一両

杞子，五錢

黨參，五錢

大棗，十個

Yen Wo

燕窩

Admittedly, under less glamorous scrutiny, this is no more than bird spit soup, but it has the most wonderful properties for the human body. It clears the lungs, stops coughing, clears phlegm, treats headaches, and cools the body.

There are many different grades of bird's nest, depending on how large the pieces are and how much they have been cleaned. The best grade is called the Golden Thread Bird's Nest.

The bird's nest should be soaked for a minimum of twenty minutes. It expands quite a bit, so you don't need to use more than a couple of ounces per person. After soaking, it should be thoroughly cleaned by removing any bits of feathers that may be in the water. Then rinse and strain the bird's nest thoroughly. Cook in a double boiler for three hours.

Depending upon the style, you can add different ingredients. For a sweet soup, add brown sugar. For a richer broth, cook with slivered chicken breast, and add a little soy sauce.

Cordyceps Stewed with Duck

Although duck is not part of the Scholar Warrior diet, the traditional recipe has specified duck for centuries. It is said that cordyceps is comparable to ginseng and that it is worth four times its weight in silver. Furthermore, duck and cordyceps combined is said to be equivalent to an ounce of the highest grade ginseng. However, if you are strict in your diet, you may substitute chicken for duck.

If you like, you may braise the bird first to brown it and seal in the flavor. Stew together with the cordyceps until well done—at least an hour. You will notice that the cordyceps comes bundled with string. Be sure to untie it before cooking.

This formula is often used to build the lungs, warm the kidneys, dissipate phlegm, stop bleeding, and fortify the jing and qi.

Dong Chong Xia Cao (Cordyceps): This is the dried fungus that grows on the larvae of certain caterpillars. Within each bundle are two distinct parts: the grub, and the upper portion of fungus. It is sweet and warming, and enters the lung and kidney meridians. It is used in cases of cough and consumption, impotence, pains in the loins and knees.

金絲燕窩

冬蟲草保鴨

Dong chong xia cao

冬蟲夏草，五錢

BEGINNINGS

BUILDING BLOOD

Fortifying blood is crucial for women. The old adage is that men must build their qi (because their store of jing to produce qi is limited) but women must build their blood (because they lose it during menstruation). For a woman Scholar Warrior, supplementing her body after menstruation and childbirth is part of her overall practice. The formula for childbirth is called the Thirteen Treasures; monthly supplementation can be accomplished with the following formula.

Angelica with Lamb

Angelica is often dubbed the "woman's ginseng," for it is considered especially tonic for women. It is one of the premier blood fortifiers in the Chinese pharmacopoeia. The recipe is simple. Prepare boneless lamb stew in an amount that you would normally eat. Clean it thoroughly, and remove as much fat as possible. Salt the meat lightly, and blanch it, if you like. Simmer together with the angelica for a minimum of three hours. You may use either a ceramic stew pot or a double boiler. If you stew it, cook until the meat is done. If you make this recipe in a double boiler, you should cook from four to eight hours. Drink the liquid, and eat the meat.

A woman may take this up to twice a month, and it is especially good when recovering from menstruation.

If one wants to make the formula more potent, and especially if menstrual flow is excessive, then you may also add *Rehmanniae radix*. Here are the properties of each herb.

Dang Gui (Angelicae Radix): Angelica adjusts qi and nourishes the blood. It has a sweet, pungent flavor and is warming. It enters the heart, liver, and spleen meridians and regulates menstruation. Extensive research has been carried out regarding angelica's effects on the female reproductive system, and it is often used to regulate the function of the uterus. It also has some diuretic and sedative properties.

Sheng Di (Rehmanniae Radix): There are two forms of this herb: one fresh, and the other washed in spirits, steamed on a wooden frame within a porcelain vessel, dried, and then reprocessed in this same way a mini-

當歸，三錢

生地，三錢

mum of nine times. The herb that is used in this formula is the unsteamed version. It is bittersweet and cold; enters the heart, liver, and kidney meridians; nourishes yin and the blood, regulates menstruation; and gently clears heat from the body.

Heart and Kidneys Harmonizing

This formula is used by women when menstruation causes loss of sleep, excessive dreaming, nightmares, depression, discontent, excessive sweating, tiredness, and lack of concentration. The herbalist's image for this is that the heart and the kidneys are no longer cooperating, and this is regarded as a fundamental disagreement of the body. The heart symbolizes fire, the kidneys water; these two primal elements are at odds within a woman when she experiences such symptoms.

Preparation of this formula is straightforward. Combine the herbs in a small earthenware pot, with five bowls of water. Simmer until one bowl is left and drink. The backgrounds of each herb are as follows.

Long Yan Rou (Longane Arillus): This tonic herb is derived from a translucent fruit that is said to resemble dragon eyes. The pulp is dried for medical use, and is sweet and warming. It enters the heart and spleen meridians. Supplementing the heart, nourishing the spirit, tonifying the spleen, fortifying the blood, this herb is frequently used in cases of amnesia, insomnia, and deficiency of the qi and blood.

Shou Zao Ren (Zizyphi Spinosis Semen): This is jujube seed. It is sweet and sour, neutral in property. It enters the heart, spleen, liver, and gall bladder meridians. These seeds nourish the liver, calm the heart, and counter insomnia.

Bo Zi Ren (Thujae Orientalis Semen): This dried seed is sweet, pungent, and neutral. It enters the heart, liver, and kidney meridians. Its tranquilizing powers are most useful here, as it calms the heart and spirit and aids in digestion.

Dan Shen (Salviae Mitiorrhizae Radix): This dried root is bitter, mild, and cold. It enters the heart and pericardium meridians. Blood is its main area of action: it cools, nourishes, and enhances circulation. It also counters irritability.

心腎雙交

Top: long yan rou
Right: shou zao ren
Bottom: bo zi ren
Center: dan shen

龍眼肉，三錢

熟棗仁，五錢

伯子仁，三錢

紫丹參，三錢

BEGINNINGS

Onion Whites with Liver and Egg

This recipe builds blood, clears the eyes, nourishes the kidneys. The scallion whites are thought to make the yang qi flow. The bulbs of green onions are considered to be pungent and mild, entering the lung and stomach meridians and dispelling pathogenic factors, promoting blood circulation, and building yang. The liver enters the liver meridian. The egg enters the heart and spleen meridians. All these ingredients may be bought in a grocery store and need not to be purchased at an herb store. Quantities used should be according to your taste.

In broth or water, simmer about eight scallion whites (including the roots, but with no green parts) together with about a quarter pound of sliced pork or calves' liver. Hard-boil the egg beforehand and add it to the soup at the last minute. Cook for only a few minutes after adding the liver so that the meat will not be overdone.

BUILDING THE LIVER

After the kidneys, the liver is considered the most important organ to supplement. According to the herbalists, the liver stores blood whenever one is at rest, and when one is active, the liver regulates the quantity of blood that the heart will circulate. During sleep, a significant amount of blood is stored in the liver and thereby enriched.

This important organ is regarded as being particularly vulnerable to stress. Prolonged anger or depression will weaken it. Similarly, if there is some physical dysfunction in the liver, it will make a person excessively angry or depressed. When this happens, one is regarded as having an excess of "liver fire," and this is often shown in bulging or red and inflamed eyes and bad temperament.

Antelope Horn Soup

Place sliced ram's horn with *gou teng* on a sheet of cheesecloth, and wrap securely. Cook with meat and red jujubes for one to one and a half hours.

葱白猪肝鷄蛋湯

保肝

羚羊角勾籐瘦肉湯

Below, on dish: cong bai, scallion whites

Below dish: egg

Top: liver

葱
白

鷄
蛋

BEGINNINGS

Below: ling yang jiao
Above: gou teng
Left: hong zao

羚羊角，一錢

勾籐，三錢

紅棗，三錢

If you are overstimulated and irritable, then ... this dish... a shaved horn should help. The first dish... preventive ... ... itself. The dish of the method, simply saute, the juices... ... time the mind... to less two dispel the stress.

This is a simple recipe to overcome herbs that have a alleviation together, they will calm ... and soothe frazzled nerves and prevent illness.

Discard the ram's horn. Eat the meat, and drink the broth. It will neutralize fire in the liver and lungs, relax the muscles, and clear the eyes. You may take this soup up to twice a month. Here are the individual properties of each herb.

Ling Yang Jiao (Antelopis Cornu): Salty in flavor, cold in effect, antelope horn enters the liver meridian. It cleanses toxic heat, subdues liver wind, and calms fright, irritated eyes, and headache.

Gou Teng (Uncariae Ramulus et Uncus): These stems of the gambir vine with fishhook-shaped thorns are sweet and mildly cold, entering into the liver and the pericardium meridians to clear heat and calm the liver.

Catfish and Rehmanniae

Catfish provides a neutral source of protein that is essential for the healthy functioning of the liver. One should use a whole catfish, and after it is thoroughly gutted and cleaned, it may be cooked with the herb as a soup for half an hour, or simmered in a double boiler for three hours. The herb should not be eaten, only the fish and the broth.

Shou Di (Rehmanniae Radix): This is steamed sheng di, as mentioned in the angelica and lamb recipe. It is sweet, mild, and warming. Entering the heart, liver, and kidney meridians, it nourishes the jing and blood and builds the kidney and liver.

BUILDING THE BRAIN AND NERVOUS SYSTEM

If you are engaged in intellectual pursuits, then it is inevitable that you will exhaust your mental energy. The herbalists have a way to replenish that as well. The first of these methods simply calms the mind. The next one fortifies the mind, and the last two dispel headaches.

Wolfberry and Jujube Soup

This is a simple recipe using two herbs that have already been introduced. Together, they will calm the mind, soothe irritated eyes, and dispel dizzi-

熟地保塘虱滋肝益腎

保腦

杞子保紅棗

Shou Di

熟地，二両

Above: qi zi

Below: hong zao

杞子，三錢

紅棗，三錢

　　BEGINNINGS

ness, melancholy, and insomnia. The jujubes are the red variety, but they should be pitted. This is easily done by pulling them apart with your thumbs and removing the pit in the center. Cook the jujubes together with the wolfberry in water or broth for about an hour. For variation, you can add a hard-boiled egg , slices of pork liver, or slices of pork heart.

Brain Tonic

This recipe uses a calf or pig brain. The brain itself should be fresh, and it must be cleaned thoroughly. To do this, immerse the brain in salt water and leave it refrigerated until the next day. The membrane that encases the brain must be removed and discarded. A toothpick is a helpful tool for pulling away the membrane. All clotted blood must be rinsed away.

Place the brain in an earthenware pot, add the herbs, meat, and water to cover. If you like, you can also add a little meat to the broth for flavor. Simmer for two to four hours. Drink the broth only. You can eat some of the brain if you like, but it is very rich. The two herbs, together with the brain, are quite beneficial.

Chuan Xiong (Ligustici Rhizoma): You will notice the three-stroke first word in this name. It is a designation for Sichuan province, for the quality of the herb from this province is the very best. These slices of the dried rhizome are pungent and warm, entering the liver, gall bladder, and pericardium meridians. It is a popular herb for invigorating the blood, promoting the flow of qi, dispelling wind, and controlling pain. It is often applied to cases of headache, tendon spasm, and menstrual disorders.

Bai Zhi (Angelicae Dahuricae Radix): This thinly sliced white root is pungent and warming, entering into the lung and stomach meridians. It removes wind, which is the cause of pressure in the head. It also controls pain and dispels swelling and dampness. It is useful in cases of headache, eye irritation, and leukorrhea.

Headache Formula

This formula is a more powerful variation of the previous one. Whereas the earlier formula is usually used as a supplement, this one is applied in

保腦湯

治頭暈，頭痛

Upper right, inside shell, and loose at lower right: chuan xiong

Left, in bundle, and loose: bai zhi

川芎，三錢

白芷，三錢

150   BEGINNINGS

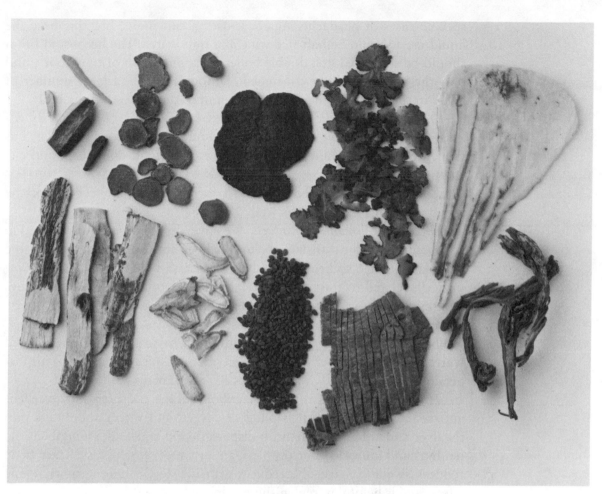

虎骨，二錢

莪朮，一錢

熟地，三錢

川芎，三錢

當歸，三錢

北芪，三錢

故紙，二錢

吧參，一錢

杜仲，一錢

蓁艽，一錢

Top row, from right to
left:

dang gui

chuan xiong

shou di

e shu

hu gu

Lower row, from
right:

qin jiu

du zhong

ba shen

gu zhi

bei qi

specific cases of headache. Again, it uses a calf brain, but this time the liquid used should be half rice wine and half water. The herbs and brain should be simmered in a double boiler for a minimum of two hours, and only the broth should be consumed. Although there is a large number of herbs in this formula, they each have an important effect on the body.

Dang Gui (Angelicae Radix) and Chuan Xiong (Ligustici Rhizoma): These herbs have already been well noted in previous formulas, but their presence here shows their importance as blood nourishers and circulation enhancers.

Chuan xiong was used in the last formula, and is excellent for the blood and controlling pain as well.

Shou Di (Rehmanniae Radix): We have already seen this herb used in connection with the catfish recipe for the liver. Its use here underscores the holistic approach to health. The herbalists assert that brain power is intimately related to the function, health, and productivity of the kidneys and sexual organs; even though this formula is for the head, other aspects of the human system must be addressed whenever relevant.

E Shu (Zedariae Rhizoma): This dried rhizome is bitter, pungent, and warm. It enters the liver and spleen meridians. An excellent agent for dispersing stagnant blood, it also moves qi and controls pain.

Hu Gu (Tigridis Os): This is tiger bone, and is considered an excellent antirheumatic medicine. It is pungent, sweet, and warm and enters into the liver and kidney meridians. It disperses wind and cold, strengthens the tendons and muscles, controls pain, and counters fearfulness. Tiger bone reduces swelling markedly, reduces arthritis, has a long-term analgesic effect, and is helpful in replenishing calcium.

Qin Jiu (Gentianae Macrophyllae Radix): This dried root is bitter, pungent, and neutral. It enters the stomach, liver, and gall bladder meridians. Among its effects are the removal of wind and dampness and the relief of rheumatism, spasm, and pains in tendons and bones.

Du Zhong (Eucommiae Cortex): It is probably because of du zhong's ability to lower blood pressure, decrease the absorption of cholesterol, and its analgesic action that it has been added to this formula.

Ba Shen (Panacis Quinquefolii Radix): This herb is also known as American Ginseng because it grows wild in the United States and Canada.

It was largely introduced into Asia via Hong Kong and Guangzhou province in the eighteenth century. Although it is classified as a ginseng, its effects are opposite to that of the more widely known red and Korean ginsengs. It is bitter sweet in flavor, and is a mild, cooling herb. Entering the lung and stomach meridians, it nourishes the yin, cleanses heat, increases salivation, strengthens the lungs, and moistens the body.

Gu Zhi (Psoraleae Semen): This dried seed is pungent and bitter in flavor. It has extremely warming properties. Entering the spleen and kidney meridians, it supplements the kidneys and fortifies jing.

Bei Qi (Astragali Radix): This herb was used in previous recipes. Here, its chief role is to build qi (the basic component of shen), increase yang, and disperse swelling.

AIDING MEDITATION

Most people think of meditation as a solely mental exercise, but the Taoists consider even that activity as one that may be enhanced through sound diet.

Frog Rice

Although brain formulas are favored by scholars and meditators alike, spiritual practitioners and people who practice qigong favor eating frog. Frog builds the original qi—the qi that first passed into your body from your parents and that you try to channel for the powers of meditation.

To prepare frog rice, clean the frog, and marinate it in wine, ginger, and soy sauce. Cook a pot of rice, and after the water has boiled to the surface of the rice, place the frog and the sauce on top. Cover again, and let the rice finish cooking. Eat both the frog and the rice.

Mi (Oryzae Semen): Rice enters the spleen and stomach. Along with the frog, it builds the center of the body, where the original qi resides. Rice also enters the lung meridians and replenishes qi; combined with the frog, it builds more qi for meditation.

打坐

田鷄大補元氣

Frog

田
鷄

BEGINNINGS

RECOVERY AFTER ILLNESS

Illness is something that happens to all of us. Even though we as Scholar Warriors can minimize the incidence of sickness, there will still be occasions when work, stress, or weather will overcome our efforts to stay healthy. When this happens, it is important to seek out a competent physician. Medicine exists for us to use. Doctors have the skill to heal us, and we should avail ourselves of every resource when ill. But after treatment, the following methods will help you to fully recover.

Black Bean and Catfish Soup

Both the black bean and the catfish are good sources of nutrition; jujubes help to build blood, and citrus peel strengthens the spleen and stimulates your appetite.

The beans and herbs should be cooked in water or broth until the beans are soft. Then add the catfish, sliced into steaks, and simmer until the fish is done (should be no more than twenty minutes). Both the soup and the ingredients may be eaten.

Hei Dou (Glycine Sojae Semen): Black bean may be bought as a grocery staple in food markets, but you may also buy it at an herb store (or by mail order) if you are unsure at first. It is a black soybean, sweet in flavor, neutral in property. It supplements deficiency of blood, clears vision, and nourishes jing.

Hong Zao (Zizyphi Fructus) and Chen Pi (Citri Leiocarpae Exocarpium): Both these herbs have been discussed, but you can see how gentle yet effective they are by their use in this restorative formula. You need not use a large amount of chen pi in this formula, two or three pieces is enough.

Squab Soup

Squab is considered a great delicacy, partially because of its restorative properties. It is a nutritious food, yet it is not as fatty as chicken. In contrast to the last recipe, which concentrates is on the blood, this formula provides protein with herbs for the liver, kidneys, and jing.

復元

黑豆保塘虱

白鴿湯

Center: *hei dou*

Around rim: *hong zao*

(Not shown: *chen pi*)

黑豆，二両

紅棗，十個

陳皮，一錢

BEGINNINGS

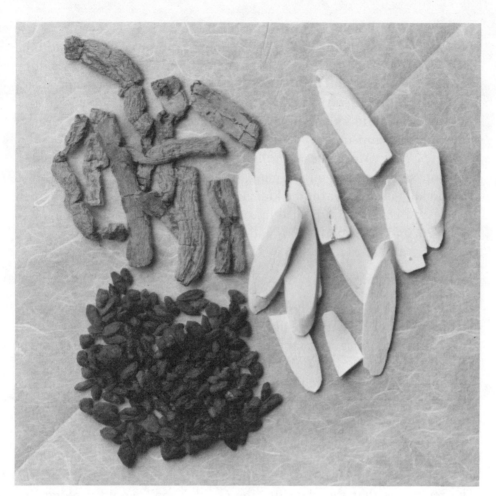

Lower left: *qi zi*

Upper right: *huai shan*

Upper left: *ba ji tian*

杞子，三錢

淮山，三錢

戟天，三錢

The squab should be cleaned thoroughly and may be cut up or left whole. Place it in a double boiler with enough water to cover and add the herbs. Cook for two to four hours. You will find that the squab will be wonderfully tender, and the herbs will make the broth nourishing:

Qi Zi (Lycii Fructus) and Huai Shan (Batatatis Rhizoma): Wolfberry builds the liver and kidneys; the huai shan tonifies the lungs and kidneys and stimulates appetite.

Ba Ji Tian (Morindae Radix): This is an excellent kidney builder. Pungent, sweet, mild, and warming, it enters the kidney meridian. It is traditionally used to warm the kidneys, supplement yang, and strengthen muscle and bone and is applied in cases of impotence, chills in the lower abdomen, and pains in the loins and knees.

Solomon Seal Wine

黃
精
酒

Although wine is generally not drunk by those advocating the path of the Scholar Warrior, it is permissible to use medicinal wines. This wine is drunk only an ounce at a time, so there is no danger of inebriation or damage to one's qi.

To make this wine, soak up to two pounds of Solomon seal in rice wine for a minimum of three months. Use the highest proof and use enough wine to cover the herbs completely. The longer the soak, the stronger the effect. This wine helps in recovery from illness.

Certain Taoists gave much credit to Solomon seal. It is said that China's first emperor, Huangdi, asked which plant would give immortality. The reply was that the plant of "the Great Yang" would prolong life. From that time, many people thought that eating this herb would help them obtain the jing (essence) of the universe. Because the root was yellow, the plant was called "yellow essence."

If you do not want to prepare this herb in wine, it may also be simmered in water for about an hour and a hard-boiled egg added at the end.

Huang Jing (Polygonati Rhizoma): Solomon seal is considered a tonic. It is sweet, mild, and warming and enters the spleen and stomach meridians. Supplementing the stomach and spleen, replenishing the qi, this herb builds jing and is used in cases of deficiency and debility.

黄精，一両

米酒

清熱解毒

車前子茶

甘蔗

EXPELLING AND PURIFYING HERBS

In general, the aspect of herbology that deals with expelling and purifying herbs is best left to the guidance of an herbalist. Yet it is important to note this facet of herbal practice because the Scholar Warrior is not simply concerned with tonifying but with purification as well. The cleaner one's body and mind, the more powerful one will be.

Plantain Seed Tea

During practice of qigong and physical exercises, a great deal of heat is built up in the system. Sometimes this heat will be trapped in the body, causing burning sensations when urinating, insufficient urination, bad breath, and pains in the abdomen. Plantain seed tea is commonly used to purge the body of this excessive heat. To make it, simmer the seeds gently in a large pot of water for up to an hour. Strain out the seeds, and use the liquid as a beverage.

Che Qian Zi (Plantaginis Semen): This plant was very plentiful, growing along the roadsides and on horse and cow paths. Thus it received its name "seeds in front of a carriage." It is sweet and cold in property. It enters the liver, kidney, small intestine, and lung meridians; it is this ability to enter so many meridians that makes it effective in purging heat throughout the body. It also regulates water metabolism, clears vision, disperses phlegm, and controls coughing.

Sugar Cane

Here is a plant that does not need extensive preparation! One may either chew on the cane itself or drink the juice, which is available commercially.

Gan zhe, Saccharum officinarum, is useful in cases of excessive heat, bloating, water retention, rashes, pimples, dry throat and coughing, pain in the eyes, and dehydration.

The photograph shows dried sugar cane, which can be simmered in water for one or two hours. The fresh cane or the juice is far superior.

車前子，五錢

甘蔗，五錢

PORRIDGES

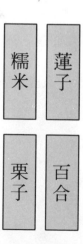

In traditional Asia, a white rice porridge is the staple of the morning meal. It is easy to digest, bland, nutritious, and filling. In normal meals, slices of pork or preserved egg are added for flavor. What is less known is that there is a whole series of herbs and other meats that may be added to porridge for medicinal purposes. In this way, a Scholar Warrior modulates well-being on a daily basis through the simple ingredients eaten for breakfast.

Making the porridge is simple. Rice should be rinsed repeatedly until the water runs clear. The quantity should be very small, about a rice bowl full to a large pot of clear water. Cover the pot, and gently simmer for two hours until porridge is formed. The herbs added to the rice change the medicinal properties of the porridge.

The type of rice used is important. Some people use only glutinous rice, and this yields a very soft, pastelike gruel. Others, preferring more texture, will add up to half the amount in long grain rice. Purists say that the cover should never once be lifted during the two hours, nor should the porridge ever be stirred.

Finally, no matter what you use in the porridge, be sure to add a few slivers of fresh ginger to your bowl. Rice porridge is very cooling to the system, and the ginger will help harmonize it.

Nuo Mi (Oryzae Semen): Glutinous rice is listed by the herbalists as a tonic. It is sweet in flavor and enters the spleen, stomach, and lung meridians. It replenishes qi and contains both starch and protein. Depending on the effect that you want, you may make your porridge according to any of the following recipes.

Lotus Seed Meal: Tonic to the spleen, stomach, and appetite, it is also astringent in cases of diarrhea and dysentery. You can either buy the seeds ground up, or grind it yourself. Add about a handful to a pot of porridge.

Chestnut: This nut is tonic to the kidneys and strengthens the loins and legs. You can buy chestnuts dried, but it is better to use the fresh nut, about a handful to a pot of porridge.

Lily: This herb is known as *bai he* (*Lilii bulbus*). It is sweet, cooling, and moistening and enters the heart and lung meridians. Bai he is used to

白粥

蓮　栗　百
子　子　合

moisten the lungs, control cough, quiet the heart, pacify the spirit, and balance urination, and it is regarded as an excellent yin tonic. It may be used in porridge whole or ground into a flour. A handful is enough.

Jujube: We have already seen the great usefulness of this herb; it is not surprising that it can be added to porridge as well. It is a good blood builder. Use about ten per person. Wash them well, and cook them until they are soft. Save the water. Add more water, and begin to cook your porridge. In the meantime, peel the jujubes and mash them. Add them to the porridge after the rice has begun to expand, and then let it cook until done.

Wolfberry: A handful of qi zi (*Lycii Fructus*) is beneficial to the blood, the liver, and the eyes.

Lamb: Sliced lamb, about a half pound to a large pot of porridge, builds the kidneys, builds yin and strengthens yang, supplements the digestive system, regulates urination, and stops cold sweats. It is also an excellent restorative after illness. If you find the "gamey" flavor of lamb offensive, several slices of ginger added with the meat will balance the taste.

Snow Pears: These are the so-called Asiatic apples that look like a cross between an apple and a pear. They may be eaten as a fruit, of course, or they may be used in porridge as an herb. Snow pears are also available dried. They dispel heat, disperse phlegm, calm the heart, and dispel thirst. This formula is especially useful in cases of dry cough that produce yellow or brown phlegm, and it is soothing to the digestion. Simply cut two pears into slices, and cook with your porridge. If you use the dried slices, a handful will do; they are very sweet.

Barley: This porridge counters arthritis, dispels heat, circulates qi, and purges water retention in the lower limbs. It enters into the spleen, lung, and kidney meridians. Cook a handful with your porridge.

Fish Bladder: Fish bladder, *yu biao jiao* (Ichthyocolla), may be bought in markets. It is white and puffy. It builds vitality, blood, and the kidneys. Especially considered excellent for women, it is used after childbirth, against leukorrhea, and to supplement women whose diets are poor.

It is sweet in flavor, neutral in property. It enters the stomach meridian, nourishes yin, subdues yang, builds the liver and kidneys, and balances the sexual organs. Cook with your porridge, about the equivalent

紅棗

杞子

羊肉

雪梨

苡米

魚鰾膠

Upper left: hong zao
Lower left: qi zi
Center, both fresh and dried: yi li
Right: da mai

以米

雪梨

杞子

紅棗

Yu biao jiao

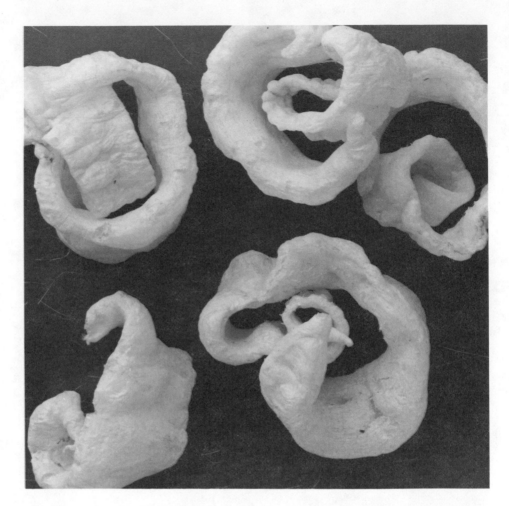

魚
鰾
胶

BEGINNINGS

of a rice bowl in volume to a pot of porridge. If you need to cut it up, soak the fish bladder in water until it softens.

TEAS

There are a great variety of teas, and a Scholar Warrior should know how to use them as part of the daily diet. Seeing tea as a beverage from a bag is, to a tea lover, as abhorrent as jug wine to a wine connoisseur. Tea is traditionally considered a deep subject requiring a lifetime of study. There is even a scripture to tea, written by the patron saint of this wonderful drink, Lu Yu.

But we are concerned with the simplest of uses. In general, teas are divided into green, black, or red teas, flower teas, and herb teas.

Green teas are unfermented and unroasted; black teas and red teas are processed by heating in enormous copper drums. Green teas are cooling and should be drunk primarily when the weather is warm or hot. They are soothing and clean tasting, and the best is probably long jing, or Dragon Well tea, from Hangzhou, China.

Black teas are heating and are best drunk when it is cold. Their caffeine content is higher as well. Among the more famous black teas are Oolong (Bird and Dragon Tea) and the Iron Guanyin Tea, or Tie Guanyin. This last tea comes in a variety of grades, with the best costing over a hundred dollars a pound. Its taste, however, is indescribably fragrant. It is said that this tea was favored by Buddhist monks, for they found that its refreshing qualities helped them in their long hours of meditation.

Red teas are extremely heating and very strong. Their caffeine content is high, and the tea brewed with these leaves can become so dark and heavy that it upsets some people's digestion.

Best among the flower teas is chrysanthemum tea, which is simply an infusion of chrysanthemum flowers. Known as *ju hua* (*Chrysanthemi flos*), it is sweet, bitter, mild, and cooling. It enters the lungs and liver meridians and disperses wind, heat, and toxins, and clears the eyes. Another flower tea that is known for expelling excessive heat is honeysuckle tea, known as *jin yin hua* (*Lonicerae flos*). It is sweet and cold in property, enters the lung,

鐵觀音

烏龍

龍井

Left: ju hua
Right: jin yin hua

菊花　金銀花

Bo he

薄荷

BEGINNINGS

stomach, heart, and spleen meridians, and is often used to cool fevers, dispel toxic swelling and heat, and treat skin eruptions.

An herb tea that can safely be used by anyone, and is readily available in the West, is mint tea. Known as *bo he* (*Menthae herba*), it is pungent and cooling. It enters the lung and liver meridians and dispels wind and heat and cleanses the throat.

Teas, used properly, are the final supplement you need as a Scholar Warrior. With the herbal recipes to supplement your regular meals and teas as refreshing drinks, you are well on your way to using diet and herbs to build the strongest foundation of physical health.

薄
荷

晉陶淵水乃傳林之書渡新縛六僑
嘉譽高山法師居廬山送客不過虎溪道之良而丑過往肆如釋尼之
過虎溪因松與吳世僅為三笑圖一日陶陶三人語言語黃念石覽送

且圖畫吳媒拯華

THREE
LAUGHING
FRIENDS. Kao
Ch'i-p'ei (c. 1672–
1734). Qing dynasty.
Asian Art Museum of
San Francisco, B65
D56.

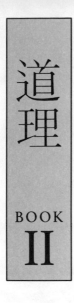

道理

BOOK

II

Without the proper understanding of philosophy,
There cannot be an understanding of the Tao.
Without going beyond philosophy,
There cannot be a realization of the Tao.

PHILOSOPHY AND ISSUES

6

Tao gave birth to one
One gave birth to two
Two gave birth to three
Three gave birth to all things.

TAO

GROUNDING YOURSELF
PHILOSOPHICALLY

THERE ARE MANY STYLES of Taoism, for there have been hundreds of masters in each century. They have found varying but equally valid ways of gaining their insight, and so Taoism has evolved into an elaborate and sprawling school. It is a religion to some, a body of philosophy to others, or to many people in Hong Kong, Taiwan, and much of the rest of Asia, simply a conglomeration of superstitions. But there are common elements. When one searches to the very core of Taoism, it is possible to see that Taoism is eccentric, uninterested in dogma, and seldom concerned with deriving authority from higher powers. It is based on direct observation and relies on pragmatic appeal when addressing its constituents.

Taoism declares that its beginnings are unknown, lost in history over four thousand years ago. It probably had its earliest beginnings among nature worshipers and shamans. Early humanity found the world and the harsh elements unfathomable, and Taoism sought to deal with such frightening phenomena as floods, storms, and natural disasters by integrating the human world with the natural one. Interestingly enough, Taoists never concentrated on dominating nature. They never thought this possible. Instead, they tried to understand the principles within nature and harmonize with them.

Early in Taoism's development, divination became an essential feature. On their most basic level, these systems were not so much methods for predicting the future as they were attempts to see into natural processes and events. The *I Ching* is the only main form of Taoist divination widely known today, and it takes an almost scientific approach to circumstance. It eschews any propitiation of gods or spirits. For the Taoists, the Tao and the flow of events was impersonal. They focused on understanding the principles behind that flow. They contemplated sky, earth, water, wind, thunder, mountains, lakes, fire—simple elements. But it was their understanding of such basic elements that led the Taoists to deep abstraction and great profundity.

Though some people think of Lao Tzu (6th century B.C.) as the "founder" of Taoism, this is not true. His *Tao Te Ching* is considered by many masters to be a compilation of previous writings, and many of the concepts refer to already well established ideas. Lao Tzu did not write in a vacuum. He clearly made references to other writings and ideas and addressed himself to the social problems of an already advanced civilization. Taoism began much earlier than Lao Tzu, and it has an unbroken history through his time and into ours.

Taoists are empirical. They test their beliefs in the world, and everything they believe is up for questioning and reexamination at any time. Such a lack of absolute assertion delights its adherents and confuses those who require spirituality to be authoritative and based on beliefs in reincarnation, an afterlife, and powerful gods. A quick examination will reveal that Taoism cares little for these elements and does not need them to justify its point of view.

Reincarnation and the promise of a life after death are two of the most

I CHING (YI JING) The *Classic of Change*, or *Book of Changes*. This is one of the principal texts of divination and embodies many of the Taoist attitudes about the Way.

TAO TE CHING (DAO DE JING) This has been variously translated as *The Way and Its Power, The Taoist Virtue Classic*, and so on. A book of eighty-one poems attributed to Lao Tzu, it sets down his final thoughts about pursuing the Way as he was about to renounce the world entirely.

LAO TZU ON A
WATER BUFFALO.
Anonymous, undated.
Bildarchiv Foto Mar-
burg der Philipps-
Universitat, Marburg,
Germany. Lao Tzu
was a librarian in the
imperial house of the
Zhou dynasty. Lao
Tzu tried to put forth
a better way of life,
but eventually tired of
his struggles and left
on a water buffalo in a
westward direction.
According to legend,
the gatekeeper begged
him to stop and write
down his philosophy
for posterity. That
writing is the *Tao Te
Ching*.

common elements in religions. Though the Taoists speak of these concepts, they privately admit that these parts of Taoism were installed centuries ago to attract lay followers and to compete with the other strong religions in China, Buddhism and Islam. An elaborate doctrine of gods, rebirth, and otherworldly rewards proved to be much more comforting to the populace, but inwardly, the Taoists never relied on a concept of heaven and hell. Where were these two places? At a time when people could barely conceive of planets, were heaven and hell anything more than fantasy?

Quite bluntly, they said that there was absolutely no proof of heaven and hell, and that furthermore, there was no proof of reincarnation. A leaf thrown into a river might be found downstream. How is a soul thrown onto the wheel of transmigration to be found? The Taoists declared that they could find no evidence of reincarnation, so they refused to rely on it. Even if reincarnation existed, one still had to start all over, from birth to infancy and on to maturity, without any conscious control over the knowledge and skill gained in previous lifetimes.

Furthermore, the Taoists asserted that life itself had no guarantees. They wanted spirituality to address itself to that, not urge people to go further into even more uncertain territory. No one knew what was going to happen to them in the next month or the next year. When people traveled even here on earth, they could not even predict with any reliance what would happen. If they could not even tell what would happen when they went over the most distant mountain range, then how could they possibly speculate on a heaven no one could show them, or an afterlife that tore one's soul asunder and plopped it into a body somewhere else in the universe? No. The skeptical Taoists wanted to do everything in the here and now.

Some Taoists even turned this fierce skepticism toward the gods themselves. You may find this strange, because there are many Taoist temples that shelter a bewildering pantheon of gilded and brightly clothed figures. But though there are gods in temples, and although religious activities are one of the obligations of Taoists, the development of elaborate temples was an almost political movement meant to help Taoism survive against the attractiveness of Buddhism and Islam. In their own private thoughts,

THE THREE PURE ONES. Anonymous, undated. Bildarchiv Foto Marburg der Philipps-Universitat, Marburg, Germany. On the right is Lao Tzu. He is the teacher of the Jade Emperor, the celestial ruler, who appears in the center. On the left is Original Being, who represents the principle of primordial origins as well as renunciation; though he is most qualified to govern, he has renounced that responsibility in order to devote himself to cultivating the Tao.

Taoists realized that there was much more to cosmology than a bureaucratic pantheon in the sky: the Tao preceded all things, and it was Tao that gave birth to the gods, not vice versa.

Even among priests and monks, devoting oneself to clerical duties was not considered essential for insight. Perhaps a particular person needed discipline, and so constant tending to an altar, temple, and worshipers might provide just the right method of restraint. But in the end, the Taoists believed that wisdom comes from self-cultivation; service built personal character but was not considered the ultimate means to attain wisdom.

In short, the Taoists eliminated the usual basis for religion. The ultimate justification for spirituality was not in the promise of an afterlife, not in the gods, not in ritual, and not in clerical authority, but in the honest and personal exploration of this life and this time. Taoists were the mavericks of the spiritual world. They did not care for conformity, or for the attitudes of the herd. All they cared about was the honest search for the truth and the direct experiencing of the Tao.

TAO, THE DARK MYSTERY

The early sages postulated Tao as the ultimate nature of all things, and this is still the best starting point for understanding Taoist philosophy. Tao is of a scope more vast than our imaginations can conceive. It is in the space between heaven and earth, is heaven and earth itself. It preceded all things and will last far beyond the disintegration of our world. It is as close to absolute and eternal as we can imagine.

We may speculate about the Tao, give it elaborate descriptions, but the images we employ are merely metaphors. The ultimate nature of Tao itself is not possible for us to grasp because our minds are inherently dualistic. We are children of beauty and ugliness; we dwell in the midst of contrasts and extremes. When given the choice between the nameless and the nameable, we gravitate toward what we can identify. The Tao, however, is both nameless (nonbeing) and named (being). Within the depths of Tao, existence and nonexistence come together; no distinctions exist. Time becomes circular or even irrelevant. Our minds cannot function in such a realm. We cannot see where there is no contrast. We cannot know white without black, upper without lower, left without right. In Tao, both white and black stand in the same place. This is why Tao is elusive, indescribable, nameless—strangely colorless and flavorless.

It is precisely this confounding area where duality is neutralized that Taoism most enjoys. Taoists call this paradoxical mystery the nameless. They say it is the nameless that gives birth to the named (meaning all things conceivable, hence all things dualistic). All things come from Tao the nondualistic. Tao gave birth to us, surrounds us, nurtures us, supports us. It is the mother of all life, not in the sense of some mythical goddess, but as the summation of all the life-giving processes in the universe. The entire universe, with its explosions, its deaths and births of stars, its evolution, its expansion and contraction—all things from the most distant points in infinity to the very point of our own hearts share Tao as mother.

Tao is not a substance. It is all substances. Tao is not space, but it encompasses all spaces. Nothing changes or moves without Tao. Tao is something active, moving. Tao is process, a tremendous expansion and contraction, a constant tide between existence and nonexistence. Yet,

WU MING
Nameless. Nonbeing. The Taoist name for nonexistence.

YOU MING
Having a name. Being. The Taoist designation for all of the conceivable universe.

XU
Emptiness.

GU SHEN
Valley spirit.

TUO YUE
Bellows.

though it moves, its movement is not something tangible like the wind. With the wind, we can say that there is something there. We can feel the breeze; we can examine dust particles in the stream of air; we can measure changes in temperature. Nor is the movement of Tao exactly like water. We can touch the cool liquid, see the glimmering stream, measure the volume of its flow. But Tao is much more than that.

Think back to the Taoist statement that the nameless gave birth to the named. What is nameless has no duality, for it cannot be defined. Anything with duality must be tangible and understandable; all tangibility has causes and origins. Whatever has an origin cannot be absolute, for there is always something preceding it. Only that which has no dualism has no origins, and so may be considered absolute. The Taoists call this absoluteness *emptiness*.

This may seem contradictory. How can we conceive of anything real as being empty? But this is precisely what the Taoists assert. In fact, they value emptiness highly. They assure us that emptiness is positive, productive, and nurturing, and they use concrete images to help us understand this point.

Fond of taking their examples from nature, Taoists use the metaphor of *gu shen*, "the valley spirit." A valley supports life, feeds the animals who live there, and provides fertile earth for agriculture. It can do this only because it is empty. It accepts the flow of the river because it is most low and most humble. It receives the warmth of the sun because it is wide and not filled with anything to block the light. It brings forth life because it supports all who come to it.

But the quiescent nature of the fertile valley may still leave the idea that emptiness is limited to being receptive, or that it is somewhat static. Nothing could be further from the Taoist concept of emptiness. Perhaps the most graphic description of emptiness as something active is the metaphor of *tuo yue*, "the bellows." This is a basic Taoist image, full of rich connotations. The Taoists have been associated with metallurgists, blacksmiths, potters, and alchemists since their earliest beginnings—all people who understood how to use emptiness.

What makes bellows work? For the Taoists, it is not the wood, crossbars, and leather but the space between. Without that expanding and contracting emptiness, the bellows could not perform their function. Bellows are the very idea of emptiness put to practical use; the Taoists love to take the abstruse and yoke it to a practical task like firing a furnace. Emptiness is not an abstract term to them. Taoists even see the space between heaven and earth as a great metaphysical bellows: the supreme emptiness through which Tao flows. Heaven represents the male, and earth represents the female, and their interplay is the movement of emptiness. The Tao itself moves back and forth between heaven and earth, going in and out between the nothingness of nonbeing and our world of existence.

The valley bears life; the bellows makes the flames leap higher. Heaven and earth come from the emptiness of Tao, the world issued forth from Tao. Each one of us is a child of the Tao. The Tao is our mother, and as long as we are in her embrace, we are safe. Yet who was mother of the mother? Where is Tao's source?

The Taoists declare that the source of all things is an even greater emptiness. Being can only come from nonbeing. As long as the source of the world is defined as coming from some material phenomenon, or as long as it is thought of as the creation of gods, then the question of where that phenomenon or that god came from is left open. But emptiness cannot be transcended. Nothing else precedes nothingness, so it is logically the beginning point of Tao.

Taoists have many ways to indicate this supreme emptiness. They sometimes call it *hun dun*, "chaos." They sometimes refer to it as the limit beyond all limits, *wu ji*, or "limitlessness." It is impossible for humans to enter into this primeval nothingness, or to know it. We have corporeality. We have existence. We have identity and individuality. As soon as we entered into this emptiness, time, our minds, the Tao, and anything else that was of our world would be negated. We cannot absolutely enter into the supreme emptiness and return; we can only know it from afar.

Neither emptiness nor the Tao were created by anyone. They are a primeval reality that well precedes gods and human beings. The Taoists use the term *xiang di*, "image preceding god." Gods are only a small part of Tao's coming and going. It is thus nature, the universe, and Tao that human beings must seek to integrate themselves with, not some lord in the sky. Heaven and earth as the Taoists perceive them are impartial, without

HUN DUN
Chaos, the primeval state of the universe.

WU JI
No limit, limitlessness, no barrier. Emptiness.

XIANG DI
An image in front of God.

consciousness, and without any beings to direct events. They simply exist and move according to Tao. Life functions without intention, without thought, without bias. Heaven and earth have no conscious sense of themselves or what they do.

The Taoists sum up this "creation" of our universe with characteristic simplicity: emptiness produced Tao. In turn,

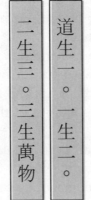

Tao gave birth to one
One gave birth to two
Two gave birth to three
Three gave birth to all things.

XUAN
Dark, profound, mysterious, abstruse.

ZHAN
The dark color of deep water. Profound. Deep.

The Taoists do not speculate much more than that. When they realize the limits of intellectual investigation, they cheerfully admit that they don't know any more and are equally sure that no one else will ever know either. We are simply here in this world. We cannot truly explain why we are here or what we are supposed to do here. The Taoists only observe that we must live in harmony with nature and in that living contemplate the Tao for an understanding of ourselves.

Tao. Tao the supreme, Tao the inescapable. Look into it, and all your human references go slack. Try to plumb it, and the brightest light fails to return. That is why Tao is called *xuan*, the deepest, most abstruse mystery. Tao is the mystery of all mysteries. They say it is like *zhan*, the deep, dark color of water, the flowing softness of the most vast of all oceans. This mystery does not act with self-consciousness, yet all things owe their existence to it.

WU WEI

As the Taoists say, "Tao does not act, yet there is nothing that it does not do." This paradoxical statement is the summation of one of Taoism's most important concepts, *wu wei*. Wu wei means nonaction, not-doing. But it isn't merely a fancy way of saying doing nothing. The wu wei—nonaction—of Tao is that it acts without conscious thought. No one is "up there" planning things. No one is deciding anything. Tao simply goes about its business silently.

Both in the sense of the emptiness of the cosmic bellows, and in the sense that there is no conscious action, the Tao is said to be empty, yet all things are accomplished by Tao. Wu wei is the emptiness that accomplishes. The Taoists have many examples to amplify this point. Take a flute. What makes its beautiful music? It is the hollowness of its center and the holes along its side. Or look at a wheel on a cart. What makes it useful? It is the open hole of the hub that fits the axle; the emptiness of the wheel gives it its usefulness. A house is not a house without the emptiness of windows and doors. A pot is not useful without its open interior. A well gives water only because of its deep opening. Emptiness is useful.

The Taoists observe that wu wei characterizes the movement of Tao. But they also believe that wu wei should apply to human endeavor. If human beings followed the way of the Tao, if they behaved according to wu wei, then they would be in harmony with the natural order. They would not violate their inner nature, and they would get along with other people. It is because most of the world does not live through nonaction that we have all the tragedy of human existence.

Wu wei means acting without conscious thought. But we must be very careful here. We certainly all have met people who are thoughtless, who never think before they act, who, in fact, barely have a notion of what is going on at all. Yet this is not wu wei; it is confusion, ignorance, and abdication of involvement. Other people borrow the concept of wu wei and make it a superstition. They don't do anything, especially when confronted with a serious decision, and let whatever happens happen. They'll trust in the universe, or Tao, or some other presence in the ether to live their life for them. But this is not wu wei either. True living of wu wei is to

WU WEI
Not acting. Actions with no reverberations. A symbol also of the temporal, impermant nature of all things.

live in accord with Tao and to attain a state of such perfect understanding and insight that all actions are spontaneously correct. There is no scheming; there is no selfish motivation; there is no conscious desire to impose your will on others or on nature; there is no emotionalism; there is no irrational behavior; there is no acting according to trends, or what priests say, or what society says, or what divination says. There is only acting, yet there is nothing that you do not accomplish.

Wu wei may seem contradictory to the path of the Scholar Warrior, but this is not so. When one is not mature in one's field, then naturally one has not reached the mode of nonaction. Only when one is fully mature in one's field is there the possibility of wu wei. For example, a warrior who has truly mastered all the necessary skills no longer thinks of technique or strategy. The skill of such a warrior has become more subtle than reflex. During a fight, there is no sense of self-preservation, no sense of cruelty, no sense of the self, no sense of the need to dominate the other person. There is only spontaneous action. At this high point, such a warrior may truly be said to be empty.

An artist who is fully developed no longer needs to pause to think about what colors to mix. The brush moves nearly automatically. There is no conscious thought, only the absorption in creativity. There is no will; there is no planning. Such a state was much admired by Chinese artists. For such a person, there could never be a bad painting, never a mistake, for the artist proceeded only as nature would. There was true wu wei, and all strokes were spontaneously correct.

A master musician might practice scales, but in performance, there will be no thought of how the fingers are moving, no determination to make a great performance, no worry about how to read the music. There is no separation between performer and performance. Again, this is perfect wu wei: the emptiness that accomplishes all things.

How is this wonderful state of spontaneity to be achieved? Through another key Taoist concept: *jue xue*, or "give up learning." Giving up learning is how we return to our inner good and true natures and how we attain wu wei. The Taoists felt that society violated true human nature. Civilization distorted the inner spirit with its artificial standards, its tiresome etiquette, its pandering to human perversions. Intellectualism, the

JUE XUE
To give up, or transcend learning.

temptations of knowledge, wrecked a person. The Taoists asked, "What's the difference between a yes and a no? Are they really so far apart?" It was their way of rejecting the artificial distinctions of society.

"Give up learning." Ah, but did they say when? If merely giving up learning was enough, why have Taoists always been among the most highly educated people of their time? If education was bad, why did they have over a thousand volumes in their canon? Why did they open schools? Why did they give discourses? Why did they serve others? Clearly, they do not mean that learning should never be undertaken. What they do mean is that learning should not become the tool of selfish egotism. When they say to eliminate sagacity, they mean to eliminate the veneration of stupid old men, but they continue to value wisdom. When they say to discard knowledge, they mean to avoid using one's ingenuity to take advantage of others. When they say to eliminate benevolence, righteousness, and morality, they mean that we should not adhere to the empty and phony forms of these things. When they say to give up learning, they mean that we should transcend technical details and enter into a creative state in which our actions are deeply intuitive and correct.

This "correctness" is the correctness of nature. Nature is never right or wrong. It simply is. If there is an earthquake, it may cause terrible devastation to us, but we cannot say that the earth was wrong. If a river floods, breaking our dikes, we cannot say that it has done wrong. If the seasons proceed in their own way, we cannot accuse them of being selfish; nor can we exalt them for their generosity. The phenomena of nature alternate in their own way, and we conform to them as best we can. In the same way, if one is in tune with the Tao, one does not do things except from a deep motivation tied to one's integration with the Tao.

The Taoists assert *bu zheng*, or "noncontention." Again, they do not mean that we should expend no effort. They mean that we should not be going out there and striving unnaturally for great achievements. For human beings will inevitably strive to hold on to the extreme edges of life. They want a great deal of money without losing. They want beauty but not ugliness. They want immortality, not death. They want fame, but never disgrace. It is this stubborn and selfish grasping for extreme advantage that leads us invariably to failure. Hoarding gold and jade only invites

BU ZHENG
Noncontention.

robbery. It is far better to let matters proceed naturally. If your life is so wonderful that good fortune comes your way, take it in stride. Don't strive for further triumphs. If disgrace comes your way, likewise take it in stride. Don't plunge into self-destructiveness. Those who do not contend commit no wrong.

Eliminating learning and noncontention bring us constantly toward wu wei. But these are ideals that cannot be achieved all at once; we are imperfect, and we are already tainted with the poison of society. We must develop gradually, following a natural path until we understand and come to embody wu wei. That is why it is said,

> When learning, increase daily.
> For Tao, decrease daily.
> Decrease, and decrease again
> To arrive at nonaction.

Wu wei in daily life, then, will come only when one has wisdom and maturity. After we have lived life fully, perhaps traveled extensively, come to know ourselves and others intimately, then it is a simple thing to respond to life spontaneously. We do not need to scheme, to plan, to plot strategy. We act with unconscious insight, and without doubt. Like the ideal artist, we would only act as nature itself would have acted, so we cannot make any mistake.

WHEN THE SUN SETS, THE MOON RISES

We have spoken of Tao's emptiness—its wu wei—as the movement between heaven and earth, the movement between being and nonbeing. This movement of Tao is summed up by the word *fan*, or "returning." This means not only that Tao returns to its source, the great emptiness, but also that it returns from that source to our world of existence. It is in this constant returning—this back and forth movement—that polarity is established. With polarity come opposites.

The great polarity generated by returning is called yin and yang, words now familiar in the English language. Yin and yang are the Taoist terms for opposites. They are light and dark, hard and soft, outer and inner, male and female, hot and cold, positive and negative. According to legend, early Taoists formulated this idea from looking at a hillside. Where the sun struck the southern side, they called yang; where the hill was in shadow they named yin. There was no sharp line of demarcation between light and shadow. They blended in a blurry line, a shadow edge. One might even say it was impossible to determine exactly where one began and the other ended. Neither could exist without the other: they defined each other. Without that contrast, without the mutual definition of the two, neither could exist separately. Light could only exist with darkness. You cannot have one without the other. As each moment passed, the edge between light and darkness moved—a graphic display of yin and yang.

FAN
Returning.

Beginning with these simple, concrete observations, the Taoists built their philosophy on yin and yang and eventually extended it into abstract principle. One of their premier observations about yin and yang was that all phenomena are relative. Something may be yang in one context, but yin in another. For example, the moon would be considered yang because it is bright when compared to utter darkness. However, when compared to the sun, the moon would be considered yin because its brightness is less than the sun's. Let us go back to the Taoists as they observe the hillside. No two of them will see the exact same proportion of yin or yang as they gaze at the hill. One standing in full sun would say that the hill is predominantly yang. Another, standing on the shadowy side, might conclude that the hill is nearly entirely yin. A third, standing directly at the edge of the shadow, might declare a nearly even balance. None of them would be incorrect. It all depends on the point of view. The Taoists may well have been the first to ask, "Compared to what?" They cannot see anything in our world as absolute. The entire universe, with its constant and dynamic motion, is an ongoing play between yin and yang. Since the universe is infinite and has no fixed points, there is no absolute point of view; there is only an observer whose observations must forever be considered subjective. The universe that the observer is viewing is relative to where the observer stands, and it would have already changed in the very next moment.

YIN YANG
Duality, the polar opposites inherent in all existence.

Another crucial observation was that yin and yang could never be in balance. Sometimes they blend; sometimes they oppose each other; but they are never completely equal. That would be stasis, and the Taoists do not observe stasis anywhere in the universe. There is always some very tiny bit that is off center, out of balance. And it is this tension that allows for the ongoing movement of things.

This variance between opposites is seen as part of every human being. A person is yin and yang in varying proportions. You are yin and yang. You have two sides to your brain, each one of different character. You have left and right, upper and lower, inner and outer, mind and body, and so on. Qi is paired with blood, and the emotions, yin, are paired with reason, yang. Our personalities have both masculine and feminine qualities. We are profoundly dualistic, with a never resolvable tension between the extremes. It is this tension, this fusion, that animates us.

But this tension extends even into our psychology and character. As long as people are composed of both yin and yang, they cannot totally forsake any single aspect of themselves. You cannot be totally good, and you cannot be completely evil. Of course, you should try to be good at all times, but you should understand your bad thoughts or actions. A Taoist who understands this simple doctrine thus has no use for guilt, fanaticism, or dogma. Dogma is unnecessary. Philosophy and religion are not perfect. Sometimes, you may even have to do something dreadfully wrong that is terribly right for a particular moment. Yin and yang mean relativity. Once wu wei is achieved, even immorality may be the Tao. That is why Taoists "give up learning" (of limited societal definitions).

Guilt is only for those who are unable to accept their own actions. Instead, an understanding of yin and yang allows one to shape one's personality solely in regard to Tao rather than by society's or religion's definitions. Even if one makes a mistake, one understands that there is a certain inevitability to it. The fanaticism of the ascetic who seeks to eradicate some supposedly unacceptable part of himself is irrelevant. Give up sagacity. Accept yourself as you are. You will not remain the same forever, so why be troubled by some part of yourself? If you practice the way of the Scholar Warrior, you will be disciplining yourself while you explore all the parameters of your personality. The proportion of yin and yang and the way the two combine will change too. As you practice, bad things will drop away, but there will be new stages to face too. There is no reason to crazily try to erase or create something. Progress comes naturally.

So yin and yang are relative and in flux both in nature and in each person. But the Taoists felt that there was a discernible order to the alternation between the two. They saw that yin and yang alternated in cycles. Turning their eyes from the hillside where they observed the interplay of light and shadow, the Taoists looked to the sun and the moon. Their observation about the cycles of existence was profoundly simple. They said: "When the sun sets, the moon rises. When the moon sets, the sun rises."

By this cogent observation, they were able to describe the totality of cyclic change. It was important to the Taoists to determine how the Tao moved through the world of phenomena, because it was by understanding this that they sought to integrate themselves with Tao. Looking beyond their assertion that the movement of Tao is in returning, and elaborating on the observation of yin and yang, the Taoists became even more specific about the alternation between polar opposites.

Taking the cycles of the sun and moon as their example, they formulated these simple but all-encompassing views about change:

> What is to be reduced is first expanded.
> What is to be weakened is first strengthened.
> What is to be abolished is first established.

As the *I Ching*, or *Book of Changes*, puts it: "Whenever any action reaches its extreme, it begins to change into its opposite. When something has reached its nadir, it begins to ascend toward its zenith. When something has reached its zenith, it will inevitably begin to descend toward its nadir." Here is the observation about the sun and the moon expressed as abstract philosophy.

RELATIVITY MEANS NOTHING IS PERMANENT

Coupled with the relativistic view inherent in yin and yang, the Taoists also included in their view of change that nothing is permanent. This is a crucial point, for it supports the idea of emptiness; it supports the idea that all is change; it supports the idea that human beings should not contend and strive to hold on to things (because they will invariably change or fade away). The Taoists said, "A rainstorm does not last a whole day. Heaven and earth's works do not last, how then can man's?" Thus, though Tao proceeds through nonaction to accomplish all things, none of these things last. They are all subject to change.

One of our biggest mistakes is thinking things will last. We tend to act as if we will live forever, especially when we are young. We procrastinate; we fail to plan for the future; we ignore our health. We pursue our relationships with the vain hope that "love will last forever," and we are never quite prepared for the death of loved ones. We wail pathetically at funerals, and what we are in fact crying about is not the "misfortune" of the deceased but our own fear and lack of preparation for death. We do not understand wu wei—that nothing in life lasts.

The Taoists, of course, are not the only ones who notice the fragility of life. Many people have noted the passing of the seasons, the erosion of even a granite mountain, the deaths of animals. The works of civilization fall into disorder. Great monuments crumble; bridges fall; the forest quickly reclaims what people abandon. In human relations, temporariness is also the rule. Parents die; lovers leave; children grow up and wander away. Many people notice that nothing in life lasts, and they find it sad.

In fact, if we consider a moment, we are quite lucky that nothing is permanent, that misfortune, illness, boredom, bad weather, governmental mismanagement, and a host of other irritations do not last longer than they do. Bad things do not last, and that is important to remember when we face them. But good things don't last either. They are here for us to enjoy, but we should not be affected when they pass away. We should, in fact, remain impartial to all things.

The Taoist views change and the temporalness of life as being useful. If nothing lasts, one can take advantage of that fact. This odd reaction to something that many find depressing is reminiscent of the legendary meeting between Buddha, Confucius, and Lao Tzu. The three sages were standing before a large urn of vinegar, symbolizing life. Each in turn dipped his finger in. Buddha tasted and pronounced it bitter. Confucius tasted and pronounced it sour. Lao Tzu tasted and pronounced it sweet. The Taoist is a person who seeks to turn all things to advantage. Even the impermanence of life, which others find bitter or sour, the Taoist makes into something useful. They noted that a great tree must still begin as a sapling. A journey of great distance still proceeds from a single step. Why dwell only on the final outcome? There is more to life than that. Any event begins from something small and grows large. It may pass away, or it may be transformed into some other object or force. If we can follow this, our endeavors will take on the inevitability of natural occurrences. That is using temporalness to one's own advantage.

Toward this pragmatism, the Taoists take note of the following principles regarding the movement of circumstance.

Act when matters have not yet emerged, or when things are still small. To the Taoists, it is a great shame to act too late. They seek to act while things may still be affected. If you wait too long, a situation gets out of control. If you address it right away, then you can direct it or suppress it with ease. This principle has ramifications for many areas of life. For example, if you are raising children, it is easy to establish certain parameters when they are young. But once they get older, it becomes harder and harder to do. The process of self-cultivation as a Scholar Warrior is similar. If you find yourself indulging in some new bad habit, then the time to act is in the very beginning. "Nip it in the bud," is a common saying.

In the workplace, we have many occasions to practice this ideal. If you have an assignment, it is easy to do it if you act in a timely fashion and get the right people to contribute their parts at the right time. If you miss a step, it becomes difficult to go back and correct it later. And if your timing is off, you miss your deadline. Something that would have been simple becomes difficult because you did not act while matters were small. A personal relationship is also similar. If you establish the proper understanding from the beginning, then the course of the relationship will go more smoothly.

The time to act is when there is nothing yet to do. This maxim underscores the last point, but it is more specific about timing. A Scholar Warrior acts long before the common person even perceives that there is a situation emerging. That is why the acts of Scholar Warriors appear to be so miraculous. They are able to perceive a situation and act upon it long before others even know anything is happening. By the time others know, the force of the action is too great to oppose. It takes experience and an understanding of how actions proceed in order to do this.

The fragile is easily dissolved, the minute easily dispersed. There are two sides to this observation. One is in regard to something that you want to destroy. The other is a warning about your own activities. In the first case, the advice is to destroy that which you oppose as early as you can, even "when there is nothing to do." For all things are fragile in their beginnings, and those things that are tiny can be easily scattered. A common example is a seed versus a tree. Which is more easy to uproot? Of course, the seed is easy to dig up, the tree difficult to pull from the earth. In the same way, if you are in a political situation and you perceive potential opposition, the correct way is to undermine your rivals long before they have had the opportunity to organize themselves. However, if you are entering a situation that is already mature, you can see that you are already too late. Things are no longer fragile or minute. You thus have to use force to change things, and the Taoists advise against this. That is why they say, "Plan the difficult task when matters are easy," and "The time to govern is before there is disorder." Whatever your endeavors, it is best to act early, when things are small, and if you are confronted with a large and long-standing situation, start something new, create a new context. What you start may include the original situation you wanted to address, but the new context will be so much wider and more far-reaching that it will render the old one small. Only then will you be able to affect the original situation according to the rule of acting while matters are small.

The second point, about the fragile being easily dissolved, is a warning about your own plans. When you are starting any venture, it is going to be fragile and minute. Until it takes root, it can be easily swept away. It is important to protect it from opposition if you want it to last. Only if your venture is protected in its early stages can you go on to complete your plans.

If you manipulate things when they are small, great things may be accomplished. It is really because Scholar Warriors understand how circumstances naturally progress that they remain unopposed. If they have their timing correct, if they have selected the proper course of action, and if they protect what they have planted until the proper time to come forth, then they cannot help but be successful. For example, if someone is establishing a new business, they must exhaustively plan their products, meticulously establish their system of distribution, and carefully prepare all their accounting procedures in advance of announcing their product. Let's say they have to subcontract to a manufacturer. If there is a mistake early on, they can fix it without much expense. But if they have to make a recall two years later, the mistake will be quite costly, even ruinous for the company. A farmer is another example. To have a successful crop, a farmer needs to do things at the right time. In and of themselves, each of these things will be quite minor. Perhaps they might include tilling, applying fertilizers, planting, weeding, controlling insects, and so on. Unless the farmer does each of these little things, there will be no bountiful harvest. But if the farmer *does* do everything correctly, the crop is bound to come. Can you make a plant "ungrow"? No, you cannot, and so the farmer's small manipulations at the proper times lead to a big harvest.

Once it has been established, balance is easy to maintain. The beginning is the most crucial time, and it is also the most difficult. Once things are started in the proper way, they can proceed according to a momentum of their own. Let's go back to the example of the farmer again. Once the crop is established, there is very little to do except water it and safeguard it from disaster. The farmer has done the job, has started things going, and now has to leave things alone to develop. The farmer's timing must be impeccable, yet much of what is required is to leave things alone. That is what the Taoists mean by wu wei, or not-doing. They don't mean the complete negation of action; they mean the timely application of the proper actions.

Once things have started, they should proceed naturally. If you have set things in motion according to the laws of change, then you should not interfere. Such intervention goes against the laws of noncontention; it violates the natural development of events. Don't be like the rice farmer who destroyed his plants: he killed them by pulling on them, thinking that would help them grow faster.

If we add this to the philosophy of change stated in the *I Ching* about things changing to their opposites when they reach their extremes, then we will be able to follow, and to a certain degree manipulate, events in life. If we could isolate one single set of events, we could see that they follow a certain parabolic curve. At the beginning, and on ascension, the course is easy to adjust, the direction simple to alter. But after the peak has been passed, the curve is set, and decline is inevitable. The trouble is that single events cannot be isolated; they come pell-mell, and their beginnings are often obscured. That is why even wu wei requires skill.

Know the ways of yin and yang. Understand that life occurs in cycles. Note the way that change occurs by the transformation of opposites. Act at the right time. In this way, the sage may never be opposed.

THE TAOIST

DAO REN
A Taoist.

We have spoken of the mysteries of Tao, the central concept of emptiness, and the relativity of yin and yang. Each of these ideas is meant not just for intellectual discussion but for outright realization. But if these ideas are truly meant to be implemented, what must the person who does so be like?

Taoists have always been among the outcasts, the strange ones, the iconoclasts. Conservative members of religious orthodoxies have criticized them as difficult, erratic, and uncooperative. Confucianists—those staid people so concerned with upholding the etiquette that binds society together—were frequently scandalized by the Taoists' unconventional behavior. Yet they were also prevented from discounting Taoism altogether because of the learned character of Taoist masters and the brilliant discourses these teachers gave. The orthodox were frequently amazed by what the unorthodox could do. In a legendary meeting between Confucius and Lao Tzu, Confucius professed not to have understood the Taoist, yet likened him to a dragon.

One who has entered the mysteries of change can truly be called a Taoist. Such a person, man or woman, is described as subtle, mysterious, dark, penetrating, deep, unrecognizable, and obscure. These Taoists do not display their talents or their understanding. They feel the pulse of Tao completely and do not care to have any distractions from that feeling.

Once they are found out by the populace, they disappear, or act crazy, in order to be left alone. It is said that such a person has "no mind."

Aside from the eccentricity that most people find disturbing about the Taoist, the idea of "no mind" is one that gives many people trouble. It may be easiest to say "intention" here. The Taoists have no intentions. They strive for wu wei, and in such a context intending to do things has no place. It should be evident that they do indeed act according to the rules of change that were noted earlier, but that type of action is on a wholly different level from the planning and machinations most people use. Their type of action is only that which is in accord with Tao. They know what to do not by analysis, but by abiding in a state of simplicity that allows them to mirror the Tao perfectly. For the highest Taoists, their inner mirrors are bright: they reflect perfectly without adding or subtracting one bit from the reflection.

This simplicity of character is symbolized by the word *pu*. Pu refers to a raw block of wood, not carved, not cut, not affected in any way by human designs. It has no shape, no identity. This is the natural state that the Taoist tries to return to, a state in which there is no identity, no worry, and no extraneous thought.

The Taoist compares being like a block of wood with the unsullied innocence of a child. A child has no identity. It does not know its own name, does not care for fame or fortune, does not know shame, guilt, embarrassment, or sin. A child may commit some harm accidentally, but never intentionally. That is why the Taoists refer to *ying er*, or "the infant." They take the infant as a symbol for the state of pure innocence and emptiness they seek. In being like a block of wood, the Taoist strives for a pure self free of the marks of society. In being like an infant, the Taoists trust themselves solely to the Tao. They follow it without hesitation, like an infant heeding the call of its mother.

Do bad things happen to Taoists? Yes, misfortune comes to them as much as it comes to anyone else. Being a Taoist is not exemption from the troubles of life, and the Taoists will not try to pretend that following the Way will make them rich, happy, or powerful. What it does is give them a way to follow that will help them survive, harmonize, and participate. When bad things happen, they don't lament them. They go through bad

WU XIN
Wu means no or non. *Xin* is heart, mind.

PU
A block of wood. The uncarved block. A symbol of pure, untouched simplicity.

YING ER
An infant. A symbol of innocence and lack of conscious scheming.

times with their essential nature intact. Just as a block of wood floating on a stream comes to a waterfall without any fear, thought, or altering of its nature, so too do Taoists go through disaster. The block of wood will still float after going over. The Taoists know that their inherent nature will remain intact, even in times of misfortune.

Water is an image very much favored by Taoists. They say that the highest good is to be like water. Nothing is softer than water, yet it can overcome the hardest of rock. The Taoists admire water because it conforms to whatever confronts it yet always seeks its own level. Whether as rain, or ice, or steam, or river water, it maintains its own character. Even if water is dirtied, the mud will eventually settle out, leaving clear water. Water may cut through stone; it may flood towns; it may bear the weight of heavy ships; but it does so without thought or planning or knowledge of the rules of society. Though it may overcome all things by being soft, what is important is that its softness is its inherent nature; by being itself, it completes all things.

The Taoists were always highly educated. They believed in giving up learning, but they believed in doing so after they had some learning to give up. The images of water, infants, uncarved blocks, and perfect mirrors meant that there had to be no blemishes or obstacles to the inherent inner nature. While learning was an obstacle, ignorance was a barrier as well. So the way the Taoist proceeded was to remove ignorance through education and travel, and then remove the education. Doing otherwise was not to attain the state of wu wei, it was just to remain stupid. That is why the maxim was "Decrease, then decrease again." First, decrease ignorance. Then, decrease learning.

Taoists who had attained such a high state were said to have realized the Tao. They had attained the skill of acting much as a force of nature, and their achievements had acquired inevitability. They acted without thought of social standards or self-gain. It was said that actions in less than this perfect mode degenerated into benevolence, morality, charity, and righteousness—in short, socially motivated modes of acting that were not necessarily sincere, understood by the actor, or perhaps even appropriate to the situation. Taoist virtue means having no intentions. It means having wu wei.

SHUI
Water. The word shows the rivulets of a stream.

Did the Taoist have any social responsibility? Oddly enough, yes. Although the Taoists rejected the notion of society as an evil, they did recognize that people could live together in a community. They felt that such communities should be simple, egalitarian groups of people who were content with life just as it was. Such people would live their days working to grow their food or care for their needs, but there would not be any mania for social advancement, expansion, conquering of neighbors, or warfare. They acknowledged that there had to be leaders, and that leaders had to be wise, but they saw the essential task of these leaders, aside from focusing the group on tasks like harvesting, as one of perpetuating a state of innocence among the people. The leaders were not to incite their followers to be ambitious; they were not to urge people to cultivate inequities like status or castes or to encourage veneration of priests; they would never condone imperialistic activities; and they would do nothing to make the people interested in anything beyond their lot. A life of serenity, contentment, and harmony with nature were the goals that Taoists advanced for their communities.

Theirs was an essentially agrarian vision of utopia, with natural labor, harmony with the land, and in a sense, a knowledge of, but refusal to use, machinery. When a farmer was asked why he continued to plow his fields by hand, the old man replied that it was not that he did not know about the existence of machines but that he would be ashamed to use them. Every task was a way to be in touch with the Tao, and to the purists, even machines would distance a person from the natural pulse.

At night, there would be little to do but to rest and enjoy the tranquility. Perhaps those so inclined would contemplate or meditate. This looking within was the ultimate stillness possible for a human being. When one looked within, and stilled all inner movement, then one was approaching an internalized version of the cosmic emptiness of the Tao. In fact, said the Taoists, the microcosm of our bodies is a replication of the macrocosm of the universe: Tao is inside us. Activity was compared to muddy water that is stirred up by turbulence. The stillness of contemplation allows the mud to settle down, the water, which represents the true inner nature, would then clarify, and the inherent spirit would then show with great clarity. If we stilled ourselves, gave up learning, ceased to make distinctions, then we could feel Tao within. At that point, the sage was not then contemplating the Tao: the sage was Tao itself.

HOW THE TAOIST PLANS LIFE

The achievement of inner clarity is the common goal of the Scholar Warrior and the Taoist. The methods of the Scholar Warrior provide an ideal path of progressive development: a person completes each stage of life, then makes it the stepping-stone toward the next. With each step, the previous one is naturally left behind—one tries not to go back and forth in confusion. As one gradually achieves the important point of each stage in life, one will gradually simplify oneself. In the final phases, one will begin to realize the essential emptiness of all existence.

Taking advantage of life's stages was deeply ingrained into Chinese culture. For example, Confucius said, "At fifteen, I had my mind bent on learning. At thirty, I stood firm. At forty, I had no doubts. At fifty, I knew the decrees of Heaven. At sixty, my ear was receptive to the truth. At seventy, I could follow what my heart desired without transgressing what was right." Generations sought to chart their lives by this formula.

Doctors and herbalists had their own thoughts on the stages of life. The Yellow Emperor's medical classic, *Neijing*, established the following physical phases of life:

For women:

Age seven:	The energy of the kidneys—jing—becomes abundant, her teeth change, and her hair grows longer.
Fourteen:	Beginning of menstruation, ability to bear children.
Twenty-one:	Emanation of jing is regular. She is fully grown.
Twenty-eight:	Muscles and bones are strong, hair has reached full length, and her body is vital and fertile.
Thirty-five:	Yang energy begins to decline, face begins to wrinkle, hair begins to thin.
Forty-two:	Yang begins to deteriorate in the upper part of her body, her face wrinkles, and hair begins to whiten.

| Forty-nine: | She can no longer become pregnant, circulation begins to decrease. |

For men:

Age eight:	Emanations of his kidneys and genitals are fully developed, his hair grows long, and he begins to change his teeth.
Sixteen:	Emanation of jing becomes abundant, and he begins to secrete semen.
Twenty-four:	Emanation of jing is regular, muscles and bones are strong, and he has reached full height.
Thirty-two:	Muscles and bones are strong, his body is healthy, and he is vital and virile.
Forty:	Production of jing begins to decline, he begins to lose hair and teeth.
Forty-eight:	Masculine vigor is diminished or exhausted, wrinkles begin to appear, and hair begins to whiten, especially at the temples.
Fifty-six:	The force of the liver deteriorates, his muscular strength declines, secretion of semen is exhausted, jing diminishes, kidneys, testicles and physical strength deteriorate.
Sixty-four:	Loses teeth and hair. Bones and muscles decay, posture is no longer upright, and virility is at an end.

The Taoists felt that one who practiced the ways of the Scholar Warrior and of the Tao could extend the periods between these stages (but not indefinitely). If they knew qigong, knew how to exercise, and had attained philosophical understanding, then they could prolong their lives. Those who lived in harmony with the four seasons, withdrew from society to wander, and understood the profundity of wu wei could live even longer.

The Taoists did not take the numerology of the ages literally, but sought a more flexible means of planning their lives.

They divided the stages of their lives according to the images of the seasons. Spring is birth and childhood. Summer is youth. Autumn is adulthood and independence. Winter is withdrawal into contemplation and preparation for death. By integration with each season, and by preparation for each coming season through careful self-cultivation, the Scholar Warrior makes magnificent accomplishments along with measured progress toward ultimate self-realization.

We all have to pass through childhood, youth, adulthood, and old age. Just as the Taoist seeks to utilize the characteristics of change and the nature of impermanence, so too does the Scholar Warrior seek to use these general stages to lend power and harmony to life. This use of structure may surprise those who expect that Taoism is merely spontaneous. Though Taoists respond to the ebb and flow of life with great sensitivity, they have an inner intention, a larger understanding of life, that makes it possible for them to respond freely to any given circumstance. All through their lives, this inner sense of pattern guides them. They may revise the images whenever they please, but they keep these alterations private. Nothing stands between their thought and Tao. They understand every stage of life from childhood to death.

Spring

Spring is the time of birth. This first moment in our lives has a bearing on what will come later. Like the instant when a potter throws a lump of clay on a wheel, that event begins all others. Although we will gradually take form, our inner nature and how centered we are can delay or improve the final outcome. Our parents determine a great deal of our early formation. They are like the potter beginning to shape a pot. The clay is wet, plastic, yet it already has its own nature. It must be shaped carefully. Whatever form the potter begins determines the future shape of the pot. Once it begins to dry, the options for change or embellishment become fewer and fewer.

The balance between parent and child is a delicate one, and parents have to know both how to set things in motion in a child's life and when to let things proceed without interference. Timing is everything. Some things not begun in childhood are difficult to instill later on. It is best to learn as much as possible, for only things that take root early can serve one through one's whole life. A young person should be taught both academic and athletic arts. Some things, like a talent for music, mathematics, languages, or certain sports can be lifelong assets only if they are established early enough. If one misses this early training, it is very difficult to go back and correct it. That is what is meant by regret for lost youth.

Children are wonderfully supple—pliant, full of talent, unblemished by the cruelties of the world and society. They should be allowed to cherish the wholeness and purity of their time. They shouldn't be rushed but should be allowed to grow at their natural pace. If parents don't understand this, or if they are inadequate to the task, or children do not apply themselves to learning, then the Taoists say that the chances for a successful life are diminished by half. If you are a parent, you must raise your children with the utmost wisdom and responsibility. It is you who must set them properly on their path. If you are someone who is now on a path, your introspection must include a frank examination of your childhood; if there are any problems from that time, they must be corrected and resolved. Unfortunately, this is a task that is more difficult as time goes by, and some things leave scars that cannot be removed except by the deepest spiritual practice.

Summer

Summer is youth, and it is the time of growth. Plants in the warmth and light grow amazingly at this stage. So too should a person grow rich with experiences, learning, and the beginnings of self-initiative. During this period, it is absolutely critical to establish certain things in your life. Skill in athletics and martial arts, strong muscles and bones, and good health are all physical things that are easily integrated into one's very being if they coincide with the body's natural growth. Scholarly excellence becomes inherent if developed when the mind is young, pliable, and not distracted with all the responsibilities of later life.

This time is also a time of experimentation, of testing. It is a time of balancing. One has to carefully test oneself and the world. The most helpful advice here is the Taoist ideal of the middle course. Taoists never adhere to the extremes in life. They eschew fanaticism and obsession. A

Taoist will try almost anything in moderation and in the context of their philosophy. At first, you will make mistakes. You shouldn't be reckless, but there will inevitably be errors in judgment that you cannot avoid. There has never been a single person, Taoist or otherwise, whose heart hasn't been broken many times. In the summer of one's life, one begins to know the sorrows of the world and to identify what one has within to cope with them.

It is never too early to consider the implications of aging. Use the positive examples of older people to see how they live their lives. Learn from their mistakes and their good characteristics. When you reach their stage, you will have ample precedent to guide you, and then aging can be positive. Aging is a force in life. The way of the Taoist is to use that force, like all such forces, to one's own advantage.

Having a master at this stage is very beneficial. He or she is like a gardener who will bring out the very best in plants. Whereas your parents take you as far as their experience allows, the master dispassionately cultivates your hidden talents. A master, in his or her wisdom, will know when to let you take your falls and when to intervene. A master will be there to provide an image of stability when your world is in constant flux and a role model as you struggle to establish your own individuality. The Taoists say that if one lacks the guidance of a true master, one will never reach one's full potential. And one who misses both the care of parents and the care of a master, the Taoists believe, will find it impossible to become a Scholar Warrior and a full seeker of the Way. There is no substitute for proper care and guidance.

Autumn

Autumn is one's middle age. It is the time when Scholar Warriors are in their prime. The old-time martial artists and scholars usually were at their best from the age of fifty on. It is at this time that one makes one's greatest achievements. The foundation that one has spent half a century establishing can now be the basis for great accomplishments.

We all have something both to achieve for ourselves and to contribute to the rest of the world. We should pass on what we know, so that others may benefit from our experience. This is what keeps the path of the Scholar Warrior from being purely narcissistic. At least in the autumn of one's life, one should use one's experience for the good of other people. Humility, service, and compassion should be qualities that even a warrior should cultivate and exercise.

Winter

Winter is the time of withdrawal and contemplation. One looks back on a life rich with accomplishments, renounces the commitments that one made earlier, not because they were bad, but because one has finished with them and done what one wanted to do. Just as the earth becomes still under softly falling snow, so too do Scholar Warriors become still in contemplation and meditation. The consider what they have done, and they consider how best to use the precious little time left to them. They resolve to go to the end of their lives with grace, dignity, and understanding. Death becomes not an unwanted companion but a presence to accept without fear.

No one who is alive can reliably claim to know death. Different people react in different ways to the idea of their own death. Some respond with bravado, some with fatalism, some with indifference, and others with deep philosophical insight. But it all comes down to one fact: death is a mystery. Despite belief in resurrection, immortality, and transcendence, no one has ever demonstrably escaped death. Though even Taoism claims to have surpassed death—part of its whole basis as a religion is the belief in personages who attained immortality through self-cultivation—there is no real proof.

Every religion tries to address the issue of death, but they often do so in childish ways. They promise heaven. They promise reincarnation. They promise that you will get to be just the same or better after you die. But just because it is written in a book, or because your kindly priest says it is so, or because some clever theologian argues persuasively for such a view doesn't prove that there is life after death. It is only a matter of faith—a faith like that of someone who believes how wonderful life was in "the good old days." We are each going to die. That defines our life. There is no guarantee of what you might find after death, so it is far better to do something great while alive. Everything is to be done for the sake of the here and now, not for vague promises of life after death.

It is this total emphasis on the present that leads the Taoists to prolong their lives through healthy living. They want to achieve all that they desire before they die. The Taoists can extend their lives through exercise, diet, herbology, philosophical understanding, and meditation. But they don't do it simply to live long or to accumulate wealth. They do it to gain insight into themselves and the truths of life within their limited time.

They try to understand death as much as possible. They perceive death as a transition, not as an ending or a tragedy. It is merely a change of status. They view life as charmingly ephemeral. They thus engage in a lifelong process of becoming dispassionate, so that they will not have any ties to life when death comes. Many old people, as they draw near to death, mention that they have nothing to live for; the Taoists agree in a positive way. If you truly have nothing to live for, then you can die peacefully. If you are unsatisfied with your life, you haven't really seen its ephemeral nature, and you will not accept being taken away. By living a life of achievement, you will divest yourself of all ties to this world, and thus leave it willingly. The only question is one of timing. You don't want to become dispassionate too soon—life will become boring. And if you don't peak soon enough, you will die before you are ready.

From death back to birth, Taoists use the metaphor of seasons to regulate their lives. They understand that failure to fulfill the imperatives within each stage will reduce the prospects for success. It is like taking advantage of the seasons—sowing when it is appropriate, harvesting when the time is right—using the natural progression of events to achieve our will. Whatever phase of life you find yourself in, judge whether to take any action by how it will accord with that phase. To fail to fully experience any period is failure; to remain stuck in one is to be warped. To be Taoist is to discern the patterns of nature and to align ourselves with their movement.

A GOAL

During the progress through each stage, setting goals is the best way to maintain focus and concentration. One determines what actions are necessary in the state that one finds oneself in, as well as determining an overall goal in life. Striving to complete and then clear these goals is not the same as the contention or ambition that the Taoists reject. Having goals clarifies one's personality, whereas contending obscures one's personality with more and more ambition to increase and hold on to the accomplishment. The way of the Scholar Warrior is to make accomplishments in order to then leave them behind. They believe that we all embody curiosities, tendencies, yearnings, and desires for knowledge. These elements must not be suppressed, but must be given full expression. If we don't do this, we will not be able to realize emptiness, for our inner need for expression will be unfulfilled. Only by the proper exercise of our goals can we clear away these elements of our personalities.

Many people say that they have trouble identifying goals. The way to do this is not to ask others, nor to ape the lives of heroes. The way is to look within. All answers are within us; we need only calm ourselves to find them. Like water that becomes clear when allowed to stand still, our natures will become clear with still introspection. We must be observant; by being aware of our own tendencies and our own desires, we can slowly ascertain what we are meant to do. We must couple this practice with reasoned experimentation. Try everything in moderation. See whether a certain direction is positive and indicates further exploration, or whether it leads to a dead end. As you envision a short-term goal and achieve it, ask yourself if it leaves you satisfied. If so, then you need not do anything more. If you want to continue, then you should follow, within reason. If you make a mistake, pick yourself up and keep going.

The Taoists believe that our inner truth is often obscured both by our talents and by our flaws. Talent must not be used to feed the ego but should be used for achievement and self-understanding. Flaws must be mastered so that they don't lead to our downfall. Only training can help us to see beyond our subjective desires and temporary fascinations. Only introspection can then help us to find our innermost reasons for living.

You are unique. No one else can understand you fully. You answer not to a god but to yourself. The Taoists say that the final judgment is before the mirror of truth, and you are both subject and judge. If this is so, then you are the only one responsible for your life, and the direction for your life must come from within yourself.

Our overall goal is nothing less than identifying the innermost purpose of life. Our lifelong quest is to identify that purpose and then use every means at our disposal to achieve it. Without emphasizing introspection and training, you cannot identify it. What are you meant to do? Are you meant to be a wanderer, or an artist, or a business person? Is a profession enough of a definition for you? Is a family important? Make your definitions for yourself, then prepare to pay the price. Nothing can be achieved without sacrifice and hard work.

Not even a sage or a master can tell you what to do in your life. Here, then, is the lie to psychic readings and tales of predestination. Life is created anew every day. You are different every day. How can anyone make predictions? How can anyone claim to know you better than you know yourself? Even if a master can look within you and read your mind, what guarantee is there that your mind will not change in the very next moment? The Tao is not fixed; your mind is not static; your personality is not immutable. Only you can look within each day and ask yourself whether you think you are on the right path or not. Only you can make plans for the future, decide if a particular goal is worth the sacrifice, or make the commitment to strive for something.

Don't expect your goals to remain unchanged throughout your life. The Tao changes constantly, and you will too. You will change as you gradually adjust to each new stage in life. Be open to such change. Don't feel that integrity lies in dogmatically holding to one course. Life will not permit rigidity. It is helpful to know where one is going, and it is wonderful to visit places—sometimes once, sometimes many times—but it is also valuable to be flexible enough to adapt to the unexpected whenever it comes up. That is the delight of life.

Face life. Don't run away from it; don't take drugs or wine to shield yourself. Don't overdramatize life; don't romanticize it. Don't project any fantasies or illusions on it. Just face it. That is the essence of Taoism.

Two of the most useful ways to maintain awareness of your goals and how they change are to travel and to keep a journal in daily life. Travel gives you new perspectives. Life's experiences are compressed into a very short period of time. Routines are impossible to keep. One is thrown back upon one's own resources and forced to confront all that comes one's way. It is easy to see how others live, how animals live, how nature changes, and then learn from all that. The world is also the best laboratory. Go out and try all your ideas. When you travel, you will quickly learn what works and what doesn't. The Taoists say that it is virtually impossible to mature without the rich diversity of experiences that travel affords.

Many people keep travel diaries, but journals are valuable every day of your life. You should note your goals, your training regimen, the results, the times you may have slipped in your discipline, and so on. Be objective in recording both good and bad; the journal should only be for your use. All too often, our perception of progress is distorted by egotism, poor self-image, or poor memory. Keeping a journal circumvents this. It is your mirror that extends back into the past, your way of making evaluations and judgments. We are nearly always aware of ourselves each day. A journal will keep this awareness objective. A Scholar Warrior is concerned only with self-perfection. Without constant and accurate judgment, such excellence is impossible to achieve.

Life isn't fair. There is no justice in life, and the sooner you accept it, the better off you'll be. There is only you, and the world, and the terrors, and the wonders, and loneliness, and happiness, and beauty, and banality. You are going to be hurt all through life. Take it. Your heart is going to be broken over and over again. Well, all right. That's when you have to have the warrior's courage. You see, there is no real reason for being a warrior, and unlike the scholar—for whom there is no ultimate justification either—the warrior accepts that without question and faces the unknown with courage and strength. Just keep your mind on your goals and persevere.

CONCLUSION

The Tao is a mystery that can be known only through persistent self-cultivation, empirical investigations and a strong determination to do all things in this present lifetime. A true Taoist goes through life buoyed by an inner purpose and an understanding of both the workings of nature and his or her own character. This inner understanding is expressed not by contentious assertion but through a unique effortlessness, wu wei.

Life is a path of four seasons, each with its appropriate accomplishments. Throughout life, the Taoist strives to simplify desire so as to eliminate all barriers to knowing Tao.

Tao is empty, but this emptiness is dynamic, productive, and positive. Only this emptiness may be regarded as absolute and constant in life, for duality cannot be regarded as absolute. Only in emptiness can there be a total transcendence of dualism; only in emptiness is there a transcendence of relativity. The Taoist strives to know this emptiness fully, in part through the simplicity of the uncarved block, and in part through the practice of meditation. Following the Tao is a journey requiring balance and care.

師
徒

7

Master and student
Walk the path side by side.
They share their destinies
Until their paths diverge.

MASTERS AND STUDENTS

THE ADVANTAGES AND
PROBLEMS OF STUDY

TRADITIONALLY, TAOISM WAS MEANT to be learned as a child learns from its family. Just as you as a son or daughter did not take formal lessons from your parents on how to be a child, neither did a student of Taoism gain the core of his or her knowledge from a book. Taoism was gained by living with the masters on a daily basis. The student, who often began studying while still a child, simply lived and grew naturally. No one had to tell the student to think new thoughts, or to be curious, or to make his or her body grow. These things come of their own accord, and the masters were there to subtly guide and to pass on their wisdom.

In the Asia of the past, masters were a bit more accessible, and it was possible to commit oneself to the study of Tao if one's heart was so moved. But nowadays, masters are fewer in number and harder to find. Modern culture neither recognizes the importance of a master nor supports masters. Moreover, with the fast pace and distractions of modern life, few people are satisfied with the patient, long-term relationship of master and student.

Further compounding the problem is the plethora of false masters who hurt their students with poor guidance. Sometimes, this malpractice is not simply bad advice, but the introduction of medicine, diet, or techniques that cause bodily and mental injuries. Even people who are uninterested in spiritual pursuits have heard about the various abuses of so-called masters, and these perverse teachers continue to prey upon the sincere aspirations of thousands around the globe. There have been many cases of teachers who have not developed fully, who have become infatuated with power, or who have fallen to material or emotional temptations. Responsibilities are greater for a master than for an ordinary person; not everyone can bear the burden. This unfortunate state of affairs leads some to question the need for a master. But rarity is not enough reason to reject the idea of a master. Just because there are many bad masters does not mean that there is no such thing as a good one.

If you truly need a master, then you must find the one appropriate for you. But the way to find a master and the standards to apply are not well known. It makes no sense to study with a master because of fame alone. The ease with which advertising and rumor make people famous overnight should give us ample reason for caution. It doesn't matter whether a particular system or master is well known or popular. What does matter is that the master is qualified and that there is a true relationship between master and student.

The most important things about masters are their proficiency in their system and their genuine compassion for and interest in their students. A male master is like a father. A female master is like a mother. Without parents, we do not have life. Without a master, we cannot have spiritual awakening. The master helps us find the way. The master is the true gateway. Those without masters but who nevertheless hold aspirations for spirituality and self-cultivation are like spiritual orphans. They can fend for themselves and still live successful lives, but whatever their achievements, they cannot compare with what they could have achieved with the guidance of a master. A master cares for students as a parent cares for children. Oddly enough, good mothers and fathers also seem to be more rare these days, so it's no wonder that people can barely accept the idea of a master.

Unlike our relationship with our parents, however, our connection with a master is voluntary. We cannot choose our parents, but we do have a say in whom we learn from. We must choose wisely. The old saying, "When the student is ready, the master will come," can also be interpreted to mean that you must know what you want from a master before you can select one wisely. Many people seek out masters when what they are really looking for is a surrogate parent. This has nothing to do with the true role of the master. You should go to a master to seek the answer to your questions, and to acquire a way of life that will serve you well. Your life is always very much your own responsibility.

The concept of a master should not be regarded as a strange Asian custom. There are plenty of analogies to the master in the Western world. Look at the world of ballet, for example. No one has become a world-class ballet dancer by reading a few books and imitating movies; being a dancer requires years of strenuous training under a good teacher. The importance of an athletic coach is no different. A good coach inspires the people he or she is training. Usually former champions, coaches impart all the secrets of their own greatness. Their students may sometimes surpass them, but true coaches never become jealous of such success. They know that these achievements are an extension of their own. What runner, weight lifter, boxer, swimmer, gymnast, or any other athlete ever became great without a coach? To paraphrase the Chinese aphorism about masters and students, "An excellent coach produces an excellent pupil."

No matter what level of the Scholar Warrior you seek to achieve, you cannot do it without a teacher, a coach, or a master. Being a great dancer or athlete is difficult, but it isn't as difficult as living a complete life in accord with the Tao. Being a world-class champion is for the very talented and well trained, but it cannot provide knowledge of what to do after retirement and what to do to face death. The task is complicated indeed, and the challenge cannot be met with a smattering of book learning and attending a few unrelated seminars. You need a coach to train you, whether you are an aspiring dancer or an aspiring meditator.

There is one way that the best masters differ from many of the coaches and athletic trainers in the world today: they never stop growing. They teach as a natural part of their own quest. But they still continue on their lifelong path. Being a coach is not a function of retiring from the arena. All too often, people teach or become coaches when they can no longer participate in their field. In the tradition of the Scholar Warrior, there have been many great women and men who were powerful fighters or accomplished scholars and who knew when to leave one field of competition and enter another. As they entered each new stage in their lives, they were able to apply their skill, discipline, and knowledge so that they continually achieved brilliance. Coach should not be a role taken when one can do nothing else. Being a master is a function of continuing greatness, not an empty role taken on to gather innocent students.

Just as you should live your life with a purpose and a goal, so too should you approach a master with specific goals. What do you want to learn? What kind of master do you want? The more adequately you can answer these questions, the greater your chances of finding an appropriate teacher. In addition, such a clear picture will help you to assess your progress through the years. You know exactly what you want, so there should be no confusion about whether you are getting it or not. The remainder of this chapter will try to identify some of the more important issues between masters and students.

WHAT IS A MASTER?

If one were to list the qualities of a master, they might be as follows:

A master is like a parent. Masters must be capable of both loving and disciplining their students. They want only the best, so they teach their students all they can. Aware of their own shortcomings, they will send their students to other teachers to learn skills they cannot themselves teach. Just as a mother and father give of their flesh to create a child, nurture with their labor to help it grow, and pass on an inheritance to

SHIFU
Master. The name applies to both men and women.

PHILOSOPHY AND ISSUES

provide for the future, so too does a master give of his or her spiritual essence, nurture with training, and pass on a spiritual legacy.

A master will have a lineage. A true master has a lineage, just as we all have a family history. As the history and example of our ancestors influence our lives, so too does our lineage influence our thinking. The master passes on this influence, so it is critical that the master has a good background and sound history.

A master, by his or her very presence, can awaken your dormant spiritual energy. This is subtle, not dramatic. You feel good, energetic, optimistic, and safe around your master. This must be experienced to be believed.

A master can answer any question that the student has. No matter what the nature of the inquiry, masters must be able to direct their student's search. That is why they must be Scholar Warriors. Only someone with a broad spectrum of experience can do this.

A master must have lived the life that he or she is advocating. There can be no intellectualizing, hypothesizing, fantasizing, mesmerizing. A master must be experienced. Anything less is hypocrisy.

A master must look healthy and vital. Eyes and skin must be clear, body muscular and lean. He or she should be fastidious in habits and glowing with health. True spirituality has a physical manifestation, for there is no true division between body and mind. Unless you can sense this in a person, that person is not worth studying with.

A master must be the right age. A young teacher is too inexperienced. An older one will be too impatient, too irritable, and too interested in completing his or her own spiritual quest. In general, it is best to begin one's study with a master who is between the ages of fifty and sixty-five.

A master inspires trust. You feel safe with him or her. It should not be a strain to believe your master. You understand that he would do nothing to intentionally harm you. Your master protects you—physically, mentally, and spiritually.

A master is three-quarters along his or her own spiritual path. Any less, and he or she is like a parent who is too young: such a master might do all right, but often makes mistakes where an older and more mature person would not. On the other hand, masters who are too close to ultimate spiritual attainment cannot communicate on a normal level. They are already partly in the spiritual realm and will have a tendency to withdraw from everyday activities. You need someone still active and vital.

There are two types of masters. One is the type who cares primarily for his or her own practice. This type of master generally is highly accomplished but will not come out publicly. Masters like these hide themselves away and train themselves for higher and higher stages of accomplishment. Sometimes, they will teach because they meet a student they feel is destined to learn their art, or sometimes they are forced to teach because of dire circumstances or poverty. To learn from such a person can be a fantastic opportunity, though masters like these can be temperamental, impatient, and as demanding of their students as they are of themselves.

The other kind is the priest or teacher. These are masters who have been trained specifically to take on a public role. Usually their own masters designate them as teachers because they are articulate, socially skillful, and able to properly represent their tradition. Inwardly, they are often motivated by strong compassion and find that helping others to learn their system is as essential as their own success. Such masters need a certain amount of charisma to hold their group together. In return, however, they usually will teach unreservedly.

Neither type is superior to the other. But as a student, it is essential that you look carefully into your teacher's character and make sure that you are compatible with his or her inner nature and personal priorities.

FAULTS OF A MASTER

There are things that a master must never do. If you observe any of the following behavior in a prospective teacher, stay away. If you are with a master who begins to display any of these faults, then you must go to his or her superiors or to their classmates. If the master doesn't respond, or is a lone teacher, you must leave.

Exploitation: A master should not use a student for any material gain or social prestige, or for any selfish purpose.

Sexual involvement: Absolutely unacceptable.

Hypocrisy: Whatever your master advocates, he or she must practice it to a level ten times higher than his or her students.

Abuse of spiritual power: A teacher may have supernatural powers, but he or she will not carelessly demonstrate or use them.

Cruelty: Sadistic treatment is not acceptable. There have been many masters who have been mean to their students. There is no wisdom in this. This does not mean that a master cannot punish students, or be firm or tough, but outright abuse is wrong.

Possessiveness: Every child leaves home. Every student has to go into the world. The master shouldn't keep a student past his or her time. A master also shouldn't hesitate to send a student to other teachers.

Inattentiveness: No matter how skilled, a master won't be any good if he or she doesn't care about you. At the same time, if master and student are not in close proximity, there can be little spiritual transmission. Long range transmissions and swamis in stadiums are not effective.

Dishonesty: How can a master awaken ultimate truths if he or she isn't truthful with you?

Failure: If a master fails in his or her own quest, or fails to awaken the spiritual in you, then that is a fault.

The entire spiritual community should acknowledge that not every master who claims that title is genuine. And though a seeker might want desperately to find spirituality, there is no reason to tolerate a poor master. Setbacks, accidents, emotional and physical scars, and sometimes fatalities come of such relationships; they never lead to anything positive.

FAULTS OF A STUDENT

Though masters may have faults, students have many more. Frequently, they wrongfully blame their masters for their own shortcomings. Among the faults of students are the following:

Faithlessness: Many parts of spiritual inquiry require enough faith in your master to at least practice what is presented. If you have insufficient trust and confidence, or are perhaps too skeptical, then you will never succeed. No one is telling you to be unquestioning. But unless you respect the system and master you are with, you will not give either one enough of a chance to take root in your life.

Commitment is of utmost importance. Commitment means that you are willing to invest yourself absolutely in your practice. This uncompromising quality isn't for the sake of your master, it is for your own sake. You are not surrendering to your master but committing yourself wholeheartedly to your own endeavors.

Immaturity: This is the opposite condition of faithlessness. There is absolutely no good reason for the type of stupid and unquestioning loyalty that has been recently seen in religious faiths. This is personal immaturity and a wish for a return of the time when parents, lord, teacher, or god was infallible and would tell you everything to do—thereby sparing you all personal responsibility. You have to have faith, but stupidity is not a virtue.

Students like these put all their trust and responsibility for spiritual growth into the hands of the master. They don't try enough for themselves. They want their teachers to do it all for them. Spiritual progress comes only from effort.

Laziness: Spirituality takes diligence, discipline, and direction. Spirituality is only as real as you make it—and you have to make it real every day. How can you do that without perseverance and effort?

Materialism: Everyone should be self-supporting. Even if you have the good fortune to be in a monastery or ashram, you should work. If you are constantly obsessed with money and wealth, there is little room in your personality for devotion, but blindly plunging into poverty with the notion that it will enhance your spiritual status is also foolish. Some do it as a way to dodge responsibilities. Others do it as an excuse to get others to support them. They are no better than the person obsessed with money. Being fixed on the idea of great wealth or great poverty is still being fixed on materialistic concerns.

Bullying: Whether a martial artist, an intellectual, or a spiritual person, you will sharpen skills and enhance perception with your training. It is inevitable that you will become superior to the ordinary person. It is a temptation to influence, exploit, or bully others. Though it is easy to see how a martial artist might take advantage of others, there are other emotional and psychological ways to hurt people as well. The wicked intellectual is more dangerous than the swordsman. In any case, one should never use one's powers to bully others. This is why masters are so careful to test their students in many ways.

Obsession: Students who do not use their abilities to harm others, may nevertheless harm themselves by trying to accumulate power beyond their calling. Whether it is temporal power, power over classmates or other people, or sheer revelry in one's own discoveries, the thrill of personal power is very dangerous. When psychic abilities come one's way, they are merely a sign of progress. They should be simply appreciated in private and put away. Perhaps in an emergency, one could use such power to save someone's life. Otherwise, there should be no outward sign that anything has happened to you. Power is a trap along the way, and if you are foolish enough to fall into it, you will never walk a whole road.

Fantasy: Another type of student is one who becomes involved with spirituality out of fairy-tale notions. Don't they realize that all that matters is their own true accomplishment? And don't they realize that some of the most thrilling tales are mere metaphors?

Poor memory: Don't laugh. Poor memory is a real problem. What good is anything you learn if you fail to remember it and practice it?

Immorality: Morality might be something to be transcended at some point, but such a stage is reached only if one has come to subconsciously embody all the principles of morality (including its contradictions). A student must demonstrate all the qualities of a saint at any time.

BREAKING DOWN EGOTISM

Perhaps the most difficult task for any master is breaking down a student's egotism. This is a very delicate matter, for all vestiges of arrogance, laziness, selfishness, and partiality to oneself must be eliminated without destroying the sense of self-worth, and without warping the personality. This arduous task must be accomplished without the teacher demonstrating any of his or her own egotism.

Many people are arrogant in their own way. Some have predatorial, even sadistic impulses. They have learned to survive by being aggressive to the point that this has become their primary mode of behavior. Others are so eager to point out the bad habits of others that they overlook their own. Still others are desperate to assert their authority on any subject available, though their knowledge and opinion is almost wholly derived from the daily newspaper. In arrogance, people sacrifice sensitivity to others, to their surroundings, and to their own inner nature. Sooner or later, the arrogant person will fail to maintain whatever achievements he or she has made at their height and will begin a downward slide. Often, they are too blind or too unwilling to change. A certain sloppiness of character emerges, and it often becomes a fundamental laziness.

Laziness is a part of egotism because important tasks are put off. "It's too hard," one reasons, or, "I know better." Straightforward laziness is almost better than the type that is accompanied by elaborate rationalization. For people who cloak their laziness in tedious arguments, the task of instilling discipline and knowledge is almost hopeless.

An even greater shortcoming is selfishness. Although selfishness is an almost universally understood character defect, it is almost just as universally ignored. Selfishness destroys compassion for one's fellow human beings and for all other creatures of this earth. Selfishness destroys love and allows the mind to be infected by greed, mistrust, and shortsightedness. Perhaps the biggest reason to avoid selfishness is that it nearly invariably leads to a hell of one's own making. Selfishness becomes a total way of life and more often than not, selfish people make a fatal mistake that leads to their downfall.

The partiality toward oneself is fundamentally dangerous to an aspiring Scholar Warrior. As long as you refuse to let anyone else into your life, as long as you refuse to accept the authority of a competent master, as long as you refuse to acknowledge your limits while trying to expand them, and as long as you continue to reject modesty and humility as virtues in your life, you will never succeed in following the Tao. The Tao cannot be pursued where there are obstacles, and the greatest obstacle is egotism.

Giving up egotism means understanding that humility can be a road to better living. Egotism is hardness—refusal to be flexible, refusal to admit other opinions, refusal to give yourself over to training. Humility is the softness that the Taoists so cherish. One who is humble goes through adversity; does not hesitate to do the difficult; and perseveres as water going into the deepest abyss perseveres. Hardness is quickly broken. Softness can conform to any circumstance, yet it never surrenders its own fundamental nature.

Here, then, is the delicate task of the master breaking down your egotism. It is to eliminate all the hardness of your personality and to cultivate flexibility—without destroying your inherent nature.

STAYING TOO LONG

It is quite possible for a child to live too long with its parents. They become "mama's boy" or the eternal "daddy's little girl." Some stay so long that they die mentally when the parent dies. In Chinese tradition, death did not separate child and parent, for the truly pious spent the rest of their lives mourning and maintaining their parents' graves. To the Taoists, these things might arouse sympathy, but they think them foolish.

In the same way, you can stay too long with your master or become too dependent upon him or her. You will never learn enough, you think. You are afraid to face the world without your master's guidance. Sometimes, masters are at fault: insecure about old age, some try to bind a few students to them to help them along.

But Taoists are more concerned with liberation than sentiment. Obviously, they don't reject the notion of filial piety or devotion to a teacher, but if these things will interfere with the progress of either a master or a student, the Taoist will establish limits. The whole idea is to grow. Remember the example of the seasons: summer is the proper time for your teachers. You must be independent for the second half of your life.

It doesn't always happen, but sometimes a student will outgrow a master in some things. This is difficult because the student should regard his or her teacher with the same reverence as before. It is like the understanding that we can now do something our parents cannot do. It is not a call for derision; it is a call for responsible behavior.

You cannot ever surpass your master in all things—if only because your master has more experience than you—and you certainly cannot expect to surpass your master in his or her chosen field. If you begin to think that you have become better than your master, then that is a time for caution. Every master has secret abilities, and if you think that you can destroy or supplant your master, you may learn your mistake in a fatal way. If you are truly better, then you should use your accomplishment to support your master and the system, have compassion for your classmates, and remain modest about your skill.

Respect must be unwavering. Simply because you may be more adept at modern things does not mean that your study is over. You are with your master to learn a way of life. As your master ages, just as when your parents do, it may be time for you to care for your master as your master once cared for you. Before you allow yourself to feel annoyed by the responsibility of taking care of an elderly person, stop to think. Without your master's devotion to you, could you even have this dilemma now?

In Taoism, there is only walking of the path. When a master and student meet, they agree to walk together. Only time will tell the duration of their time with each other. While they walk, they share; neither is to deter the other. If the student falls and cannot get up, or decides to linger by the roadside, then the master does not have to stop. The master has his or her own life to live. If, through inadequacy, the master stumbles, or reaches the end of the road and dies, then the student should walk forward without a second glance.

Our life-styles should be of our own choosing. Our lives should not be determined by any influence that we do not want. If it seems unrealistic to live the life of the Scholar Warrior—this isn't China at the turn of the century, and the post-technological world of today is so very different—it may be good to consider that we need not be the victim of our own time. What is current in society is only temporary, and we can spend our whole lives following trends without reaping anything beneficial. But the values, skills, and understanding that we gain from honest self-cultivation under a master's guidance will always be with us.

The Taoists say that this world is nothing but dust. Everything soon crumbles. The works of human beings are too easily destroyed by natural disaster, war, or the simple passage of time. Monuments to kings are long buried, plans for the greatest of endeavors seldom last beyond the memory of the generation that made them. Even the works of heaven—from a rainstorm to the stars and planets themselves—do not last.

This life is but a dream. In our waking state, we project our own values and interpretations on all the phenomena that come our way. Things that we thought we could depend on fade with the next revelation. Calculations that we make quickly go awry. The life that we thought we could have grows more distant every day. Even when we are asleep, we are only dreamers dreaming that we are dreaming.

Why then should we place our reliance on the outside world? It is far better to cultivate our inner qualities. Though we may well find ourselves nothing but dreams and dust, at least we can dream the dream we want, and at least we can maintain our skills until the time that our soul dissolves. Experience and skill are the two things that no one can take away. Is it so unrealistic to pursue the skill of the Scholar Warrior when the alternative is so unviable? "We can't practice. We're too busy. The world has changed. I have no one to inspire me. My master is too old-fashioned. It's too hard. There's no use for these skills. I'm fine the way I am." These are some of the excuses that students repeat over and over again. But they have no true validity. As long as you allow such excuses to invade your consciousness, you will be forever trapped in the world of dust.

Find the right master and train to be a Scholar Warrior. For in that training is the key to liberation. What is that liberation? It is the seeing of the dust of the world, and the understanding of how to respond to that vision.

CHEN
Dust.

MENG
Dream.

消除疑問

8

Life acquires meaning only
When we face the conflict
Between our desires and reality.

RESOLVING DOUBTS
CONFRONTING CONTROVERSY

A WIDE VARIETY OF ISSUES confront a person on a spiritual path. Problems that face us may involve our relationship to society at large; they may be shortcomings of the tradition we are studying; or they may be problems within ourselves. As we undertake the path of the Scholar Warrior, we may even find that the very way our personalities change is confusing. Actually, every difficulty is an excellent challenge. The various issues we encounter on our path should be confronted and understood. They must be penetrated through knowledge. If left unresolved, each forms a blind spot in our character. If overcome, they can become stepping-stones to higher levels of being.

Books on spirituality often seem to dwell on the rosy. But life is not that way. If a way of life is true, then it must bear up under testing and scrutiny. Problems, questions, and dilemmas arise. We should face them all squarely.

When people who have undertaken the path of the Scholar Warrior meet unexpected internal conflicts, they often leave the path. This is a tragedy. If they were prepared, they would recognize these classic conflicts and resolve them. This chapter examines ten of these important issues:

- Continuous learning
- The necessity of competition
- Finding your fatal flaw
- Discipline
- Nonviolence
- Avoiding isolation
- Relationships
- Technology and Taoism
- The nature of simplicity
- The future of Taoism

There may be many other problems that arise during your study, but the examination of these topics will give you a good foundation for coping with doubts.

CONTINUOUS LEARNING

The first feature that most people notice about the Scholar Warrior is the tremendous emphasis on skill and knowledge. They want to know if all of it is necessary.

Students often protest subjects like trigonometry, world history, and chemistry with the question, "Why should we learn this? We'll never have to use it in the real world." Unfortunately, teachers seldom have an adequate rebuttal to this mistaken notion. In the same way, you may wonder whether all the skills of the Scholar Warrior need to be learned. But they most definitely do, and in fact, they are the very minimum necessary. Learning is never wasted.

The first assumption that needs to be corrected is that learning must somehow always be "useful." If that were true, we would only need to go to trade schools, and there would be no need for poets or singers, or perhaps even physicists. No, learning is valuable in and of itself, for it allows us to wonder, to play with new knowledge, to combine it with other things we know. We all make unique bridges across the oceans of learning we have within us. That could never happen if learning were always "one way," or always "practical."

Learning satisfies a certain curiosity and interest that is innately human. We may not all want to learn the same things, but each of us has certain things that we are not only curious about but would enjoy knowing in some depth. For some of us, it might only be the melodies of popular songs; for others, it might be the measure of the universe. Fundamentally, however, we all want to learn. There have been many times that we have met someone who was supposedly dumb or "uninterested in learning," only to find that the individual was in fact interested in some body of knowledge. The desire for knowledge is innate, and unless it is satisfied and cultivated, a person will remain unformed.

Proper knowledge gives us freedom. As long as we acquire an enormous range of skills, we can be prepared for whatever life throws our way. It is impossible to predict the future. All of us, from the lowliest beggar to the highest saint, are surprised by life at one time or another. The important thing is to have the resources to confront whatever circumstances come our way.

This is why the Taoists say, "Know magic, shun magic." They mean that through the cultivation of knowledge, you can know precisely how natural calamity and human enmity can be avoided. You can know all the ways in which you might be affected and be able to meet crisis on the challenger's own terms. The Taoists do not mean that you should learn the ways of others in order to be like them, only that you should learn the ways of others to avoid being manipulated by them. For example, some people object to learning the warrior's art because they see no use for it. But one can never say with certainty that one will not need to defend oneself or defend others. If you learn how to fight but never have to use your knowledge, you have not learned in vain. There will be many times that you will have to face a situation with the assurance that you will be able to survive. You may not have to actually punch and kick, but the courage you have from knowing that you could will make you a much stronger person than one ignorant of fighting. The same is true of math, or reading, or medicine. Why surrender your rights of knowledge and action to other people, professionals or not? It is far better to be able to depend on yourself, and this is impossible without deep learning.

THE NECESSITY OF COMPETITION

Once learning is acquired, competition is inevitable. If you want to excel, you must compete. Whatever your field of endeavor, you must do well. If you make your living selling flowers, you have to make sure that your flowers are at least as fresh and beautiful as the next person's. Competition will eventually be surrendered when one reaches high spiritual attainment, but when one is starting out, competition is unavoidable. It is a fact of living.

Competition is inherent. If you are ever in a place where there is a natural disaster, you will find that people, including yourself, will revert to a very primitive mode of survival. You take care of your own. You make sure that you have food, shelter, warmth, and protection from aggressors. The veneer of civilization is very thin; our instinct to survive and compete is fundamental.

Beyond the basics of survival, you should select the arena for competition and the extent to which you strive against others. Sometimes, you may enter into an organized contest, such as a match or an athletic game. At other times, you can use competition in a wholly internal way. You can select an ideal or another person and silently try to beat them in your own training. For example, if you were weightlifting, you could train until you matched the strength of another person in the gym. Or if you were bicycling, you could select strong riders and try to keep up with them. You can even compete against yourself; by keeping a record of your attempts at a sport or any other activities, you can consistently strive to go beyond your own limits.

Warriors are concerned with the domination of others. One of the primary methods that they use to train for this is to develop an awareness of the faults of others. They scan the body of each person they meet for weakness. Even while speaking to you in a relaxed situation, they are noticing your every movement, tabulating all your flaws. They know the vulnerable points of the people they meet with such precision that the moment of combat is mere exercise. Masters cultivate their students by constant drills: Where would you hit this person (often pointing to someone a hundred pounds heavier!)? "I guess I'd just die. . ." you want to say, and then the master chides you and tells you how to do it.

A Scholar Warrior never enters a building, a room, the forest, without first ascertaining the possible sources of attack and all possible routes of escape. Eventually, the practice of noting the weaknesses of others, and the constant movement within the context of one's surroundings, becomes a reflex. They are like jungle cats, moving with supreme confidence as they stalk their prey. Total knowledge of their environment and total knowledge of their quarry make them the most feared hunters.

Our jungle is not only the jungle of society and business but also the jungle of culture, information, and psychology. Whether you are a student, a business person, an academician, a government official, or even a monk in a temple, you will find yourself in competition. Perhaps even your personal relationships are competitive. You might use Taoist philosophy, but even if you use the idea of non-action as you work toward a goal, you are competing. As long as you are in the world, you must compete, and if you must compete, you must *win*.

But once you have acquired the awareness of others' flaws, you need not poke at every one of them. Sometimes, one compassionately ignores the chinks in one's companions' armor. Constant awareness of human shortcoming can be a very gloomy way to go through life. A warrior is forever occupied with the ugly, and sometimes it is better to back off and remember the good sides to life. Eventually, observing faults will become subconscious and it need not occupy you. You will understand that you have reached this stage when you are no longer concerned with competition but are still able to respond. The awareness of the Scholar Warrior will become so complete that even you will not know how you will respond until the moment of attack. That is true wu wei. As the old saying of the warriors puts it, "If my opponent does not move, I do not move. If my opponent moves, I attack first."

The observing of faults may also be applied to yourself as a means of introspection. It is one of the ways of learning proper self-conduct. You watch how others behave and see if you yourself are guilty of the same errors. You try to correct them in yourself.

Sometimes when your master points out faults in other people, it is a diplomatic way of criticizing you; by seeing someone else's example, you are expected to draw the proper conclusion. But whether your master points it out, or you acquire the habit of checking yourself against the flaws of another, you can learn in an instant what might have taken years of trial and error to realize. As the old saying goes, "A moment of embarrassment is far better than a lifetime of shame." An extension of this habit is to read biographies and study history. When you encounter people, you are limited to the perception of the moment. But by studying an entire life from birth to death, you can search for those elements that made that life successful. Supposedly, one is to read the lives of saints for this very reason. But the lessons there are not always easy to implement, and the lives of the ordinary are just as important.

We need to compete in life because this is the surest way to improve ourselves. Competition encourages us to bring out our best qualities and to compound those advantages into superiority. Such highly developed attributes are nominally useful as we struggle to maintain ourselves in society, but more important, they give us a solid foundation for life. Eventually, you may give up competition for more refined modes of living, but the stability and strengths that you acquire will become the raw material for your new endeavors.

FINDING YOUR FATAL FLAW

We all have a fatal flaw, and we don't know what it is. This fatal flaw is the shortcoming that we don't know about or can't do anything about. It is our undoing because it is precisely in our blind spot.

SI DI
One's fatal flaw.

While you search for this flaw, you should take refuge in humility. Never put yourself first. Stand behind. Facilitate, perhaps even lead subtly, but take no credit. Whenever anything is done, let people feel that it happened spontaneously, or from their own efforts, not from your leadership. But we must understand humility clearly. Neither the houseboy attitude, the pacifist posture, nor the passive immigrant mentality are true humility. Humility is the control of egotism. Obsequiousness comes from being subjugated by others. Humility is the path to straightforward self-knowledge. Search yourself over and over. Listen to the criticisms of your masters and your classmates and to those you respect. Decide if their criticisms are valid, and if they are, implement them. Try to find every single flaw in yourself and eradicate it.

In youth, problems may seem simple and efforts heroic. Perhaps that is why warriors prefer to die young. But in old age, the horrors of growing old become constant and hard to resist. Fate never rests in its effort to undercut the human heart, and it will tirelessly try to wrest your proudest abilities from you. It will weaken your grip on your sword handle; it will make your mind feeble. You can try to use herbs, breathing exercises, meditation. But fate will close in on you again. Dying old and feeble, hobbled by the entanglements of incompetence is devastating failure. The only alternative is to eradicate all flaws. Fate may still hound you daily, but it will have fewer openings. Don't die from your own weaknesses. That is terrible. To die in the way one chooses is best of all.

In the legends, there was a Taoist priest named Bai Mei. He was reputed to be invulnerable to blows from fists and weapons alike; he was literally the sage with no vulnerable points. Even direct attacks to his eyes and groin were unsuccessful. He had only a single vulnerable point—the top of his head—which ultimately led to his death. In the warrior's way, we must all strive to close our vulnerabilities.

When the Taoists speak of the sage having no vulnerable spot, they say that a weapon will have no place to enter. Someone who has attained Taoist realization is like an infant who remains unafraid of fierce beasts. Such a person is one with Tao, and even tigers will not attack him or her. The point is that the sage has no weaknesses, no fear, because there is no sense of the self, no sense of gain or loss, no sense of desire. But most of us

BAI MEI DAO REN
White Eyebrow Taoist

do indeed have vulnerable openings in our personalities as well as our bodies. We have selfish desires that can be exploited by others. We are undisciplined or lazy, and so miss opportunities. We may be so proud that we will blunder badly because of our own arrogance. Eradicating all of one's vulnerable spots is not easy, but it is essential if one is to survive.

Every warrior dies. If you die in battle, so be it. However you live your life, so too shall you die. If you live a violent life, you will die a violent life. If you live by the sword, you must accept that you may well die by the sword. If you live by your wits, your wits may well be your undoing. Beware of hubris. For it is the single vulnerable point in your armor, even if you are as powerful as Bai Mei.

After arrogance, obsession ranks second as a common flaw. Bai Mei is a good example for this reason. He was a man who attained an extraordinary level of development but he became mad with his power. Each of us should strive for our best, but maintain balance and moderation as well. Disproportionate ambition is a tremendous liability, and it often leads us to do crazy things in our determination to dominate others.

In China, there were martial artists who achieved something called the Iron Palm. By soaking their hands in herbs, thrusting thousands of times a day into heated sand, and striking bags and boards countless times, they made their hands into fearful weapons. One slap was like a blow from an iron ingot, and the hapless victim seldom lived. But there was a price to the possessor of these deadly hands: he could not close them, and he could not feel anything. They were truly like sculpted metal in every regard.

Bound feet are also a well-known feature of ancient Chinese culture. In this practice girls had their feet bound tightly for their entire lives so that their feet would remain small. Nature, however, was not easily thwarted, and their feet doubled upon themselves, the toes folding under, the bones breaking. In extreme cases, rot would set in, and decay and death festered at the ends of their limbs. Pain and loss of circulation became part of their everyday reality—all for the sake of "femininity" and the sensual swaying that having such small feet supposedly encouraged.

There is little difference between these two ways of making human beings grotesque. But such ugliness is quite a possibility when the Scholar Warrior becomes obsessed with the idea of perfection. There is no reason

WU SI DI
Literally, no place of death. The vulnerable spots of one's body are regarded as one's death trap. When it is said that a sage has no death spots, the implication is that the sage has triumphed over death. The nature of that triumph, however, is open to a wide variety of interpretations.

to make yourself ugly for the sake of success. Drugs and steroids are not necessary. Training to the point of crippling yourself is silly. A distinction must be made between persistence and obsession. Persistence is balanced and takes a long-range view. It does not risk destruction in pushing for immediate success, nor does it allow itself to degenerate into procrastination. Obsession, on the other hand, is all drive and determination without moderation. It loses the whole in its eager grasp for the part. Whether your vulnerablitiy is egotism or obsession, strive to eliminate your fatal flaw.

If we want to survive in life, if we want to complete all of our goals and be able to resist the attacks of accident, fate, jealous rivals, and our own egotism, then we must ensure that there are no places for these attacks to enter. We must constantly examine ourselves and bolster our defenses. Only by sweeping away all vulnerabilities can we have the strength to walk the Way.

DISCIPLINE

One cannot reach the high level the Scholar Warrior demands without some sort of ambition or drive. This requires discipline, and a brief examination of the old warriors will illustrate its qualities.

Up to the revolution of 1949, there was still a great martial world in China. Masters who had perfected their skills prior to the gun's appearance in China were still alive. Metallurgy had reached its highest level, and hundreds of different schools of martial arts existed. Nearly anything was seen as an appropriate source for a style. Among the more eccentric schools that existed into the 1940s were styles inspired by such things as the Butterfly, Bee, Centipede, Sparrow, Duck, Hawk, Cat, Dog, Corpse, Demon, Fire, Earth, Metal, Wood, Water, Elephant, Camel, and Plum Flower.

Consider the Snake style, for example. In this style, best suited for thin people, the two hands imitate the darting and coiling movements of the serpent. Blocks are really slips of the twisting arm, and strikes are not like sledgehammers or battering rams but elegant, pinpoint hits with the fingertips to soft spots. The demeanor of a Snake stylist is frightening: glaring eyes and relentless pursuit are meant to intimidate the opponent. By contrast, the Elephant style uses long, flexible punches, in imitation of an elephant's trunk. Swings come from unexpected angles, and sometimes a whole forearm will come crashing down on an opponent. Whatever the style, they reflected the research and experience of generations of masters as they sought to overcome the competition of other schools.

Perhaps one of the ultimate schools was the Lost Track school. Begun by three masters who searched all of China for the best techniques of each system, and developed by ten generations of subsequent masters, this school had codified a staggering number of techniques by the twentieth century. They required mastery of some 70 sets, 108 weapons, qigong, *neigong*, and acrobatics. Their two crowning sets contained one thousand and ten thousand movements respectively. And to make sure they missed nothing, these masters even included in their repertoire the study of Western boxing, chess, weight lifting, and football. The Lost Track masters remarked that only three characteristics were necessary to be a successful martial artist: intelligence, perseverance, and courage. As it so happens, these are precisely the ingredients of discipline.

A warrior needs intelligence to learn, perceive, and plan strategy. While a novice, one must bring the utmost in mental ability to bear on absorbing knowledge. Sets demand extensive memorization; weapons require differing techniques; combat demands long experience; and knowledge of anatomy requires deep study. When fighting, an intelligent warrior never lashes out blindly with injudicious force: he or she tests the opponent, gathers information, memorizes each strength and weakness. The warrior's complete concentration will change one's thinking. One's mind becomes a warrior's mind: fierce, calculating, assertive, and always aware of everyone's weaknesses. That is what it means to beat someone before a battle: you have long ago assessed their vulnerabilities.

No one can maintain intelligence without patience, attention to detail, and fortitude. That is why perseverance is the next necessary element for a warrior. Years of grueling training to forge the body into a superb war machine requires perseverance. Split-second reactions to attack and strategy-as-improvisation are only gained with constant practice. In old

China, fighters trained by catching large logs only on their forearms, wrestling with boars and other animals, doing endless sessions of jumping and tumbling, and fighting duels to the death. Only perseverance would keep them in pursuit of their goals.

That courage is the final essential characteristic might not be surprising. Fighting demands bravery. But courage implies two things far deeper than the basic drive for victory. Courage indicates something inherent, and it indicates self-control. Warriors must have an instinct for bravery, one that they've nurtured no matter how frightened they may have been in the past. Courage should grow stronger as a fighter endures, and as such, it not only shows mastery of body and mind but triumph over fear and instinct as well.

The one underlying quality all three of these characteristics share is discipline. Without it, one could not achieve and maintain the level of dedication and transcendence necessary. People sometimes subscribe to the mistaken notion that discipline is restriction. That is not true. Discipline enables one to act. Only with discipline can one truly be all that one wishes to be. With discipline, one is able to carry out a decision free from fear, doubt, ambivalence, and laziness. Being a warrior means being disciplined. Training is discipline. Fighting is discipline. Discipline is freedom.

The control that comes from such inner strength eventually becomes ingrained in the personality. In the case of the warrior, it is expressed through movement. When a warrior fights or performs, there is a terrible beauty, the unmistakable dance of the predator. Intelligence, perseverance, and courage, densely alloyed with discipline, then shows itself. Warriors do not think, do not consciously move. They let movement take them over; they become movement. At the ultimate stage, the warrior is transformed into his or her art.

Master warriors experience a mystic unity—the oneness that sages constantly refer to—in training, performance, and battle. They are not fighters, they are war itself. They do not imitate the movement of an animal, they become that animal. Their minds and bodies cease to have any separation. The mind is cleansed of doubt, the body is free from any blockage.

This transcendent quality is what separates warriors from simple murderers. Killers kill in confusion, lust, greed. Killers are not in control, they do not understand their actions. Whether killers are accidental aggressors, sadistic bullies, journeyman executioners, duped soldiers, ambitious generals, arrogant politicians, or fanatical religious leaders, they very likely have no sense of discipline, of form, of oneness with training, action, and movement. This is not to say that the act of killing people is less grave for a warrior. But warriors readily accept any consequence of their deeds. Stained with sin, they nevertheless remain true to their path in life. Their sense of control is so complete that it dominates their conscience and soul.

The warrior of old differs greatly from today's military person. A warrior's technology was always the warrior's own mind and body. Training was for higher skill, not more efficient mechanization. Combat and death were personal, never so long-range that one's opponent was completely unknown. And there was always an equal chance: every time a warrior attacked, he or she was exposed to counterattack. Confident in their skill, obedient to their own code of ethics, mind and muscle attuned to their highest state, warriors relied on a virtually shamanistic merging with their own inner force. No matter what your field of endeavor, whether career or spirituality, this is the level of discipline to attain. Only with it are we complete.

NONVIOLENCE

One of the greatest stumbling blocks in accepting the way of the Scholar Warrior is the prevailing contemporary mind-set against violence. No one is more opposed to senseless slaughter and stupid aggression than Scholar Warriors. They have devoted all their efforts to attaining perfection. Why should they demean themselves by butchering those who cannot even defend themselves? No, the Scholar Warriors may fight among themselves to improve their skills and to maintain the standards of their society, but the mere abuse of others is not part of their purpose.

The idea of nonviolence has become terribly warped, to the point that it is in itself an abuse of mind and patience. Gentleness and the injunction against harming others is part of virtually any creed, but the ideal of nonviolence is now something perverse and far from its original idea. Nonviolence has become a political tool. It has become a rationale for exploiting others. It has become the basis for mistaken self-destruction. People have even borrowed the Taoist terms for noncontention, yielding and softness, and enlisted them as support for nonviolence.

But yielding is only a single term. If one understands the concept of yin and yang, how can there be yielding without assertion? One cannot be yielding forever.

The opposite of nonviolence is not violence but action. Simply because one accepts the moral principle of not harming others unnecessarily does not mean that one should degenerate into a spineless wimp. Some people who consider themselves nonviolent somehow translate this to mean they should be incredibly passive. They are so busy being gentle that they become procrastinators and weaklings with too little drive to make anything of themselves. The Scholar Warrior knows how to be dynamic as well as quiescent.

The ideal of nonviolence has often been defined as the total refusal to do any violent act toward any living being. Even the mosquito must be spared and honored. But there is no fairness and there is no justice in this world. Those are human concepts and function only in the world of ideas. All ideals suffer in the confrontation with reality. There is no paradise, and there are no utopian ways of conduct. There are only principles and the ironic sorrow that comes from trying to live according to those principles. The Scholar Warrior, though a gentle person, will not hesitate to act dynamically—perhaps even violently—when appropriate. Nonviolence is only possible in personal situations, and then only when the practitioner is operating from a position of strength. In other words, Scholar Warriors are nonviolent because they are in control of the situation. They don't need to turn the other cheek because no one is going to slap them in the first place.

Warriors are not simply aggressors. Warriors are also champions, defenders, protectors. Who among us has not needed a protector at one time or another? Who among us would not protect others? A Scholar Warrior is not the same as a "Scholar Killer" or a "Scholar Maniac." A Scholar

Warrior is an intelligent person who is neither soldier nor cannon fodder. A Scholar Warrior is capable of perceiving right and wrong in an all too gray world and is just as capable of defending on the basis of that unstinting belief.

"A warrior is not martial. He does not exhibit his prowess," is a Taoist injunction against pride, bullying others, and abusing power. It doesn't mean that power must never be used. It must sometimes be exercised. When it is called for, however, the Scholar Warrior always seeks to steer the middle course and avoid extreme actions of any kind. Nonviolence is an expression of compassion. But there must be appropriate times for all expressions. If we are in the position to be merciful, then we must. When it is necessary to act in a way that is decisive or aggressive, we should not hesitate to do so. The Scholar Warrior would urge you to be gentle but to be prepared to defend yourself and others. Be the pacifist with a sword. Most important of all, do not be so arrogant in your nonviolent beliefs that you fail to know your enemy.

善
為
士
者
不
武

AVOIDING ISOLATION

As you practice the ways of the Scholar Warrior, you will become a rarefied individual. You will become more sensitive. As you seek to perfect yourself, you may be less tolerant of those who do nothing to discipline themselves, and you will seek out as companions primarily those who are more sympathetic to your way of life. Perception will increase, and you will easily see the mediocrity of others.

But you must guard against isolation. Though your path may be perfect, it nevertheless is no guarantee against being destroyed by others. You may not want to live according to the ways of others, but you must remain familiar with them in order to protect yourself.

Not knowing others well was the mistake of Chinese warriors during the Boxer Rebellion of 1900. They thought that Taoist ritual could protect them from gunfire. That tragic error was symptomatic of the larger arrogance of Chinese culture and the naive refusal of the Chinese to accept the superiority of Western warfare. The entire country paid for that mistake with constant war in the first half of the twentieth century.

Unless protected, it is even a mistake to become a renunciate in a temple, ignorant of the events of the outside world. You have no guarantee that the world will not someday come flooding in on you. It might be something as petty as vandalism. It might be something as monstrous as world war. No god will protect you. No faith will spare you. Throughout history, throughout the world, there has not been a single real incident of the gods coming to rescue their believers. The rivers of the globe have run red with the blood of martyrs; the earth has been made fat with the broken bodies of the faithful. How can we say that mere belief will protect us? Countless millions have died because of that fallacy.

Therefore, follow the ways of your devotion, but don't be naive. You must always know your enemies. You must always be able to protect yourself. That is the only way to preserve your faith and live in peace.

The Scholar Warrior's life is built around strategy. You plan each phase of your life using the cycle of the seasons. You learn all the arts from the best masters so that you possess skill in great measure. You eliminate your vulnerabilities through rigorous self-examination and persistent training. You know the weaknesses of your opponents and realize that almost everyone may be an adversary at one time or another. If you do all this, you can be a mover in almost any situation, not necessarily by being first, but by being best. That is what the sages mean when they say, "I move last, but arrive first," and "Though the superior one is behind, he leads nevertheless."

RELATIONSHIPS

Traditionally, ideal Scholar Warriors had no personal relationships as we think of them today. Their deepest relationship was probably with their master, and their masters were usually at pains to make them independent of this tie. Naturally there were some others who had families and spouses, but even among them, the ideal of the Scholar Warrior as a lone champion was still very strong.

The elite Scholar Warrior was celibate. Whether man or woman, they believed that sexual relations depleted jing and qi. Furthermore, emotions were regarded as liabilities in a lifetime of carefully planned strategy. These people did not marry. A marriage took commitment and time, energy that they felt was better devoted to self-perfection.

This attitude caused a rift between the Scholar Warrior and the ordinary person, who proclaimed them selfish. The Scholar Warriors retorted that they saw no nobility in sacrificing themselves to spouse and children. Aside from the loss of jing and the matters of pregnancy and nursing, a child was at least a two-decade-long commitment—too great a chunk to subtract from the Scholar Warrior's lifelong strategy.

Women Scholar Warriors especially considered pregnancy a liability. They not only refused to submit to it but found ways to circumvent menstruation through herbs and exercise. They believed that though a woman had a vastly greater amount of internal energy than a man, pregnancy would reduce her reserves by half.

Loneliness was a topic that was never traditionally discussed, but they must have faced it with their usual stoicism. Certainly, the Scholar Warrior was seldom alone, for teachers and classmates were almost always around. Attitudes toward relationships and sexuality were different from those of our contemporary society; having a lover was not thought as important as it is now. There was a tremendous amount to be learned, enough that there was barely time to be lonely. But when Scholar Warriors became old, they had to confront the inevitability of old age.

Some circumvented this possibility by dying young. They simply avoided the winter of their lives. It was far better, they said, to go to the gods in the full beauty of their prime. In their opinion, old age was shameful: it proved that the person had taken no risks and had lived life as a coward. Other warriors did, through the sheer brilliance of their skill, live to old age. Yet their heartache was often unmitigated, even in a time when supposedly the elderly were venerated.

One such example occurred during the 1930s when an old master was wounded in a duel. When he sought out his children to shelter him during his recovery, he found that they were all too busy to bother with him. They had their careers, and they had their families, and they did not want to bother with a foolish old man who still engaged in the feudal practice of dueling. He felt that his eyes had been opened.

Before he had completely recovered, he received another challenge from a formidable opponent. It would not be shameful to die at this man's hand. He went to the duel, and when the moment came, he did not even bother to block the fatal stroke. The poem that he left behind made all the other Scholar Warriors weep:

> In youth, a leaf on the tree:
> Fresh, vibrant, beautiful.
> In old age, a leaf in the mud:
> Ground unnoticed beneath the heel.

No matter how many victories you may count during your time as a Scholar Warrior, it will be impossible for you to avoid the issues of loneliness and old age. There are only two ways to face it: to arrange your life so impeccably that you will be supported and surrounded by the friends and allies you need, or to enter fully into the Tao. This requires achieving a state of mind in which all ordinary emotions and needs are transcended. This may not be as easy or as wonderful as it sounds, but we will examine this in detail toward the end of the book.

Relationships and the Scholar Warrior is an issue that cannot be neglected. It is a question of balance. On one hand, excessive emotional involvement, overindulgence in celebrations, and the potential depletion of sexuality will undermine anyone. On the other hand, a life of complete involvement with the path of the Scholar Warrior without ever planning for the inevitable decline of old age is shortsighted. Therefore, one must strike a balance between the two, and that equilibrium is up to each individual to determine according to his or her capabilities. There is no right or wrong here, only the personal choice that is up to each of us to make.

TECHNOLOGY AND TAOISM

The Tao ultimately manifests itself only outside society. But Taoism—the system of knowledge about the Tao—is not wholly outside society. There are priests, and there are lay practitioners of high standing, who still live in the common world. The central concept of the Scholar Warrior is that of providing a functioning path through society while still keeping a passage open to the Tao. Today, that means Scholar Warriors must confront the issue of technology.

In the past, people lived closer to nature. The culture was agrarian, and it could not help but be affected by the rhythms of planting and harvest, the cycle of the seasons, and the overwhelming quality of natural disasters. Since the industrial and technological revolutions, however, people have lived more distant from the pulse of nature and have created a world centered on human society rather than on the natural environment. Nowhere is this more apparent than in our civilization's deep involvement with technology.

The sheer intimacy of electronic communication, through video, film, telephone, fax, computer linkages, and other instantaneous media yet to come, has changed the way society operates. Information is now accessible to any person in unprecedented amounts. Knowledge may be accumulated, processed, stored, and rearranged with the help of sophisticated personal computers. Schoolchildren are learning to use electronic media at an increasingly early age. There is no way to function effectively in society without knowing and using these various forms of technology.

The probable Taoist response would be to pronounce it all trivial, the overwhelming madness of self-centered human beings. They would declare—and rightly so—that all this is a violation of nature, and that this staggering magnification of the worst aspects of the human mind will only lead to more disaster and a further alienation from the Tao. They would point out that this continual emphasis on information will only distance us from our innermost voice, drowned, as it were, in innumerable digital impulses. The individual will become lazy, unable to function independently of machines, and this mania will lead to physical deterioration as well: continual exposure to electrical fields disperses the qi; staring at a video display depletes the eyes; and reliance on stored memory makes the mind lazy.

I remember a young lady who came to my master after having visited his home temples. She showed him pictures of different monks. He recognized them, including one who she said had an ambition to computerize the Taoist canon. My master simply shook his head. The books were meant to be read, he said. The calligraphy was written by the enlightened saints themselves. The strength of their qi was so strong that even the particles of ink lined up in the strokes as if they were magnetic filings responding to a mighty current. Only by being there, reading the actual handwritten manuscripts, could a student even begin to comprehend the hints from the ancient sages. It was not the words so much as the experience that mattered; by computerizing it all, one was admitting a powerful poison into Taoism and missing the actual value of the writings.

This young monk was also shown in another photograph posing with his own master. It was immediately apparent that there was a vast difference between the two. The master stood upright, with muscular, deeply veined arms that looked like the gnarled trunks of trees. His face was bearded, but his eyes were bright, clear, and calm. He had a gentle smile. Although my own teacher recognized the master as a formidable martial artist, the man looked like a simple and kindly elder at peace with the world. His student, in contrast, had rounder, softer flesh. He did not have the hardened musculature of his teacher but sat on a rock in a casual way, one hand draped on his knee as if copying the pose of models. His face was full, but there was a hint of determination in his wide jaw and furrowed brow. He looked ambitious. Here was one of the classic differences between the generations: the elder at peace with the world, for he came from a time when there was actually little distraction, the younger one facing great distractions, vast sources of information, more competition for success, and a much wider range of options.

In my master's time, a young man born into the merchant or peasant classes had no choices for a career. A young man born into the warrior or aristocratic classes had only three choices: government official, military man, or priest. By contrast, any young person today has an amazing number of choices in careers, hobbies, entertainment, technology, and even living places. What is more confusing is that the social and economic viability of these different things shifts almost from month to month. Today's Scholar Warriors and today's Taoists need to address themselves to the problems of today's world.

All of Taoism assumes at base that the human being is already at variance with the Tao, and that all the techniques of Taoism have been to help individuals regain the harmony with Tao that should have been natural. Taoism has always been the method of awakening people from the illusions of the world. Well, now there is more to awaken from. Had Lu Dongbin been alive today and on his way to the examinations, his induced dream would undoubtedly have included computers.

See Chapter 12 for a more complete discussion of Lu Dongbin.

Like Lu, we must all still awaken. But now the dream is more complex. Though the world may be illusory, though it may be a cesspool of degradation, and the ultimate answer may still be to get out of it, we must still do something in the meantime. There has to be a well-reasoned response, and there has to still be that road left open to freedom. Even after Lu Dongbin joined his master, he had to undergo years of training. Today's training has to confront the question of technology.

There is no reversing the use of technology. It is here to stay. Perhaps there is no logical way for it to fit in with the natural order of things. Perhaps the masters are right, and there will be no resolution until humanity destroys itself and the earth is left to lie fallow for thousands of years. But that is not really very helpful to us now. We are living in a technological society, and we must use it.

One of the initial approaches we can take is to ensure that whatever technology we use will not endanger our health. Excessive amounts of electricity will disperse the body's qi, so one should undoubtedly limit one's exposure and take steps to prevent or mitigate the damage caused by staring into a video display monitor. For a meditator, even the amount of electricity flowing into a house can be disruptive. We have to use electricity and computers and electronic communications devices. But we should limit our exposure and make sure that there are times we can get away from them.

Actually, all these machines are really quite neutral. They cannot function without a human being to program them. If you have religious or spiritual or creative values, you will inevitably apply them to your machines. They are only an extension of yourself. No matter how sophisticated your communications technology, the question still remains whether you have anything significant to record or to say.

It is we who assign significance to information. We have to process that information for our own purposes. If your technology functions as an extension of your mind, then what could really be wrong? But value and understanding will never be replaced by any machinery that we make, and we must strive to develop and maintain those faculties within us. Though the speed and the pervasiveness of technology challenge us to keep our equilibrium, we must do so. This signals the dominance of spirit over the mechanical.

The highest sect of Taoism deals with sorcery. In many ways, this was the technology of another time. Technology is our sorcery today. There were good sorcerers and bad ones, just as today there are creative uses of technology and evil uses. Our basic human struggles have not actually changed, only the venue.

It is important to use technology solely as a tool. It is like a warrior's weapon; the warrior is not in the weapon. Weapons are merely tools. If they lose them, their skill does not abandon them and they do not care about the tool lost. They fight on, they keep their wits about them. In the same way, technology is merely something that we use. When we are without it, it should not affect the nature and the goals of our spiritual inquiry. When we sit to meditate, we don't need the computer, and there is nothing wrong with that. We don't need hammers, plows, threshing machines, bridles, candles, scriptures, and all the other products of civilization either, but that doesn't mean that there aren't proper and even "Taoist" uses for these things. A Taoist is not afraid of being a craftsperson and would look upon technology as a type of craft. If kept in that context, there is little harm in technology. Use it, but remain detached from it. Some day, you will have to leave it behind.

THE NATURE OF SIMPLICITY

The study of Tao should not be hurried, and you should never be anxious about it. The minute you feel that way, you are far from the Tao. The Tao may move swiftly at times, but it never rushes. It moves at exactly the pace that is required. So too should our pursuit of the Tao. It should be leisurely, yet we should not miss any stage in life or leave anything undone.

The Taoists say that when a person is ready to learn of the Tao, he or she will find the way to learn of it. Those who aren't ready will never even hear of it. Still less, they may hear of it and never remember that they have. When you are ready—or as the masters express it poetically, when your destiny is right—you will meet the master who will guide you to Tao.

You will bump into your master on the road. Maybe this road will only be the figurative road of life, but the best way to meet your master is by seeming accident. You have heard of the Tao, yet you are going about your own business when you meet someone who can show you what you want to learn. If you have the good fortune to meet your master but then ignore the occasion, the master will not care. You may never meet again, but that is Tao.

If the two of you do find some rapport, then the two of you will continue along the road for as long as is appropriate. There is a wonderful sharing quality about being with a master: a sharing of knowledge, a sharing of experience, and a sharing of support. That precious connection can seldom be lifelong, however, and when it is time for the two of you to part, it will be impossible to oppose the event. But whether it was for a day, or for decades, your time with your master will be a special time in your life: your master will help you find simplicity.

Tao has to be sensed with the totality of one's being. It has to be followed, lived, and absorbed. You can't always be with Tao. Sometimes you will be isolated from Tao just because of the way you are thinking, or because of distractions in your life, or because the Tao is just somewhere else at the moment. That's all right too. But if you remove what divides you from Tao, you will have fewer blockages. This process of simplification is one of constant flux, however. Your own needs and your own desires must be worked out. To do that, you need education, and you need to live an active life. But you shouldn't think of those things as part of an acquisition process. You aren't just learning more; you aren't just doing more; you aren't just trying to cram more and more into your narrowing life. You are doing all these things precisely to leave them behind.

PU
Simplicity.

Do them; satisfy your involvement in them; and when you are ready, they can drop away like ballast from a balloon. Each thing that falls away opens wider the access to Tao.

It's a delicate process to learn, complete, and then transcend as a means to know the Tao. But in today's society, and with today's active pursuit of self-gratification, there are few alternatives. You have to simplify to know the Tao. There is no shortcutting; you've got to know what you are leaving behind to leave it behind.

When you can live your life free of stress, when you can just sit there without any anxiety, when you live a simple and carefree life—perhaps just growing your own food and enjoying each day—then you are close to the Tao. You will have no ambition to do anything other than what you are doing. The Taoists say that farmers are often good examples for Taoists. They live a natural life close to the pulse of the seasons and the earth, and they are contented. Probably, they never even heard about the Tao, yet they are more Taoist than some priests. It is precisely because they are not even aware of being Taoist that they are most Taoist of all.

Yet it is important to manage this process of simplification. If you go too quickly, you will find yourself indifferent to the world before you are ready. For example, the path of the Scholar Warrior is one of sacrifice and spartan training. Whatever vices you may have are discarded when you begin on the path. Smoking, liquor, coffee, drugs, poor habits—all are chopped off in the search for self-perfection. You may even begin to forsake pleasures like chocolates, sweets, and favorite foods without the intervention of masters or friends. Stripped of socialization and the notion that certain foods or forms of entertainment are fashionable and sexy, and left alone to choose, the body and mind gravitate toward what is good. That is why Lao Tzu says, "Give up learning," meaning give up the unwise teachings of a shortsighted society. But you will be giving up pleasures that once seemed to provide part of the meaning of life and many things that once excited you will seem hollow and flat. You may be simplifying, but you shouldn't do it faster than you can adjust.

Self-perfection may be wonderful, but sometimes it will seem terribly without feeling. It will be like an exquisite vase in a museum. Without doubt, it is of rare beauty and utterly flawless, but there is something in its form that seems distant. Its appeal is abstract. People who read the philosophy of Taoism and are attracted to the ideas of emptiness and wu wei immediately try to practice these in their lives. They don't realize that when you truly attain a state of emptiness all social definitions will become meaningless. You will not be interested in career, family, lovers, perhaps even your own existence. You will care only about unity with Tao, but in Tao there are no distinctions, no good, no bad. You will not have any preferences, so all your interests and even your very sense of individuality will dissolve.

That is why it is important to pace your progress on the path. If you feel that your life is becoming meaningless because of your spiritual path, it is because your progress is outstripping your ability to adjust emotionally. Don't rush to full realization—because at that point, everything becomes meaningless.

It is far better to practice the ways of physical purification, sound philosophy, and spiritual practice with moderation. Although you must make sacrifices, make them when you understand them fully. Within reason, try a little of everything in life. Enjoy what the world has to offer, but don't invest it with great passion. Just enjoy it for as long as it lasts. Indifference will come soon enough. Why worry about your status? Simplify. And simplify yet again.

THE FUTURE OF TAOISM

The Tao is eternal. As long as there are human beings, there will be a Tao to contemplate. Whether we follow it or not is up to us, but unless we do, we will be lost in turmoil and confusion. Even when we follow it, there will be difficulties, but we will not view them as such. Like water, we will accept a level course or a precipitous drop with the same equanimity. After all, we understand that all is emptiness, and that establishes not nihilism, not aloofness, but perspective. This type of inner Taoism is of the heart.

The Taoism of the Scholar Warrior will not have such an assured future, for it is strongly tied to the culture that generated it. That Chinese culture generated Taoism has long been the focus for various kinds of provincial attitudes. The old Chinese don't want to share Taoism with the West, and Westerners either regard Taoism as another Chinese enigma or grasp it eagerly, thinking there must surely be an answer there for them. In fact, it really doesn't matter anymore. The Chinese culture that gave rise to Taoism no longer exists. Most of the masters are dead. The temples have been made into hotels. Power lines and factories stand on land once held sacred. Books have been burned. The youth want blue jeans and radios playing the latest popular songs. Although there are a few people who are interested in Taoism, they cannot practice in the old ways. In spite of their sincerity, they have a different spirit, a different outlook. Times are irrevocably different.

All over the globe, we are saturated by a contemporary culture of materialism, instant communication, and electronic luxury. Advertising bombards us with pulsating music, sexual imagery, and the urgent appeal to involve ourselves more and more with gadgets, objects, and new fads. Nothing old is ever good enough. Each season, we must throw out the old and buy "new, revolutionary" products. Old ways, we also throw out for the sake of whatever new thoughts and attitudes come along. We think in terms of decades, and at the end of each one, we declare that era over with and look forward to a wholly different one. What use is there for a tradition, let alone a tradition that urges contentment, acceptance, self-discipline, and inward contemplation?

The ways of the Scholar Warrior will not survive in their most literal form. But we need to adapt the old ways, because they will remain the surest road to a successful life. This success is not a success of prestige and wealth but of understanding life at a level underneath the shifting currents of civilization.

A part of our lives, our bodies, and our psyches functions as part of nature. Just as no human manipulation has altered the number of days in a year, or altered the seasons, or altered the orbits of the planets, so too a primeval level in all of us is not changed by society. That is the level that the Scholar Warrior and Taoism must address. Our aging, our thinking, our urges, our sexuality, our wonder about the universe, our need to find a reason for our existence, our imperative to know ourselves, and our own mortality will always need examination and action. It is here that the way of the Scholar Warrior excels. Because these questions will always exist, there will always the need for a tradition that has the answers.

中多不付一深代地得院
年人注未吳偉設周健成
勾染門中吶年年閒
位中春付徔忆九
華言

王瑑

THOUSAND TREES
ON AZURE PEAKS.
Wang Chien (1598–
1677). Dated 1668.
Qing dynasty. Asian
Art Museum of San
Francisco, B69 D2.

坐功

Look within.
All answers are there.

BOOK

III

MEDITATION AND
TRANSCENDENCE

導引

9

Open the Eight Meridians
And you attain the pathways
To immortality.

DAOYIN

THE BRIDGE FROM EXERCISE TO MEDITATION

ONCE ONE HAS PROGRESSED on the path of the Scholar Warrior, experienced a rich life of travel and exploration, clarified one's inner purpose, and attained the level of skill one finds satisfying, one must begin the process of looking into Tao itself. This is done through the practice of meditation. The Taoists call this "entering stillness." This stillness is tantamount to the emptiness of the Tao, for in stillness there is a gradual reduction of all the functions of the body and the everyday mind. Like mud slowly settling in water to leave clarity, so does entering stillness allow a revealing of one's inner nature. The power of the Scholar Warrior is transformed into a perfection that reveals all things.

A lake, when undisturbed, mirrors heaven perfectly. In the same way, the holy aspirant seeks to still the mind so that it too may mirror heaven perfectly. As long as we are still, we are free of the filth of society, our own egotism, and our own perversions. In stillness, there is a transcendence of all the learning, all the skills, and all the ambitions we may have. We look within, and there is Tao; there is quiet. There finally, after all the grievous sorrows we undergo in the name of fulfilling ourselves as human beings, is the tranquillity that we seek.

How many of us can truly say that we are ready to glimpse tranquillity? We say we are tired of the stress in our lives, tired of frustration. We repeat to ourselves over and over again our dreams for the "good life," yet they seldom include the simple realization of who we are and why we are here. But the Scholar Warrior who has seen the futility of life and has realized the limits of human learning by trying with every resource to break those limits is ready for tranquillity, ready for stillness.

It is ironic, in a way, for we strive for years to measure the length and breadth of this universe. Only when we have satiated our yearnings do we come back to simple sitting, simple appreciation. We travel far and wide on the ocean of knowledge only to realize that the simple answer is right here within ourselves.

Look within. That is the true teaching of Taoism. Still yourself and look within, and all answers are inside you. For example, a highly accomplished Taoist adept once searched everywhere for the Tao. He spent decades of study under famous masters, and he still did not realize the Tao. He acquainted himself with all the wandering ascetics, the magicians, the hermits, and the soothsayers, and he still did not realize the Tao. He went to all the sacred mountains, did all the ritual sacrifices, memorized all the scriptures, and he still did not realize the Tao. Finally, he heard of three ancient sages who had already cast away their attachments to the world. They lived on one of the most remote mountaintops in China, close to the borders of Tibet. It took him great effort to scale the peak. The masters were there when he arrived, and they received him serenely. Mustering the utmost in sincerity, he explained that in spite of all his strivings, he had not realized the Tao. The sages smiled. "Close your eyes," they told him gently. "The answers that you seek are inside you." That, of course, was the one place that the aspirant had not searched, and after he closed his eyes, he attained the realization that he so deeply wanted. The same is true of each of us. We travel to satisfy our everyday minds. If we want to see the Tao, we must look into ourselves.

That is why it is said, "Without going out my door, I can know the world. Without looking out my window, I can see the Tao." These sayings do not mean that you can spend your whole life indoors; they mean that the ultimate knowledge of the Tao is not to be gained by external means.

Meditation, it should be cautioned, takes a day to learn and a lifetime to ripen. It is not that the actual method is so difficult; it is that it must be investigated gradually. The muddy water of our lives takes a long time to settle down—and we are forever stirring it up again. In addition, both our personalities as well as the Tao change constantly, and meditation changes too. The more complex we are, the more difficult it is for us to attain inner clarity. "Decrease daily," say the Taoists.

There is a method to learning meditation. Like anything else in life, it must be built on a firm foundation. The life of a Scholar Warrior is but a part of that foundation. Serious accomplishment in qigong is another, for breath is the gateway between body and mind. It is both an automatic and a voluntary function of the human body. It mirrors our minds perfectly. When we are frightened, our breath quickens. When we are concentrating, our breath slows, sometimes even stopping without us thinking about it. When we sleep, our breathing is unlike any breathing we use while awake. By controlling and then channeling our breath, we lay the groundwork for meditation.

Daoyin is the name of a higher classification of qigong. Its function is not only to consolidate the health of the practitioner and maintain the circulation of energy through the bloodstream and meridians, but also to bridge the gap between the physical and the spiritual.

Within the set of daoyin exercises are beginning meditations and visualizations. In this perspective, the training that you have done so far— purification, diet, exercises, herb use, and philosophy—forms the basis for this new stage. In order to make your breakthrough here, you will have to integrate all that you are as a Scholar Warrior. You will not be successful if you have neglected any area of your development. But if you do all that

DAO YIN
Both dao and yin have connotations of lead-ing and guiding. The function of daoyin is to channel one's inner energies.

is necessary, and if you practice this set every day for at least a hundred days, you are virtually guaranteed to open your meridians and gain greater insight into yourself.

At the heart of daoyin is enhanced circulation through the Eight Meridians. These Eight Meridians especially used by the Taoists are conceived as a system separate from but mutually dependent on the twelve medical meridians. People are sometimes confused because sources disagree as to the exact routing. I cannot defend these discrepancies, except to say that different masters have different insights about the exact routes the meridians take. In this sense, meridian meditation is not so much the self-examination of specific anatomical facts as it is the *awareness of energy flow and function*. As long as one understands this, and as long as one becomes aware of the flow of energy within oneself, there should not be too much confusion.

Another related potential stumbling block is the little-known Taoist practice of bridging meridians. The Taoists do not see any meridian as being a wholly closed system; they believe that they can direct energy to any point along a meridian and then send it through a connecting meridian, or even through flesh where no documented meridian exists, and continue on along another meridian. As you explore daoyin, you will see that this practice is quite common.

Visualization of the meridians is quite important, but as you do this, there will be sympathetic movement along other meridians as well. Thus, if you know the routing of the famous Macrocosmic Orbit, you may be surprised that daoyin does not contain a complete and conscious circulation through all eight meridians. It advocates visualization only where physical movement is not enough to move the energy through, or where visualization along one set will not stimulate sympathetic movement in other parts of the body.

Upon examination and practice of daoyin, you will see that the set begins by stimulating the lower dantian, the source of all your physical energy. It then concentrates on strengthening the kidneys and establishing the wellsprings of jing. Only then does it begin the process of circulation throughout the body.

Here then is the set.

NOURISHING THE DANTIAN

1. Face the east. Stand with your feet shoulder width apart. Place both hands in front of you at waist level, with one palm on top of the other. Both palms face up. Your hands should not touch your body, but should be about five inches away. Hold this concentration for three minutes, concentrating on the dantian. Try to feel heat and movement in this area.

2. Inhale while lifting the palms upward.

3. Maintaining the same inhalation, lift to the level of your throat and then turn your palms outward so that thumbs are downward. Continue to push over head. As you straighten your arms, your palms will push overhead.

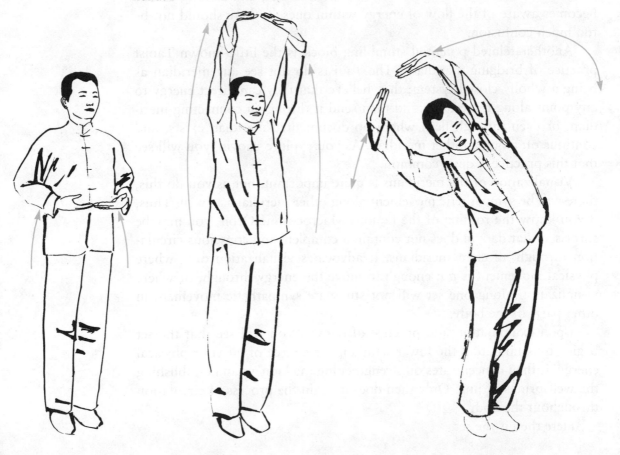

4. Lean to the left and exhale; lean to the right and exhale again without taking any breath in between.

5. Lower your hands to your sides. To repeat, join them together at the dantian and repeat from step 2.

6. Begin with six rounds and gradually increase during daily practice to twenty-one repetitions.

BUILDING QI IN THE KIDNEYS

1. Stand with your feet shoulder width apart, hands at your sides. Relax your whole body. Think of the dantian until you feel heat and movement, or concentrate for at least three minutes.

腎臟調氣功

2. Inhale, and, extending arms to the side, lift both fists to shoulder level. Base of the thumb should be facing upward and enclosed in the fingers.

3. Hold your breath, and keeping arms extended, stretch to the left, allowing your left arm to move toward the ground and your right arm up. Concentrate on your right kidney.

4. Return to the center position, and exhale. Do not lower your arms. Then inhale.

5. Hold your breath, and stretch to the right. Concentrate on your left kidney.

6. Return to the center position and exhale as you lower your arms. To repeat, begin again at step 2.

7. Begin with six rounds and gradually increase during daily practice to twenty-one repetitions.

DEVELOPING THE GATE OF JING

精
門
順
氣
功

1. Stand with your feet shoulder width apart, hands at your sides. Relax your whole body.

2. Raise your hands in front of you and rub them briskly together to warm them.

3. Immediately place them on the front of your body, preferably on bare skin, just above the waist. Feel the heat penetrating into your body, and imagine that it is being drawn to the kidneys.

4. Rub your abdomen with each hand in a circle, first going in an outward direction twelve times, then reversing twelve times.

5. Bending elbows back, lift both fists to the side to chest level with an inhalation. Use reverse breathing (see page 98 for a review of reverse breathing). Imagine your heart bursting into flame. With practice, you will actually feel a warm sensation in this area.

6. Open your fists and, palms down and fingers pointing in, press them down in front of you as you exhale. Imagine that the flame in your heart is plunging into each kidney with your simultaneous exhalation and pressing downward of the arms.

7. Repeat from step 2.

8. Begin with six rounds, and gradually increase during daily practice to twenty-one repetitions.

DEEP BREATHING

1. Sit facing the east. Your back must be straight and your hips relaxed. Your legs may be crossed, your feet pressed sole to sole, or you may sit in the lotus position if you are able. No matter what position you adopt, your knees must touch the ground (for stability), and you must eliminate any stiffness or tension. (See page 289 for illustrations of cross-legged sitting.)

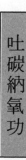

吐碳納氧功

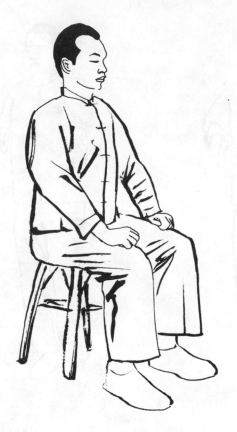

If you have some trouble, try elevating your buttocks with a cushion while your knees remain on the ground. Frequently, elevating the body about six inches is enough to sit comfortably. If you still cannot sit in this way, sit on the edge of a chair with your genitals free of the edge. Again, your back must be straight and your body relaxed and comfortable.

Your shoulders should be relaxed and lowered, and your palms should rest comfortably on your knees.

2. Bring the mind to the dantian, and inhale deeply and slowly through your nose. At this point, your tongue should be touching your upper palate, and your mouth should be closed. At the same time, close and lift your anus, and keep it lifted for the duration of your inhalation. Imagine that all the air you are inhaling is flowing gently to the dantian. The more you inhale to the dantian, the more you should relax and even

extend your lower abdomen slightly. (You must only extend the abdominal area below the navel. Do not exaggerate this, as you can permanently stretch your abdominal wall, and it will then sag in a most unsightly way.) Inhale until you cannot inhale any more.

3. Place the tip of your tongue onto your bottom palate, and open your lips slightly. Exhale slowly, imagining that all the air is leaving your dantian. At the same time, slowly release your anus. Your exhalation should be as long as possible, and you should try to expel as much air as possible from your body. As you exhale, simultaneously pull your abdomen inward and upward, so that at the end of your exhalation, you will have pulled all your muscles as far inward as possible.

4. If saliva forms during this exercise, you must swallow it in a gulp. The Taoists call this the Jade Nectar, and regard it as having highly beneficial properties.

5. You can practice this by number of repetitions, using the same number you are using for the preceding postures, or you can practice it for a set period of time. Twenty minutes is the recommended duration for this exercise.

OPENING THE CENTRAL MERIDIAN

The central meridian, or chongmei, runs from the perineum to the level of the throat. In some texts, this channel is imagined in a straight and plumb line that rises straight up from the perineum. In other texts, it is described as rising from the tail bone up through the center of the spine. It is thus the equivalent of the spinal cord or the *sushumna* as described in Indian yogic texts. The former is the recommended path.

1. Sit facing the east. Use the observations about posture that you learned in the previous method.

2. Bring the mind to the perineum, and inhale deeply and slowly through your nose. At this point, your tongue should be touching your upper palate, and your mouth should be closed. At the same time, close and lift your anus, and keep it lifted for the duration of your inhalation. Imagine that all your energy is rising in a glowing stream up chongmei.

潜
冲
神
功

The more you inhale, the more you should pull in your abdomen and raise your diaphragm. Inhale until you cannot inhale any more. At this point, your energy should have reached the level of your throat.

3. Place the tip of your tongue onto your bottom palate, and open your lips slightly. Exhale slowly, imagining your energy is slowly sinking back down chongmei. Your exhalation should be as long as possible, and you should try to expel as much air as possible from your body. At the same time, slowly release your anus. As you exhale, simultaneously relax your abdomen, and at the culmination of your exhalation, your lower abdomen should even be slightly bulging. Do not exaggerate this to the point of undue stretching of the abdominal wall or excessive pressure on your intestines and bladder.

4. If saliva forms during this exercise, you must swallow it in a gulp after your exhalation is complete.

5. You can practice this by number of repetitions, using the same number you are using for the preceding postures, or you can practice it for a set time. Twenty minutes is the recommended duration for this exercise.

OPENING THE MICROCOSMIC ORBIT

任督二脈功

This next posture helps to open the famous Microcosmic Orbit, one of the central Taoist meditation methods. The orbit is a circular linkage of two meridians, the renmei and dumei. Dumei begins at the perineum and rises up the back of the body, over the crown of the head, and down to the upper palate. Renmei descends from the lower palate to the perineum. Connecting them and circulating energy through them conforms with the Taoist beliefs that everything in the universe must move, and that perpetual conservation lies in circulating, cycling, and recycling of energy.

These meridians are not normally open to the conscious transmission of energy, however, so this posture first attempts to send the energy through using both breathing and isolated muscle contraction. These contractions not only attract the energy but are also a way to focus the mind on the crest of the energy.

1. Sit facing the east. Use the observations about posture that you learned in the previous method.

2. Inhale slightly and lean forward, forcing all your breath steadily out of your body. Pull your abdomen in tightly. This should take about two seconds.

3. Stay leaning over, and without changing your position or inhaling, abruptly relax and even distend your lower abdomen while tilting your hips upward and forward.

4. Bring the mind to the perineum, and inhale deeply and slowly through your nose. As you begin your inhalation, you should slowly straighten up. At this point, your tongue should be touching your upper palate, and your mouth should be closed. At the same time, close and lift your anus, and keep it lifted for the duration of your inhalation. Imagine that all your energy is rising in a glowing stream up dumei. The more you inhale, the more you should pull in your abdomen and raise your diaphragm.

Make sure that your mind is focused on the crest of this rising stream, for you must perform specific muscle contractions as you raise it. As the energy passes each segment of the Microcosmic Orbit, do the indicated contraction. As it progresses to the next segment, you may relax the previous section as you begin to contract for the next one.

As the energy begins its ascent, contract and lift the anus, and tilt your hips slightly upward and forward.

As the energy passes through your lower back, contract your abdomen a bit more than the ongoing contraction, and push your lumbar region backward. Try to straighten your lower back. Inhale until you cannot inhale any more.

As it passes between your shoulder blades, you should be sitting upright and your chest should be contracted inward, your shoulders rounded, as if you are pushing against your upper back from the inside out.

As you continue to inhale up through the neck, pull your chin in and thrust your head upward. Though your eyes are closed, they should begin to roll upward in your head, as if to look at the crown of your head.

Continue to inhale up to the crown point, called the Hundred Meetings Place, or baihui. At this point, your energy should be fully at this spot, and you should just be comfortably completing your inhalation. Your neck should be fully stretched (so that your head is lifted high above your shoulders), your anus fully closed, your body upright, your tongue pressed tightly to the upper palate, and your eyes rolled upward as if to look at this point from inside your head. Hold your breath and this position for as long as is comfortable. When you are beginning, try holding it for only a few moments, and over a long period of practice, perhaps months or even years, increase the duration of this breath retention for up to ten seconds. Do not hold your breath any longer than this except under the strict supervision of an experienced teacher.

5. When you are ready to go on, mentally direct your energy from baihui down your forehead. You are still holding your breath. Follow the progress of your energy with your eyes. As the energy comes to the tip of the nose, open your eyes slightly and focus strongly on the tip of your nose. Imagine that you are thrusting your nose forward, and even flare your nostrils in order to attract your energy to this point.

6. Bring your energy inward to your upper palate, and imagine that it is entering the tip of your tongue. Place the tip of your tongue onto your bottom palate, and open your lips slightly. Exhale slowly, imagining your energy is slowly sinking back down the renmei, first through your tongue, through its root, down to just below the surface of your throat. Again, you must use muscle contraction to facilitate the flow of energy downward.

As you exhale and pass your throat, contract your neck muscles. Relax after the energy has passed.

As the energy passes your sternum, thrust your chest out slightly and pull your shoulders subtly back.

As it passes down your solar plexus, slightly bulge only this region outward. As you exhale further downward, simultaneously relax your abdomen, and at the culmination of your exhalation, your lower abdomen should even be slightly bulging. Do not exaggerate this. At the end of your exhalation, you should have reached the perineum again.

7. If saliva forms during this exercise, you must swallow it in a gulp after your exhalation is complete.

8. This procedure should be practiced in rounds of twelve repetitions each. Begin with twelve circulations. As your practice progresses, add another twelve when you feel ready to go on. Finally, do a full thirty-six rounds when you feel you are ready.

THE MICROCOSMIC ORBIT

This is the same route as the preceding method, only it does not use the muscle contractions to the same degree. By this point, your energy should be flowing freely, so that it only needs the mind to guide it through the channels. High-level masters only need to *think* of the flow, and the energy immediately obeys. The even greater masters, however, do not even bother with the formality of the Orbit. They will their energy to flow to a certain point, and it arrives there without the master being conscious of the route it took. This is the instantaneous oneness of mind, energy, and body that we must all seek.

靜坐神功

1. Sit facing the east. Use the observations about posture that you learned in the previous method.

2. Bring the mind to the perineum, and inhale deeply and slowly through your nose. At this point, your tongue should be touching your upper palate, and your mouth should be closed. At the same time, close and lift your anus, and keep it lifted for the duration of your inhalation. Imagine that all your energy is rising in a glowing stream up dumei. The more you inhale, the more you should pull in your abdomen and raise your diaphragm.

Make sure that your mind is focused on the crest of this rising stream. Let it rise through these points: the tailbone, mingmen (the Gate of Life), the diaphragm, the top of the shoulder blades, the neck, the base of the skull. Continue to inhale up to the crown point, called the Hundred Meetings Place. At this point, your energy should be fully at this spot, and you should just be comfortably completing your inhalation. Your neck should be completely straightened, your anus fully closed, your body upright, your tongue pressed tightly to the upper palate, and your eyes rolled upward as if to look at this point from inside your head. Hold your breath and this position for as long as is comfortable. When you are beginning, try holding your breath for only a few moments, and over a long period of practice, perhaps months or even years, increase the duration of this breath retention for up to ten seconds. Do not hold your breath any longer than this except under the strict supervision of an experienced teacher.

3. When you are ready to go on, mentally direct your energy from the Hundred Meetings Place down your forehead. You are still holding your breath. Follow the progress of your energy with your eyes. As the energy comes to the tip of your nose, open your eyes slightly and focus strongly on the tip of your nose.

4. Bring your energy inward to your upper palate and imagine that it is entering the tip of your tongue. Place the tip of your tongue onto your bottom palate, and open your lips slightly. Exhale slowly, imagining your energy is slowly sinking back down the renmei, first through your tongue, through its root, down to just below the surface of your throat.

Continue to exhale down the renmei toward the perineum. As you exhale downward, simultaneously relax your abdomen, and at the culmination of your exhalation, your lower abdomen should even be slightly bulging. Do not exaggerate this. At the end of your exhalation, you should have reached the perineum again.

5. If saliva forms during this exercise, you must swallow it in a gulp after your exhalation is complete.

6. This procedure should be practiced in rounds of twelve repetitions each. Begin with twelve circulations. As your practice progresses, add another twelve when you feel ready to go on. Finally, do a full thirty-six rounds when you feel that you are ready.

BRINGING ENERGY TO THE PALMS

1. Sit facing the east. Use the observations about posture that you learned in the previous method.

2. Bring both hands together above your lap, fingers touching, palms open and facing upward. While slowly raising them to the level of your throat, inhale using reverse breathing and imagining the energy rising up chongmei.

3. Turn your palms over, and press down to your lap (but don't touch your legs), while exhaling and letting the energy descend chongmei.

4. Repeating step 2, bring both hands upward again.

5. With your hands at the level of your throat, separate your hands, palms out. Exhale, but keep the energy concentrated at the base of your neck.

6. Inhaling constantly, push both palms outward until the elbows are straight. At the same time, contract the stomach and anus tightly, and

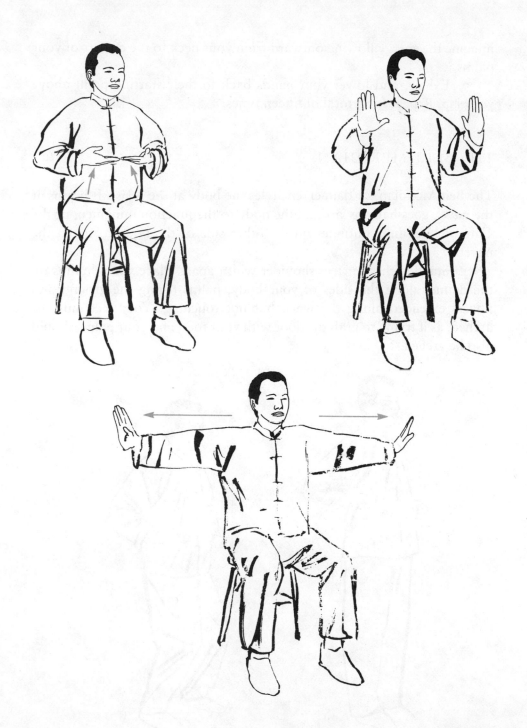

imagine the energy flowing outward from your neck to the centers of your palms.

7. Exhale, and lower your hands back to their starting point above your lap. Repeat for a total of fifteen times.

THE BELT MERIDIAN

The Belt Meridian, or daimei, encircles the body at the waist. It begins at the navel, goes halfway around the body to the junction mingmen, or the Gate of Life, and continues on the other side of the body to rejoin the navel.

1. Stand with your feet shoulder width apart. Place your thumbs on the daimei along the sides of your body, palms facing the ground and fingers extended along the waist but not touching. Your feet must be arched, as if trying to grab the floor with your toes, and your palms should also be arched.

2. Exhale, relax the abdomen as you learned in the reverse breathing exercises, and move into a partial squat.

3. Inhale, and straighten up slowly while lifting the genitals and the stomach in reverse breathing.

4. Repeat steps 2 and 3.

5. This exercise may be performed by number of repetitions, beginning at fifteen, or it may be done for a set length of time. If you elect to do it by time, begin with five minutes, and work up to fifteen minutes. When you feel heat rising up your sides toward your kidneys, you will know that the exercise is working.

STANDING MEDITATION

1. Stand with your feet shoulder width apart. Raise your arms directly out to the sides with the palms down. Hold this position for three minutes, breathing normally. Try not to think of anything in particular.

DAOYIN 271

2. After three minutes, exhale and lower your arms.

3. On inhaling, immediately raise your arms again. Exhaling, continue to hold your arms out, but this time, your palms should face outward. Hold this position, breathing normally.

4. After three minutes, inhale fully and exhale out to the palms. Inhale again, and exhale as you lower your palms. This completes this posture.

SENDING QI TO THE KIDNEYS

1. Stand relaxed, with feet shoulder width apart, arms at your sides.

2. Inhale and raise your arms to the sides to shoulder level, palms facing down.

3. Exhale and twist to the left, turning palms perpendicular to the ground, thumbs up.

練腎注氣功

4. Inhale, and turn palms down as you return to the starting position; then continue to twist to your right while exhaling.

5. Inhale, and return to the center.

6. Exhale, and let your arms descend to your sides. As soon as they are almost there, squat down with one knee up. (It doesn't matter which one. Most people alternate.) Clasp your hands around this knee.

7. Looking directly forward, hold this position, and do two rounds of reverse breathing.

8. Then inhale as deeply as possible, imagining all your breath filling the kidneys. As you are inhaling, pull against your knee, but resist this pull with your leg. Gradually drop your chin slowly to your chest as you inhale, and round your back. Pull your stomach in. Try to feel your kidneys bloating up with energy.

9. Even when you can no longer inhale, hold your position and force one more breath.

10. Exhale partially and relax.

11. Continue to exhale as you stand up.

12. Repeat from step 2 for fifteen rounds.

SENDING ENERGY TO THE LEGS

This form incorporates the Macrocosmic Orbit. Although the main point of concentration is on the legs, the creators of this form evidently felt that no conscious effort had to be made to bring the energy to the hands (because so much of the previous set does this). By this point, they felt that the built-up energy would automatically "spill over" into the arm meridians as the exercise was done.

This is a standing meditation posture. All the circulation of the energy is done by sheer mental concentration alone, making daoyin a more advanced and demanding type of exercise that begins to breach the realm of true meditation.

1. Stand facing east with your feet shoulder width apart and your hands pointing out to the sides. Your arms should be held slightly away from your body. Relax completely.

2. Beginning at the perineum, and using reverse breathing, inhale up chongmei to the level of the throat. Exhale back down.

3. Using reverse breathing, inhale again up chongmei, but at the level of the throat, consciously direct the energy across the throat to link up with renmei.

4. Begin to exhale down renmei. Exhale slowly, and maintain your reserves of breath, for you will have to exhale a long time.

5. When the energy reaches the dantian, tilt your hips up and split the energy into two streams that continue to descend along the top of your thighs. As soon as the energy has passed into the legs, you may relax your hips.

6. Continue to exhale all the way down to the ankles, then the instep, and finally, directly through the foot to the yongquan, or Bubbling

Well points. Hold your breath, though you have exhaled completely by now, and concentrate strongly on these points. Arch your feet to enhance your effort. Hold from two to fifteen seconds, according to comfort. There should be no struggling for breath, only a simple pause.

7. Begin to inhale slowly. You will have a long way to inhale back up, so be sure to inhale slowly.

8. As you inhale, the energy ascends up the inside of the foot, loops around the ankle, rises up the inner calves to the inner thighs. The two streams of energy join at the perineum. Here, lift your anus tightly and tilt your hips back, as if you could straighten your sacrum. Send the energy up the back as you do during the Microcosmic Orbit (in fact, you will link up with the Microcosmic Orbit from here on). After the energy passes into your lumbar region, you may relax your hips, but continue to employ the anal lock.

9. As you continue your inhalation, let the energy pass through these points: the tail bone, mingmen, the diaphragm, the top of the shoulder blades, the neck, the base of the skull. Continue to inhale up to the crown point, called the Hundred Meetings Place. At this point, your energy should be fully at this spot and you should just be comfortably completing your inhalation. Your neck and head should be fully stretched upward, your anus fully closed, your body upright, your tongue pressed tightly to the upper palate, and your eyes rolled upward as if to look at this point from inside your head. Hold your breath and this position for as long as is comfortable. When you are beginning, try holding it for only a few moments, and over a long period of practice, perhaps months or even years, increase the duration of this breath retention up to ten seconds.

10. When you are ready to go on, mentally direct your energy from the Hundred Meetings Place down your forehead. You are still holding your breath. Follow the progress of your energy with your eyes. As the energy comes to the tip of the nose, open your eyes slightly and focus strongly on the tip of your nose.

11. Bring your energy inward to your upper palate, and imagine that it is entering the tip of your tongue. Place the tip of your tongue onto your bottom palate, and open your lips slightly. Exhale slowly, imagining your energy is slowly sinking back down the renmei, first through your tongue, through its root, down to just below the surface of your throat.

Continue to exhale down renmei toward the perineum. As you exhale downward, simultaneously relax your abdomen, and at the culmination of your exhalation, your lower abdomen should even be slightly bulging. Do not exaggerate this. At the end of your exhalation, you should have reached the perineum again.

12. At the perineum, you may rest and take a few normal breaths if necessary, but eventually, you will be able to simply repeat the exercise from step 2.

13. This procedure should be practiced in rounds of twelve repetitions each. Begin with twelve circulations. As your practice progresses, add another twelve when you feel ready to go on. Finally, do a full thirty-six rounds when you feel that you are ready.

OPENING THE UPPER GATE

This is a sitting form that strongly opens the meridians of the face and head. It concentrates all the energy on the baihui, or Hundred Meetings Place.

　　1. From the preceding posture, sit facing the east. Use the observations about posture that you learned in the previous sitting techniques.

　　2. Beginning at the perineum, and using reverse breathing, inhale up chongmei to the level of the throat. Exhale back down.

3. Using reverse breathing, inhale up dumei. When the energy comes to your shoulder blades, raise your arms up to the side, elbows bent, and fists at ear level. Continue to inhale upward without stopping.

4. At the niyuan, the point directly on the center of the top of your head, split the energy into two streams that descend above each ear.

5. Continuing to inhale, loop around the back of each ear to just in front of the lobes.

6. Continue to inhale as energy moves out to the corners of the mouth.

7. From there, inhale energy up to the temples.

8. Continue to inhale as energy moves over the top of both eyebrows, and join the two streams of energy together at the center point between the eyebrows. From the perineum to this point should have been one breath. From here on, there will not be any physical breath.

9. From the center of the eyebrows, mentally force the energy up over the crown of the head in a glowing stream while pushing upward with your palms (fingers pointing inward) and rolling your eyes upward as if to look directly at the Hundred Meetings Place. Concentrate all your energy at that point.

10. Hold your breath as long as is comfortable. Begin with at least two seconds, but hold no longer than fifteen.

11. When you have reached your limit, make the sound "ahh!" while releasing your hands to fall to your sides. Imagine that all the energy built to a climax at the top of your head is suddenly released and is cascading down your body in all directions. You should imagine this energy as not a mere flow, but a waterfall mighty as the tallest one you have ever seen. Although the energy is released sharply, it will take about five seconds to descend. Your arms should match this pace.

12. Let the arms continue to lower back to your thighs. Rest if necessary, and repeat from step 2.

13. This form builds a great deal of pressure in the head, so it is not recommended for anyone with high blood pressure or headaches. Begin carefully with no more than three repetitions, even less if you notice any pain or dizziness. Gradually increase your repetitions to a maximum of twenty-one.

OPENING THE FRONT GATE

1. Remain seated. Your hands must be on your kneecaps, thumbs at the edge of the fold, and fingers covering the "eyes" of the knee (these are the two little dents just below your knee cap).

2. Beginning at the perineum, and using reverse breathing, inhale up chongmei to the level of the throat. Exhale back down.

3. Using reverse breathing, inhale again up chongmei, but at the

MEDITATION AND TRANSCENDENCE

level of the throat, consciously direct the energy across the throat to link up with renmei. Exhale down to the dantian.

4. Hold your breath and concentration there, and squeeze your knees twelve times.

5. Inhale up the dumei, and hold your breath at the *zhongwan* point (at the solar plexus). Squeeze your knees twelve times.

6. Exhale up the dumei, and hold your breath at the *yingbu* (at the tip of the sternum). Squeeze your knees twelve times.

7. Inhale up dumei and hold your breath at the Heavenly Well point (the pit of the throat). Bring your hands up to your head, thumbs on your temples and fingers cradling the back of your head. Squeeze twelve times.

8. Make the sound "ahh!" while releasing the hands out to the sides. Imagine that all the energy is suddenly released and is cascading down your body in all directions. Imagine this energy as the mightiest waterfall you can imagine. As the energy descends for about five seconds, lower your arms at the same pace.

9. Let the arms continue to lower back to your thighs. Rest if necessary, then repeat from step 2.

10. Do eighteen repetitions.

LOWER GATE YIN TRAINING

1. Stand facing east, with your body relaxed and your arms at your sides.

2. Imagine energy rising from your perineum to each kidney while your arms rise out to your sides, palms up.

3. Holding your breath, and keeping your attention on your kidneys, squeeze your thumbs inside your fists twelve times.

4. Exhale, and press your palms back down to your sides while sending the energy back down in the same V pattern to the perineum and from there out to the front of your thighs and down to the yongquan, or Bubbling Well points. Hold your attention there briefly.

5. To repeat, bring your attention back to the perineum and repeat from step 2. Do twenty-one repetitions.

下關陰功

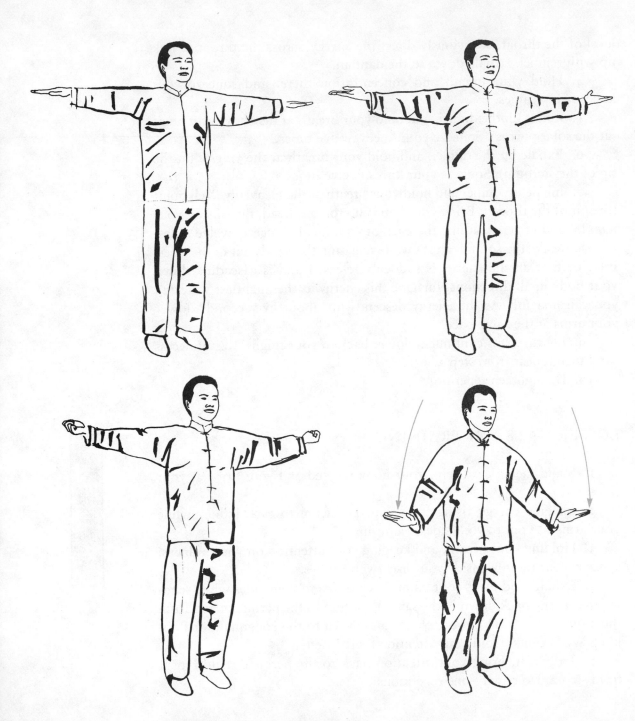

SENDING ENERGY TO ALL FOUR LIMBS

There is no special concentration on meridians in this form. By this time, your body should be completely primed with energy and there should be circulation regardless of whether you are directing it or not. This form, by movement alone, will direct the flow of energy out to all four limbs.

1. Stand facing the east, and let your body relax completely.

2. Squat slightly, and bending your elbows, bring your palms face up to your sides at the level of your dantian. Concentrate on your dantian, and try to feel heat and movement in that area.

3. Inhale, and squat lower while pulling your palms up to the level of your pectoral muscles and pushing your elbows back.

4. At the lowest point in your squat, turn your palms over and stand up while exhaling, pushing down with your palms in front of you, fingertips toward each other but not touching.

5. Repeat again from step 3, completing twenty-one repetitions.

Once you have practiced the entire set of daoyin for at least one hundred days and have gained proficiency at it, you can divide the set into two parts: standing and sitting. You can elect to do the standing postures one day and the sitting postures the next in alternation. Or you can choose to do the standing postures in the morning and the sitting postures in the evening as your meditative exercise.

Each of the daoyin postures can also be practiced singly for short periods of time. For example, if you are doing a great deal of mental work, you may want to especially use the Opening the Upper Gate exercise. If you have poor circulation to the legs, you may wish to use the Sending the Energy to the Legs exercise. However, such practice of single postures should be undertaken only after you achieve basic proficiency in the entire set, and only in combination with the practice of other qigong at other times of the day. Do not focus on one exercise to the total exclusion of all the others. Once you have mastered a particular weakness, you should return to balanced practice of the entire set.

Five of the exercises are Taoist meditation practices in their own right: Deep Breathing, Opening the Thrusting Channel, Opening the Microcosmic Orbit, the Microcosmic Orbit, and Sending the Energy to the Legs. You can use them as individual meditation practices, or you can use them as a prelude to other meditations that you may be practicing. For example, any meditation that you may know from your own teachers can be enhanced by doing the Microcosmic Orbit first. It will prime the energy of the body, circulate it through all the centers, and aid you in entering a contemplative frame of mind. Daoyin is one of the most important of Taoist practices, and it contains a great variety of techniques that you can use in your own life.

打
坐

10

Enter stillness.
This is the ultimate goal of meditation.

MEDITATION

THE HEART OF TAOISM

THERE IS A WORD, *guan*, that has an interesting double meaning. In ancient interpretations, the word meant contemplation. In modern times, it came to designate a Taoist temple. The left side of the word represents a heron. Standing in the water patiently, sometimes capable of a singular stillness, with unblinking eyes and perfect balance, the heron symbolized concentration, stillness, and great patience. The right side of the word is the character for seeing, thus underscoring the idea of vision. It is another way of saying, "Look within."

Just as there is a picture of a heron involved with contemplation, so too is meditation a natural activity. The Taoists say that most animals meditate—only human beings are foolish enough to have forgotten it. The crane stands very still for hours. The cat sits unblinking. The monkey

GUAN
As a verb it means to look, to view, to contemplate. As a noun it refers to a view, a lookout, a Taoist temple.

perches on a high branch, utterly unmoving. The tortoise stands on a rock, stretches its head to the sun, and holds that position without strain. The snake coils up and holds its own still vigil. All creatures know meditation. Human beings, however, learn knowledge, so they no longer know what is natural.

It really shouldn't have to be that we "learn" meditation. It's just that we have so obscured ourselves and live so unnaturally that we have to go back and correct our deficiencies. In the beginning, we need to follow a method. After many years, we may be able to meditate without a form, without a procedure. Then we will be as natural as the waiting heron.

People's motivation for learning meditation varies. Some want power; some want a way out of their predicament; some think that it will make them more spiritually perceptive. Indeed, the range of different types of meditation seems to correlate with this. There is not simply one type of meditation but many types, which vary in method, result, and motivation. There are meditations for martial arts; there are meditations for health; there are meditations that will make a thinker more effective. But meditations with a motive only lead to potential problems, for as long as one has a motivation, one may well become enamored of a single stage of development and neglect to go on to higher stages.

The best motivation for meditation is no motivation. That is wu wei. There shouldn't really be a reason why you want to learn meditation, for it cannot truly be used for profit. It is something that you do, pure and simple. It isn't something that you do for the sake of something else like money or love. It is something that you do, and that is all. If you are a beginner and you are trying to learn meditation for a reason, it is all right if you have some initial reason. It is far better to get started than not to start at all. However, you will eventually find that meditation has no exploitable qualities. If you do not find this out soon enough and you continue to go for quick results and tangible power, then you will be lost forever. It is only after you let go of your motivation for profit that meditation becomes successful. In this sense, it melds perfectly with the injunction to give up learning. It is the opposite of how we normally do things. We usually do things "for a reason." We do things because they are to our advantage. But in meditation, we don't even glimpse any of its wonders until we give up all our reasons and all our expectation of results.

Leave behind the normal human motivations, and meditation begins to flower. Surrender all your desire for gain, and all things come to you. The more you want success in meditation, the more surely it will elude you. The more you desire to experience the ecstatic tales of bliss and supernatural sensations, the more surely you will find it the dullest activity in the world. Just sit, and wait, and practice with the perseverance of the heron, and you will slowly find the way.

It is just when you have given up trying, just when you stop caring about whether meditation will lead to anything, that you will truly begin to see the profundity of meditation. You will go more deeply into yourself. You will find increased power of concentration. Your understanding of life will gradually begin to clarify itself. Answers and intelligence far beyond your apparent capability will arise in you unexpectedly. These signs will manifest themselves subtly—remember how strangely flavorless the Tao is.

All these things, and more, will come to you out of meditation, but you cannot want them. These are not reasons to begin meditation. These are only notations of what might happen to you. Even when you get these powers, ignore them. Keep them tucked away somewhere in your mind, or visit them only whenever you practice. Take them casually as signs of your progress, and do not fall into the temptation of abusing them. If you try to exploit what you have learned in meditation, the outcome can only be disastrous. The abilities might disappear and be impossible to recapture; your meditation would then be but a meaningless ritual. If the abilities remain and become even greater, that would be no less disastrous; you would be forever a slave to your temptations. Disdain the fruits of meditation, and the tree of your inner progress will bloom all the more richly. All you need to do is to wait, and meditate, and wholeheartedly embrace the wonder of this simple endeavor.

This is true faith. This is the faith that waits patiently; this is the faith that is firmly rooted in belief. Unfortunately, faith is little understood nowadays. It has become synonymous with a demand for blind allegiance to a god or an ideal or for unquestioning acceptance of doctrine. But that is not true faith; that is mere slavery. True faith is the ability to wait and to engage in an activity for its own sake.

How comical it is to talk so much about something that is silent! The true sages never speak, for how can quiet be described, even in whispers? Yet if no one ever talks, then few people will know that this path and this method even exist. Practice the ways of meditation. It will not be a barrier to misfortune or natural calamity, but it will give you profundity far surpassing your most exaggerated imaginings.

Meditation is best done under the instruction of a master. Not only will you be instructed, but you will be disciplined into practicing every day. The best type of practice for a beginner is to meditate along with your master. In the field of your master's energies, you cannot help but bloom into the flower of meditation.

Like everything else in Taoism, meditation begins from a very simple premise: sit and look within. Ever thorough however, the Taoists begin to cultivate their students even from the first moment of sitting.

POSTURE

XING
Form, posture.

To meditate, you must first adopt a posture. Physical discipline is the way the body is made neutral for contemplation. In a sense, the purpose of all the martial arts, breathing, stretches, and daoyin has been to train you for this simple act of sitting.

If you are unconvinced that a meditative posture is necessary, then you need only put yourself in a darkened room and do nothing. Typically, you will become bored. You will shift around, trying to get comfortable. One side or another of your body will feel tight. You'll fidget, think about trivial things. Adopting a meditative posture helps to control the problem. It puts your body into balance, and effectively harmonizes it with the endeavor at hand. Eventually, sitting in a meditation posture will become an associative signal for your entire being: each time you arrange yourself into position, you will slip quickly into a meditative state.

Sitting should be relaxed and your posture comfortable. Your chin

CROSS LEGGED SITTING FOR MEDITATION

PROPER METHODS OF ALIGNING ONESELF FOR MEDITATION

should be held in, head as if suspended by a string, spine straight, shoulders relaxed. If sitting cross-legged, the legs should be in the lotus position or the half-lotus position. If you have touble maintaining a cross-legged position with your spine straight, you can elevate your buttocks with a small cushion. You can also sit on the edge of a chair. If you do so, then you must ensure that the genitals are unimpaired, because the body's energy must be free to flow without restriction. A helpful technique is to center yourself by imagining two triangles. The first one is a right triangle. Imagine that its base extends from the base of your spine straight out in front of you; it ends at a point where your eyes naturally fall when you look down at the floor. Now imagine a perpendicular line rising from the base of your spine to the top of your head. Finally, connect the two end points with a diagonal line. This image will help you to align your spine. The second triangle goes out laterally. If you imagine an isosceles triangle whose tip is at the center of your head, and whose base is to the left and right of your body, then you will be perfectly balanced laterally as well. It is in this totally stable and properly aligned posture that true meditation can take place.

You should be able to hold this position effortlessly. The Taoists do not believe in patrols by elder students who will punish someone if their meditations falter. They do not feel that meditation should be forced, and it is for this reason that it is a practice taken only as the culmination to efforts as a Scholar Warrior. All the problems in discipline, posture, vitality, and motivation are worked out years before a student ever sits on a meditation cushion. Then everything truly proceeds in an effortless fashion.

The body, as you know, has innumerable meridians. The major ones have their terminal points in the fingertips. The hands and fingers should be given some form to take, so that the mind is controlled, the body stilled, and the meridians sealed to allow no energy to escape during meditation. At this stage, you should not be concerned with the specifics of hand positions, for the doctrines surrounding these gestures are extensive. As a beginner, you need not pay specific attention to these doctrines. Pick a hand posture that seems attractive to you.

The place where you meditate is also important. It must be a serene

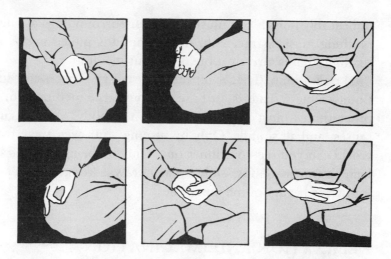

place, one where you feel elated and safe. Caves or huts of recluses were the best places; if they were sites where others had attained their enlightenment, that was even better. But for the majority of us, such places are only ideals; we will have to content ourselves with quiet rooms. The room should be clean, dust-free, and well ventilated and given over solely to one's own meditation.

If you have the luxury to have a room in your home devoted only to meditation, no one else must enter that room except you. Perhaps there will be paintings on the walls, a vase of flowers, a few favorite books, a picture of your master, a personal altar, if that is your inclination. There should be no electricity coming into the room, as this disrupts your inner flow.

Some people like incense when they meditate. The sages say that the sense of smell is the last of the senses to be overcome. Fragrance pacifies this wayward sense. But it can also become a crutch if you are unable to meditate without it. Meditation is an endeavor to be independent, so incense should be something you can take or leave. If incense helps you to meditate, then there is nothing wrong with using it. But if it is a distraction, then it would be far better not to have it.

Silence is indispensable. Many people imagine that they live in a very quiet place until they begin to meditate. Then the neighborhood seems unbearably noisy! You must have your surroundings as silent as possible. Nothing must distract you. If your mind is pulled away by the slightest rustling, that is already a break in your meditation.

Look within. That is all the Taoists say is necessary for true insight. Enter stillness. That is, at base, the only true method. But to do that, all other things must be made neutral: the body, your environment, your senses, and all sounds. Only by turning your eyes away from the outside world can you see your inner one. Only by being in utter silence can you hear the inner sounds. Only by withdrawal from the outer world will you know the beauty of the inner one.

RELAXATION AND IMAGINATION

Relaxation is an imperative prelude to all breathing exercises and to meditation. You should relax your body completely, part by part if necessary. You must also relax your mind by putting aside the worries of the day and by looking forward to your practice with an open attitude free of anxiety.

Relaxation does not mean loss of control. Relaxing your body doesn't mean letting it go limp. It means dispelling all tension, and allowing the inherent energy of your body to flow freely. In this sense, relaxation releases energy. If you have been practicing all the other stretches, qigong, and daoyin, the proper relaxation of your body will already induce the energy to flow into the proper channels.

But energy may be stepped up or down, and though the qigong practitioner may learn to send extraordinary amounts of energy through selected meridians at will, the subtlety of control demanded in meditation is even greater. This control cannot be a forced effort but must be natural, almost casual. As soon as you will it, the energy is there. The simplicity of this is gained only with relaxation, and that relaxation comes as the crowning point of much training.

In the beginning, your energy will not focus by itself, and your mind will not be accustomed to directing energy. This is why early techniques focused on movement, stretching, visualization, and use of herbs. Whenever you took different postures during practice, the energy of the body spontaneously took on the pattern dictated. Only gradually was the mind brought into play, thus avoiding any objection on its part. But now, the mind must be fully brought to bear and must take precedence over the body.

The first phase of using the mind requires using the imagination. Meditation is not possible for the unimaginative, the stupid, or the dogmatic. Meditation requires a plunging into the creative, a suspension of the everyday logical mind that stands in the way of our efforts. It is only when we go beyond this petty, rationalistic mind that extraordinary experiences become possible. This does not mean fantasy or silliness: an artist needs imagination, yet the painting is quite real. A gymnast tries for a new maneuver that she imagines, and thereby pushes back the boundaries of her sport. A surgeon will not dare to try something new without imagination, yet he will save lives nevertheless. Imagination and creativity are fundamental parts of our meditation. In a sense, we are using it to create ourselves.

Every meditation technique begins with some sort of visual or aural guide to help bring you into a contemplative state. Some methods use both. Although the ultimate aim of meditation is the complete emptying of oneself, this is not possible for a beginner. They need a procedure. Looking at a chart, gazing at a statue, sometimes looking at a natural scene like a flower, a rock, or the sky, are all parts of meditation exercises. Visualizing pathways of light or complex patterns within the body is another way. Chanting of prescribed syllables also induces a deeper state of consciousness. You keep doing it and you keep doing it, and one day, though you are doing the same thing, you will feel different. You will not be able to describe it later, and you may not even be able to recall it properly, but when you meditate again the next day, the same feeling of something being deeper will be there again. That is when the preliminary methods of visualization and sounds have become so internalized that they lead you to a true meditative state. When imagination reaches a state of intensity like this, it becomes concentration.

CONCENTRATION

In the beginning, meditation will seem a little foreign. You might even wonder if anything is actually happening. In fact, as long as you are trying, and are engaged in the process of self-observation, you are meditating. There are many grandiose claims and descriptions made of meditating. These come from ignorance, from sincere but misguided attempts at encouragement, or from the very rare experiences of high masters. But it is a little like the descriptions of adult life that you might have heard during your childhood: your own subsequent experiences were doubtless quite different.

So it is only actual personal experience with meditation that will be meaningful. All the stories are meant to give hints of what might happen to you. They also warn of pitfalls so as you confront them in your actual meditation they can be avoided. But pay attention only to the message. It is like a fairy tale. If we absorb the message, then we are wise. But if we go out and attempt to live the fairy tale, we are foolish.

With the stilling of body and mind, concentration begins. Normally, our minds are scattered, for they must constantly sort through the many sensory impressions that we receive each moment. They are busily engaged in adjusting their view of reality and planning for the future. When there is a task at hand, however, we focus on the task. We must do this to engage in our everyday living.

But during meditation, we give up our scattered modes of thought and focus on the task of concentration. Concentration means that the mind is focused. When you practiced daoyin, and you had to focus on the Microcosmic Orbit, this trained your concentration. When you brought your energy to the Hundred Meetings Place, and held your breath at that single point, you were concentrating. In the same way, meditation involves intense concentration to achieve higher states of consciousness.

It is a mistake to think of concentration as static. Often, religious texts will describe concentration as the mind absolutely focused on a single point, thus implying that the mind stops and is held. True meditation is not always like that, but is dynamic. A better description might be absorption. The mind becomes absolutely absorbed in the inner task.

MEDITATING TAOIST; stoneware altarpiece. Ming dynasty. Asian Art Museum of San Francisco, B70 P4. Note the bracket that encircles his body and on which one hand is resting. This is a meditation crutch and is used by Taoists to prevent falling during long periods of meditation.

But concentration is effort, nevertheless. According to the Tao, actions requiring effort still fall short of high practice, since they originate from a finite source of energy. It is only by linking with the infinite that we can tie in with an inexhaustible source. As you practice meditation more deeply, you will reach a stage at which concentration is no longer necessary. You slip directly into a meditative state, and whatever the focus of your meditation, you will simply be there without any effort. There will be no outside interference. Even sounds that occur outside during your meditation will not be heard. Your breath and heartbeat might even stop, but you won't be concerned. All there will be is total absorption in meditation.

This will be a significant point in your progress. When you experience it, you will have no doubts about it. You will know total absorption and a complete and splendid integration with something wholly beyond what you can imagine. This will, in fact, be one of the best ways to know what it is to transcend the self, for such absorption cannot take place unless we neutralize ourselves.

The moment of absorption might last for only a short time. Perhaps it will not come again for many days. Don't look for it, and don't be discouraged. Just go on as before. In its own time, absorption will come again, only deeper and more profound. Then you may have many mediocre weeks before the next time.

That is all fine. Even when meditation is simply ordinary, it will be wonderful. It may take you some time to see this perspective. You may even have to wait until you have not meditated for some time to see how precious it was while you were in it. There will be highlights, of course, but by definition such highlights cannot happen all the time.

DIFFERENT EXPERIENCES

When you learn meditation in a class, there will be times when your master and your classmates will discuss what has been experienced. This happens especially during certain meditations that focus on philosophical inquiry, or that direct students to search for particular places in their bodies or in space. You are supposed to come back and describe what you have seen. Then the master tells you whether you are going in a meaningful direction or simply hallucinating.

When I sit in class and listen to the accounts of my classmates, it is absolutely fascinating to hear that no one's experience is the same. We are all sitting in the same room; we ar all practicing the same exercises and meditation; we are all being guided by the same master; yet not one of us has an even remotely similar experience. Some people's are very dramatic, with visions of fire and water. Some frankly say they see nothing. Some experience the surfacing of certain psychological problems; others dutiful-ly experience the exact pattern of the meditation and no more. Sometimes, my master simply tells someone he or she is experiencing delusion; this tends to be especially those who have elaborate visions of heaven and hell and hobgoblins and great conflicts of power. Those who become sleepy or who experience very little are told that they are not adequately investing themselves in their meditation. Nevertheless, the interesting fact remains that no one experiences the same thing. From day to day, you will not experience the same things yourself. Meditation is different every day.

If you look at your journal, you will confirm this easily. On successive days, you will have all sorts of different experiences, yet by and large you will find that there is a gradual deepening to your practice as the months go by. Because no two days are alike, you should not take any one day very seriously. If you have a magnificent session full of seemingly mystical sensations and revelation, just record it in your book and wait. It is likely that the next day will be quite different, perhaps even dull. If you experi-ence a day when your meditation is terribly boring and you are very sleepy, record that too, and then let it go. Like the Tao, it is not the indi-vidual components so much as the overall process and the whole that is most important.

During meditation, more than at any other time, you will experience not only how different you are from your classmates but how different you are day by day. The Taoists accept this and simply follow it, and by doing so, they go very far in entering the Way.

There is very little reason to discuss your meditations with anyone. Certainly, you should not go around advertising that you meditate, or that you have had a certain experience. It is useless, anyway, because even if you are speaking to someone who also meditates, it is unlikely that you have had the same experiences. Meditation is personal.

THE GOLDEN LIGHT MEDITATION

JIN GUANG
Golden Light.

This meditation for beginners involves visualization, concentration, and absorption. Its purpose is to strengthen your immune system against physical disease and your aura against more subtle pernicious influences. It is a way of purification.

1. Take the sitting posture you learned during daoyin. Calm your mind completely. Your eyes should be almost closed and focused on the tip of your nose. Take eleven breaths, using natural breathing. Inhale slowly through your nose, and open your lips slightly to exhale. Keep your anus closed throughout the whole meditation, and keep the tongue to the roof of your mouth.

2. Take another eleven slow breaths. When you inhale, imagine that you are inhaling light and purity. When you exhale, imagine that you are exhaling dark smoke and toxins.

3. Take another eleven slow breaths. When you inhale, imagine that you are inhaling light and purity. When you exhale, imagine that you are exhaling light and positive feeling. Try to radiate this goodness, and imagine it going to everyone around you, and all the living beings in the world.

4. Imagine a ball of light at the perineum. Hold this concentration for a few moments.

5. Imagine a ball of light at the pineal gland. Hold this concentration for a few moments.

6. Connect the two spheres with a thin strand of light.

7. Slowly expand the strand to the size of the little finger.

8. After a comfortable period, expand the strand to the size of the thumb.

9. After a comfortable period, expand the light to the size of a staff.

10. After a comfortable period, expand the light to the size of a column.

11. After a comfortable period, expand the light to a cylinder around the body.

12. Shape the light into an egg shape that encloses the entire body.

13. Imagine the light penetrating the body from all directions. If there are any black areas, concentrate more light there until all dark spots are gone. Stay in this state as long as comfortable.

14. To withdraw, reverse the above process until back to the strand of light.

15. Bring the sphere at the perineum up to the pineal gland. Slowly lower this sphere of light down through the body to the lower dantian. Concentrate on the dantian for one minute.

16. Take three deep breaths.

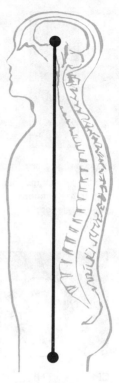

THE INTERNAL
ALIGNMENT OF
THE GOLDEN
LIGHT
MEDITATION

At the end of this meditation, it is important that you do not simply jump up. Your body and mind have entered a different phase of consciousness that will have had an effect on all your systems: your mind, your blood, your breathing, your nerves, and your muscles. At the very least, your legs and even your back may be stiff from the effort of sitting, and to move suddenly can cause cramping, aches, or muscle tears. Some meditators who know no methods of balancing themselves after meditation, but who nevertheless practice for years with great sincerity, end up with degenerated joints, hemorrhoids, arthritis, and spinal disorders.

At higher stages of meditation, where energy is concentrated strongly in certain centers, there is an added danger of the energy becoming trapped there. This can lead to a variety of problems such as pain in that area, burning sensations, headaches, dizziness, nausea, and vomiting of blood (in extreme cases), and if the energy is trapped constantly in a spot over a prolonged period of time, even mental illness can result.

In Taoist styles of meditation, there are sets of movements that are performed before getting up from the meditation cushion. These reestablish the body and bring it back to normal after the changes of meditation. No matter what system of meditation you follow, you can benefit from the following simple ways to end your meditation session.

BALANCING YOURSELF AFTER MEDITATION

CLICKING THE
TEETH TOGETHER

ROLLING THE EYES

After you have finished your meditation, sit still and relax. Then do the following exercises:

1. Take three deep breaths. Inhale strongly to your dantian, and exhale strongly (but not loudly) out through your slightly opened lips. Use natural breathing, not reverse breathing.

• Click your teeth together thirty-six times. If saliva starts to form, hold it in your mouth.

• Roll your tongue between your upper teeth and your inner lips eighteen times in each direction.

• Move your cheeks in and out to encourage the formation of saliva.

• Divide the saliva, called the Jade Nectar, into three parts.

• Inhale, then exhale to the dantian. At the end of your exhalation, swallow the first part deeply, and imagine that the Jade Nectar plunges straight to your dantian as a brilliantly glowing liquid. In your mind, you should follow this liquid all the way to the dantian.

• Repeat this process again until you have swallowed all three parts.

• After you have swallowed the last time, softly make the sound "*tu*!" This will release any air that may have been trapped in your throat or lungs during the process of swallowing.

2. You may now open your eyes if they were closed during your meditation. Perform the following eye exercises.

• Roll your eyes alternately up, then down, ten times.

• Roll your eyes alternately side to side ten times.

• Roll your eyes alternately from corner to diagonal corner ten times in a sideways hourglass pattern.

• Roll your eyes in circles ten times in each direction.

3. Warm your hands by rubbing them briskly together.

• Place one hand on your dantian, and with the other one, rub your forehead ten times. You are trying to disperse any excess energy that may still be lingering in the meridians of the head.

• Warm your hands again, and rub up and down the sides of your nose ten times.

• Warm your hands again, and rub up under your nose ten times.

• Warm your hands again, and rub up and down the sides of your face from your jaw to your temples ten times.

• Warm your hands again, and with the back of your hand, rub under your chin ten times.

4. Warm your hands by rubbing them briskly together, and place your palms over your ears with the fingers resting on the base of your skull. Flick your index fingers off your ring fingers so that they softly strike the point where your neck enters your skull. You should hear a sound like drumbeats, and this is why this technique is called Beating the Heavenly Drum. You should do this thirty-six times.

5. Warm your hands again and rub your kidneys thirty-six times.

BEATING THE
HEAVENLY DRUM

RUBBING THE
KIDNEYS

6. Warm your hands, place one over the dantian, and rub your coccyx thirty-six times.

7. Warm your hands, place them both over the dantian, and rub your dantian by keeping your arms still and simply turning your waist from side to side.

8. Clasp your hands in front of you and twist your waist from side to side. Each time that you turn, make sure that your head also turns in that direction, as if trying to look as far behind yourself as possible.

9. Return to center and rock your diaphragm and massage your lungs by raising your arms up and then down, pressing your palms to the floor.

Left
MASSAGING THE
DANTIAN
Middle
SHAKING THE
HEAVENLY PILLAR
Right
ROCKING THE
DIAPHRAGM

10. Gently unlock your legs and stretch them out. Rub your kneecaps in a circular motion ten times in each direction.

11. Massage your legs by rubbing down the top of them, then rubbing back up along the bottom. Press enough to feel some pressure and warmth. Exhale down, inhale as you pull back up. Do this ten times.

12. Flex your ankles back and forth ten times.
• Turn them out to the sides ten times.
• Rotate them ten times in each direction.
• Flick your big toes off the second toes ten times.

13. Rub the yongquan points thirty-six times each.

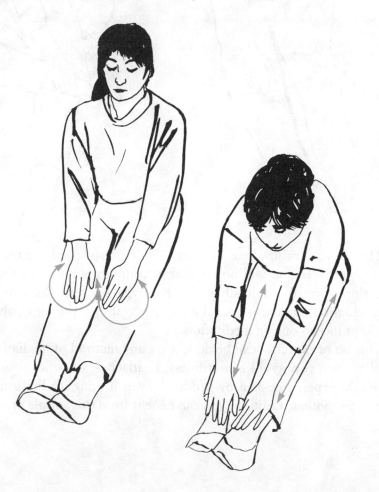

RUBBING THE
KNEECAPS

MASSAGING THE
LEGS

This comprises just one of many different styles of meditation balancing exercises. You will notice that in common with all of them is the dispersing of heat, the leading of the energy back to the dantian, and the gradual restoration of circulation, especially to the legs, which have been kept locked during meditation.

This set of exercises can be done after any method of mediation and is useful to help you avoid any stiffness, headaches, or other troubles that you might experience as a by-product. Even if your meditation practice belongs to another tradition, you can benefit from this simple procedure.

出家

11

So I sit in solitude, forgetting the year or month
While in the mundane world below,
Lifetimes and generations pass.

WITHDRAWAL

THE OPPORTUNITY TO BE SPIRITUAL

IT IS FLATLY IMPOSSIBLE to achieve personal excellence without daily solitude. We must all retreat from the pressures of our daily lives to develop ourselves. Distractions are something that weaken our inner strength, no matter how good the reasons for them may be. Perhaps our time alone will be short; it stands to reason that the benefits will be less dramatic, but better than no time alone at all. Longer periods of time alone will be more beneficial. If you can spend time away—perhaps a weekend, or a week—you will achieve much more than you dreamed possible. It is quite amazing to recognize what we feel when we are thus "in touch" with our inner selves, it makes us realize the amount of energy we waste on trivialities.

Whenever you do retreat, you should endeavor to isolate yourself completely, even to the point of avoiding training with the opposite sex. Scholar Warriors believe that attraction between the sexes is strong and prefer to leave that outside of the training time. There is nothing wrong with going back to a normal life later, but while you are training, your attention should be solely on cultivating yourself. You can be sure that all your delights and problems will be faithfully waiting for you when you come back.

Totally unsupervised isolation will not bring you results, however. It is important to remember that you are practicing a method and a way of life. Better yet, you should train under the guidance of your master, for you will then progress very rapidly. You should not fear being lonely. Instead, it is good to associate both with your classmates and with other people who are beyond the ordinary. Learn from them, for they have a wisdom that flourishes only away from the ugliness of civilization. You can be sure that these people are still out there. But they do not live in cities and teach in schools. They are men and women of wisdom in all fields. It is they who are the true Taoists, living anonymous lives as craftsmen, artists, professors, or naturalists. In withdrawal, you can learn their secrets.

In the histories of the Taoists and the Scholar Warriors, there is a long-standing tradition of withdrawal from the world. A person may withdraw for the sake of spiritual realization or may withdraw temporarily with the intention of returning after his or her training is complete. This type of withdrawal was called "ascending the mountain," for it was in the isolation of the mountains, high above turbulent society, that people thought they could best discipline themselves. These people would join a master who would train them every day for years. There was no distraction whatsoever: the only work was in support of the training area, and there was no social life, no family communication, no frivolity of any kind. For those years, the student was as good as dead to the outside world, and his or her only life was the pursuit of excellence. When it was said that some person had gone up the mountain, everyone nodded solemnly; they all knew that person would return almost superhuman. They knew that the student would inevitably excel, and that his or her reappearance in society would be like that of a god resurrected.

SHANG SHAN
To go up a mountain.

MEDITATION AND TRANSCENDENCE

Whether you withdraw for short periods of time every day for your training, or train for periods of weeks or even years at a time, you will find great benefits from being away from your everyday problems. Not only will the strength you cultivate be completely your own, but you will have a better perspective on whatever problems weigh on you. Quite possibly, they will not seem as difficult when you come back.

The best summation of this type of thinking is the poem by the South Goose Beach Taoist, quoted in the Introduction:

> Court gowns of red and purple are not attractive.
> Instead, I love white clouds embracing emerald mountaintops.
> So I sit in solitude, forgetting the year or month
> While in the mundane world below, lifetimes and generations pass.

The master is expounding on the wonders and importance of isolating oneself from the world. The first line indicates that he has already experienced the world. By mentioning the court gowns of red and purple, he is alluding to the fact that he has encountered them—in China, common people never saw members of the imperial house. Quite possibly, he wore the robes himself, but he is saying that they no longer appeal to him. He has left them behind for the sake of a natural life. He loves the white clouds embracing emerald mountaintops. His withdrawal from the world is complete; he cares only for the exquisite solitude of contemplation and is totally unconcerned with the passage of time in the mundane world.

Leaving behind the court gowns brings us to an aspect of withdrawal crucial to a Scholar Warrior: the time of complete retreat from the world should be concurrent with a renunciation of being a Scholar Warrior. You must be able to identify this point exactly. Indeed, you have been preparing your whole life for this moment. It began when you planned your life according to the seasons. The Scholar Warrior is the supreme way of life. But it is limited. If you stick to only one role in life, it is inevitable that you will experience the downfall that comes with the fading of ability and the decline of mental acuity. Only by renouncing the role of the Scholar Warrior can you avoid this. You choose to make no further achievements, seek no further glory, pursue no quests. You retire from active life for a life of contemplation. Being a Scholar Warrior was a fixed identity, a rigid role. According to the Tao, that which is rigid must someday be destroyed.

You'll know when you have reached this stage. You will be world-weary. Life will hold few surprises for you, and your ambition will have cooled to an ember. You will have completed all your quests, satisfied your curiosities, and banished regret. Quite literally, you will have done all that you were born to do. The final stage in your life is to leave behind the muck of civilization and enter the Tao.

Leaving society after finally waking to the futility of the world is a long-standing tradition. Sometimes officials would leave upon the collapse of their policies. A warrior would leave when finally weary of competition and killing. Scholars would leave after learning that their knowledge was insufficient to guide them all the way through life. In Taoist legends, there is the story of Lu Dongbin, one of the Eight Immortals. He was on his way to the capital to take the civil examinations that he hoped would lead to an illustrious career. Stopping in an inn where the innkeeper was boiling millet, he struck up a conversation with an old man. The stranger smiled knowingly at Lu's ambitions. Observing that the young scholar was tired, he gave him a pillow so that he could rest.

Lu awoke after a short nap and went to his examinations. He passed them and was rewarded with a high position in government. As the years passed, he rose higher, married a beautiful aristocrat, and became governor of a province. Upon reaching old age, however, disaster after disaster struck him: his wife was unfaithful; his children were a disappoint-

LU DONGBIN

ment; and armies of invaders were attacking his city. In sorrow, he knew that his life had passed. His hair was gray, his body broken, and the love and respect that he had yearned for had slipped away. Now the life that he had sought with such drive was about to end at the edge of a barbarian's sword. He thought back. Why did he not cherish life when it was so much simpler?

Instantly, he was back in the inn. The millet had not even finished cooking, and the stranger was still there. He realized that it had all been but a dream, but he also saw the message that had been sent to him: worldly life was futile. At that moment, he decided to forsake the path that he had begun and to seek the Tao instead. He begged his fellow traveler to guide him. For the traveler was an immortal, Han Zhongli. Through the guidance of his master, Lu eventually became an immortal.

When you are tired of being a Scholar Warrior, withdraw from the world to seek the Tao. But you must be very honest with yourself. Simply because the end result of the Scholar Warrior is the negation of that identity, it does not follow that one should never undertake that path. You cannot avoid what the Scholar Warrior offers you, because you are already a complex and socialized human being. You have ambitions, drives, creative yearnings, worldly ambitions. Mysteries confound you; places and friends haunt you. Until you can satisfy yourself that you do not need these things any longer, you cannot leave the world. But once you can, then there is no use in continuing the charade.

That is why the Taoists constantly speak of returning to a state of simplicity. How can you return to a state of simplicity unless you have experienced complexity? The masters believe that we have been ruined by education, but that education is a necessary evil. Therefore, we must become highly educated, to discharge those aspects of our personalities, and then begin to simplify ourselves. One might even say that the entire process of becoming a Scholar Warrior is an exorcism of our egotism, ambition, and socialization.

The Taoists do not care about society. They know inwardly that the pursuit of material success is doomed to disappointment and heartache, and they add that every instant when the personality is unbalanced will diminish one's health and life span. Today, even the rich are fond of saying that wealth is no substitute for self-satisfaction and the love of family. But the Taoists know that the love of family can fade with the first signs of faithlessness and conflict. Instead, the Taoists urge you to engage in self-cultivation and to be an individual. You should never hesitate to go a different route if it means that you will achieve your goals in better and faster ways. Surround yourself with the things that you like; dress the way you prefer; live the way you want. No one in the world is exactly like you. No one in the world can know you the way you can know yourself. So why should you copy other people? You could not be like them even if you wanted to. You are unique, and you must honestly pursue your destiny. This doesn't mean prearranged fate. It signifies the destiny that is your inner pattern to express. You must express what is unique within yourself. To do otherwise is to violate what is natural.

Stand as an individual, and do not conform to the ways of other people. Why follow the herd? Why do what everyone else does? Do they even know where they are going? Or are they merely aping the procedures of others and repeating the same mistakes as their forebears? To put it bluntly, everything in life changes, especially the allegiances of others. You will only wear yourself out trying to pursue the latest trends and whatever is being held up as today's ideals. There is no need to become any more involved with society than you have to. It is a necessary evil, but as with taking a medicine that is toxic, one needs to limit the doses of society one takes. When you can withdraw from the race, you should do so.

ENTERING THE TAO

RU DAO
Entering the Tao.

Once we have withdrawn from society, both by isolation and by slow but constant reduction of society's influence within ourselves, we are still left with our own sense of individuality. We may find our haven, as the South Goose Beach Taoist did, but we must then invest ourselves in ongoing purification and simplification in order to clarify this sense of individuality. This is what he means when he says, "So I sit in solitude, forgetting the year or month." He is showing us the next step in our progress.

During meditation, you turn increasingly inward. You cease to identify with the outside world and eventually cease to identify with your own body and mind. For the Taoist, thinking of oneself as the sum total of body, mind, and spirit is a mistake. As a beginner, you needed to do so, but at this advanced stage, you must drop this temporary construct. We should not conceive of ourselves as anything other than Tao. We are inherently the Tao itself; only our deep investment in physical sensation, ambition, and sense of self-existence divorces us from this true notion. We say, "I exist." In so doing, we place ourselves apart from the rest of the universe and blind ourselves to the fact that there is no I, only Tao.

We have to separate ourselves from the world's distractions in order to realize this. How can we understand the pull of the world and the pull of our own minds unless we neutralize them? The isolation of retreat will neutralize civilization. The isolation of meditation is designed to neutralize the mind itself. We have to separate ourselves from society, initially assert our individuality and independence, and then turn inward and dissolve that individuality. Dispassion for the world and dispassion toward the self are the source of liberation.

Once you overcome your sense of individual identity, you will truly enter into the Tao. Then you are the Tao, and Tao is you. You will not find any trace of yourself. You will no longer have any cognizance of yourself. You will have no individual thoughts; you will have no life or death; you will not exist. You are one with infinity, and infinity cannot limit itself by thinking like a human being. Entering into the Tao means the complete dissolution of the self. It will be like water poured into water. The once separate liquid is no longer discernible. If that frightens you, then you are not ready for this stage and should content yourself with the self-cultivation of the Scholar Warrior and exploration of the Tao on a limited level. If this idea does not frighten you, then you need only find the one who will show you the way to realization.

But what is realization? It is important to define the concept carefully, so we will know what to look for. Realization means different things to different people. Some think of realization as a final enlightenment: they strive for a perfect moment of ultimate lucidity, when understanding of all their questions will come in a single spontaneous stroke. Others believe that realization is the culmination of intensive intellectual investigation.

Still others have committed themselves to lives of total meditation, in the conviction that only this self-cultivation will bring them to the supreme perception. None of these paths is wrong. But the Taoist approach is quite different.

Most important, Taoism eschews any intellectual approach to realization. The prayer of many sages prior to their meditation sessions is this: "Protect me from intellectualizing my experiences." Though meditation is one of the most important endeavors to Taoists, they merely want to experience it and let it change them, as it surely will. But they are on guard about intellectualizing what happens to them. For them, meditation has nothing to do with the intellect, egotism, or the rational mind. The Taoists recognize that these elements will stop them from progressing. They neither rationalize nor externalize their experiences. There is no surer way to destroy the treasure of meditation. Realization to a Taoist is a total transformation on every level of being: it utilizes physical, philosophical, and meditative techniques. Spiritual progress comes concurrently with concentration on certain points and meridians. Certain states of mind and body are achieved with the help of philosophical understanding. Indeed, as a Taoist one even cannibalizes one's entire life as a Scholar Warrior and uses it as material for one's spiritual quest. In short, realization, for a Taoist, is a complete and total state of being.

This understanding is symbolized by Taoism's emphasis on longevity over enlightenment. It is not longevity in its most obvious—and greedy—aspect. The word *shou* has a special meaning beyond long life. It has a nearly sacred meaning and is such a revered term among the Taoists and the Chinese that there are over ten thousand ways to write this one ideogram. The upper part of the word represents a ploughed field, symbolizing the constant repetition of furrows turned over and over. The square box on the lower left, and the cross-shape with dot on the lower right together suggest speech and gestures. Longevity, therefore, symbolizes the repetition of years, the repetition of self-cultivation, and wisdom of speech and gesture that comes from age. The word does not imply literal immortality.

Physical immortality is not only impossible, but it is a selfish notion: it indicates a strong attachment to the self that makes realization of Tao impossible. Rather, longevity should be seen as the ideal symbol of Taoist

SHOU
Longevity.

realization because it implies an ongoing process that is in itself a state of being. Longevity is not a static thing, not a moment of spiritual realization frozen in time. It is inherent in daily life.

If we return for a moment to the very definition of the word *Tao*, as "the Way," it should be obvious that there can be many moments of realization, but there cannot be one big realization. Why? Because this would mean stasis, a stopping point, a place of supreme attainment, and this is contrary to the philosophy of Taoists. For them, all is process; all is the walking of the path; and none of it can be altered without detracting from the whole. We are here to walk the path, and that is all. If we come to a stopping point, if we come to some summit where we declare ourselves completed and totally enlightened, then we cease to walk the way. We stand still, and in standing still, we act against the Tao, which is ever flowing and ever changing. Stasis, to a Taoist, is the ultimate in misguided thinking.

Through practice and study with qualified teachers, we can all have many moments of small realizations. We will use our spiritual practice to conduct whatever investigation pleases us, and we will heap up the answers that we find for ourselves. Taoist realizations are moments in time, along with all our other moments of happiness, sorrow, mediocrity, ambition, and confusion. Why see them as special? Accept them; acknowledge them; know that they are a part of you as inevitably as any other experience. No one can possibly take an experience away from you. You know you had it; you know who you are. The security of that knowledge gives you the confidence to go on. Each moment realized will give us the skill and the understanding to face future moments. There is no time to dwell upon the beauty or the magnitude of realization, for in the next moment, the Tao has changed again. It never stands still. Understanding it can thus come only when we flow with Tao. To stop it in time, to try and take a snapshot of Tao and use that as our object of reverence, is not Taoism at all.

What are these small moments of realization like? The Taoists say that after all the methods, after all the concentration on meridians and points and chakras (Chakra literally means "wheel." Yoga believes that there are seven primary centers proceeding from the perineum to the top of the

CHANG SHOU
Long life.

XIAN
An immortal. In Taoism one could become an immortal through self-cultivation or the ingestion of an elixir of immortality. A person who has realized the Tao is also called an immortal. The word shows the symbol for person (on the left) and the symbol for mountain (on the right), thus embodying the importance that the Taoists place on ascending into the mountains in order to attain immortality.

skull. When activated in meditation, a practitioner will initally feel a spinning sensation in that area. Each chakra yields different powers.), after all the debates and philosophical discussions, after exploring the thousands of methods, it all comes down to one simple thing: illumination. Look at certain meditation methods on chakras or the dantians, for example. In Hindu, Buddhist, and Taoist methods alike, gods, animals, and other beings are imagined to be in that area of the body, and that is how the point is stimulated enough to yield up its spiritual contents. But are there really gods sitting in there? Of course not. All that counts is energy. All that counts is light. It is light that we all strive for. Once Taoists experience that, they go beyond the description of gods, beyond liturgy, scripture, teaching, learning, traveling.

The word for this shows the sun and the moon together, thus symbolizing brightness upon brightness. There is an inner light in all of us, only we do not see it. When we do, it will not only be brightness upon brightness but also yin and yang combined. When that happens, there is unity and no differentiation. Thus there is emptiness, and in this emptiness is the absolute Tao. This illumination is far beyond the realm of definitions. It is the simple purity of being and nonbeing combined.

We should remember to work toward realization not simply by persevering in the process of simplification but by going directly to this inner light within ourselves. This light is pure. This light is Tao. Why strive always to push away the obstructions? Why not try to have the light shine forth too? This is what happens when Taoists try to go directly to the core of their very beings. If they can breach their very essence, that pure light, then it will burst forth brilliantly and they can approach the rest of their lives from the point of that supreme purity. In doing so, they break the habit of always seeing themselves as separate from Tao. They are Tao itself, and live accordingly.

Taoist realization is both an inner and an outer process. The inner one is the straight and uncompromising plunging into the brilliant Tao within, boldly entering into a state in which there is neither yin nor yang, neither being nor nonbeing, only the ultimate nature of Tao. The outer one is the ongoing process of purification, simplification, and withdrawal. Both are

MING
Brightness, brilliance, illumination, clarity.

essential to progress. When one has secured both the inner and outer processes, this is called Dedao, or "realization of the Tao."

FULL CIRCLE

Cyclical movement pervades every aspect of existence. In reaching this point, we have gone through innumerable cycles, have followed the myriad changes of daily living. We have followed the Tao, and the Tao has proved to be every bit as mysterious, deep, and profound as the scriptures and the poets promised. In another way, however, we have simply come full circle. Before we entered the Tao, we were ignorant, perhaps singularly stupid. We followed the ways of the Scholar Warrior, acquired skill to face each bit of uncertainty, gained the experience and courage to overcome each of our problems and personal obstacles. Perhaps we even made great accomplishments, became powerful athletes or warriors, brilliant thinkers. We may even have glimpsed realms of unusual mystical powers through our meditations. Yet when we come to a vantage point in our path, when we come to a place where we can finally reconsider and look back on what we have done, we find ourselves back at the beginner's spot again: everything is as it was before. Only we have changed.

When one reaches a point of maturity along the path, a point after many enlightenments, many moments of illumination, one possesses without a doubt a tremendous store of experiences. But when we once again examine the Tao, we find that it is still the beautiful mystery that it has been all along; only this time, we are content to be with it, to flow with it, to stop probing it for understanding. We realize that we will never understand it in a rational way, and for the first time, that is all right. Our intellects have been exhausted in our struggles as Scholar Warriors, have been worn away by the days of meditation.

We are happy to swim in the mystery of the Tao, not being able to see the bottom, not knowing what lies beneath the surface, not seeing where the current will lead. For the first time, that is all right. We have acquired a burnished faith. This faith is not one of unquestioning obedience to some

DE DAO
To realize the Tao.

FAN
Returning.

abstract principle never glimpsed but the faith of one who has lived a long time. It is the faith of one at peace with the world.

We are happy to divest ourselves of the trappings of competition, for we no longer need them. Oh, our skills are there in our subconscious—we paid for them with our own sweat, toil, and sacrifice and they cannot be lost—and if the need arose, and we were so inclined, they might still be there in an emergency. But by and large, we do not need all the skills of the Scholar Warrior anymore. We don't need to fight, and we don't regret the fights we had. We needed to fight. We couldn't have realized this state before we became Scholar Warriors. Ignorance could not have led us to this contented state. Our minds and bodies could not have been developed, expressed, and then tamed without the crucible of competition and worldly strivings. But once we are satisfied with our accomplishments, we can put them aside.

Now all that matters is simplicity. This is what Lao Tzu meant when he referred to becoming simple again. We have created ourselves, sculpted every detail of our identity, and now we can try to transcend that. We have reached our physical and mental limits, and to go further, we need to divest ourselves of our identity. The Tao is universal. It is all-encompassing. It is everything. And if it is everything, then it is nothing too. It is all things, so it is no particular thing. So we who would know the Tao must slowly lose our individuality, our specificity, so that we may become one with all things.

Simplify yourself. After all the efforts you have made, this is the last effort. Let yourself go. Look into the Tao each day until you become the Tao. You will be a part of it more and more, until one day you will merge with it, and you will cease to exist as an individual. Your consciousness will be one with all things, and you will be the Tao. That is when you will realize your own essential emptiness.

Everything is emptiness,
Emptiness is everything.

12

RETURNING TO
THE SOURCE

THE ULTIMATE WISDOM

IN THE TAOIST PANTHEON, there is a group called the Eight Immortals. Whereas some gods are merely worshiped in temples, these gods are so widely admired that they appear in contexts from the highly sacred to the merely decorative. In the highest temple of Taoism in Beijing, the White Cloud Monastery, or Baiyun Guan, there is a separate chapel devoted to the Eight Immortals. But the group also appear in popular operas, in paintings (where they are often depicted as drunk), as decorations on porcelain, as the basis for martial arts styles, and even as names of restaurants. The Eight Immortals have permeated the consciousness of the populace for good reason. They represent an archetypal range from old age, nobility, youth, womanhood, music, art, poetry, magic, to the most profound states of worldly renunciation.

BA XIAN
The Eight Immortals.

317

THE THREE STARS
AND EIGHT
IMMORTALS
GREETING THE
QUEEN OF THE
WESTERN
HEAVENS. Embroi-
dery on silk. Qianlong
period, Qing dynasty.
Asian Art Museum of
San Francisco, B62
D28. The Queen is in
the sky, the Three
Stars are closest to her,
at the balustrade.
From the left they are
Longevity, Prosperity,
and Happiness. To
the right are the
Eight Immortals. Han
Zhongli and Lu Dong-
bin are the two im-
mediately closest to
the Three Stars. Han
Zhongli holds a fan,
and Lu Dongbin can
be recognized by the
handle and hilt of his
sword that shows over
his right shoulder.

At the heart of the Eight Immortals are two figures, Han Zhongli and his disciple, Lu Dongbin. The story of Lu's awakening to the Tao has already been recounted, and though the story of his renunciation of worldly cares is important, there are still deeper levels of significance to the relationship between the master and his student. As we consider the transcendence of the path of the Scholar Warrior, it is interesting to focus briefly on Han Zhongli himself.

He was a military man before he became a sage. During the Han dynasty, the emperor commanded Han Zhongli, then a general, to secure the borders near Tibet. This he went faithfully to do. But his army was beaten badly, and in the slaughter, he had to flee for his very life. The enemy chased him farther and farther into the high mountains, but he succeeded in eluding the search parties as he reached the snow line. He chanced upon a hermit's hut and in desperation flung himself inside.

He found a white-bearded man sitting there. The ancient one looked up calmly.

"I have been waiting through the ages for you to come," said the hermit. "I know that it is your destiny to attain immortality, and I have come to teach you the way." He thereby instructed Han Zhongli on the methods of practice, taught him qigong and meditation, and most importantly, imparted great wisdom to him. By the time Han Zhongli left the hut, years had passed. The emperor who had sent him had died long ago. Those who had been children when he left were now toothless old people. He had attained immortality, and it had seemed as if only a few days had passed. As he journeyed down the path, he paused to look back at his teacher, but both the man and the hut had disappeared.

Eventually Han Zhongli met Lu Dongbin and taught him how to become not only an immortal but a person of unusual skill as well. Lu was adept at martial arts, poetry, sorcery, and exorcism. He was the ultimate Scholar Warrior. But for a god, he had some bad habits as well. He had a mischievous, even cruel, streak. He sometimes gave the pill of immortality to undeserving beings just to see the result—often havoc on heaven and earth. He liked to play practical jokes on travelers. And perhaps most unacceptable to his master, he was a notorious playboy who could never resist seducing a beautiful woman. Lu Dongbin often irked his master

HAN ZHONGLI

with his amorous indulgences. Once when the master was ready to teach Lu a certain set of qigong, Lu did not appear, for he was busy with one of his lovers. In annoyance, Han Zhongli inscribed the set on a cave wall for Lu to study whenever he finally came. According to legend, this is how we mere mortals found the famous Eight Brocades Qigong.

Finally, in the mountains called Tian Shan, not far from where Han Zhongli attained his own immortality, Lu kept one of his appointments.

"In spite of the fact that you are immortal," said the master as he scrutinized his disciple, "you are far from perfect. Although you are adept in both the arts of the book and the arts of war, though you know the highest forms of sorcery, and though you are an immortal god, you are still not mature. You seduce women on heaven and earth, upset the natural scheme of things, interfere with people's destinies, play cruel tricks, and occupy your mind with trivialities. You hold great power, but your mind still wavers. You are supernatural, yet you have not perceived the true nature of life."

What could Lu Dongbin say? His master was right, and for the first time, he sat there somewhat abashed. Although he was a god, he still needed instruction, just as the Jade Emperor, the highest god in the entire pantheon, was himself still taught by Lao Tzu. He made up his mind to listen to his master's teaching.

"How should any person, man or woman, learn the ultimate truth?" asked Lu.

"He should realize emptiness," Han Zhongli replied. "That is the only wisdom that goes beyond skill and knowledge."

The writings that follow are based on what Han Zhongli told Lu Dongbin and what all Taoists ultimately strive for: emptiness. The teachings are recorded in Taoist scripture, but these scriptures are almost unintelligible even to a scholar, for they are codes for the oral tradition that master passes on to student. So as not to violate the rule of that tradition, this chapter represents a distillation and analysis of those teachings, not a literal translation.

The teachings are strikingly similar to the *Heart Sutra* of the Buddhist *Prajnaparamitra*. Since we know that there was intense exchange between the Taoists, Buddhists, Hindus, and Tibetans from the Tang dynasty onward, it's not unlikely that some Buddhist doctrines were incorporated into Taoism. There may even be a hint of this in the fact that Han Zhongli was initiated near Tibet. However, it's doubtful that the Taoists will admit this. They will point to the discourses on void in the *Tao Te Ching*, written long before Buddhism came to China, as evidence that the notion of emptiness arose with them. Let us not entangle ourselves in doctrinal struggles, but take what we can for ourselves. It's immaterial who thought of an idea first. All that matters is that we can gain some understanding and use it in our daily lives.

ALL IS EMPTINESS

If one looks deeply into the Taoist cosmology, one will find this apparently simple formula: Being came from nonbeing. This was expanded to a more detailed continuum. In the beginning was nonbeing, or emptiness. Into that emptiness came a thought. No one knows where that thought came from, but it set things in motion. In that first moment, qi was formed. The qi began to move and separate, and thus became differentiated into yin and yang. From yin and yang came the five elements: fire, earth, metal, water, and wood. Then the ten thousand things in the universe were generated—that is to say, everything. Things do not expand forever, however, but return to emptiness, and it is that movement of expansion and returning that is the Tao.

Han Zhongli and the Taoists who follow his philosophy state that yin and yang constitute all known phenomena in the universe. Under this category, they do not merely include physical phenomena like mountains and water or our own bodies but also phenomena we might not normally consider tangible. They include feeling, perception, impulse, and consciousness. Feeling indicates the realm of our senses. Touch, sight, smell, taste, and hearing are both sources of information and creators of reality. We want to repeat pleasurable feelings and avoid painful ones. We shape our environment, our lives, and our thoughts according to our feelings, and the Taoists include this as part of known phenomena. Perception represents the discriminating faculties of our mind. It too is part of phe-

色
即
是
空

nomena, for with it, we sort and categorize things and create accordingly. The sum total of our creations forms a thick web of cause and effect that further binds us to the world of phenomena, and this is represented by the word *impulse*. We believe that we are manipulating events, but in actuality, they form a net that traps us in involvement. Consciousness, our awareness of ourselves and the world, is above all these factors, but it is most responsible for our involvement with phenomena. Remember, it was a thought that first generated the universe—not the thought from a god's brain, just some intention, some division, some impulse. The Taoists, like the Buddhists and the yogis, regard the universe as made up not of matter but of mind. They regard all yin and yang as including both physical as well as mental categories.

All these things are mutually dependent. They are incapable of a self-generating reality. Nothing exists without having been created or caused by some other event. Everything came from something else; everything was caused by something else; and nothing can exist in this universe on its own. In fact, each thing continues to generate more and more different effects. Our reaction to the world stimulates our senses and our perceptions and causes us to act. We create new circumstances that not only engender new objects but contribute to the field of impulse as well and thicken the net of involvement. And through it all, our consciousness becomes further intertwined with the tangled web of phenomena. Through this ongoing interaction, there is only a profusion of cause and effect.

Furthermore, all things change. All things will eventually be destroyed—or not actually destroyed, as in blasted wholly out of existence, but transmuted into something else. Just as a log in a fire is reduced to ashes, so all phenomena are in a state of flux that appears to be creation and destruction. But this apparent process of birth and death is only a constant and inconceivable amount of interaction and transformation. There is neither creation nor destruction. Things are only in constant flux.

Since all of the universe is constantly changing, we cannot call anything permanent or eternal or absolute. It is precisely because there is no permanence, no truly lasting tangibility, that all phenomena are called illusory. This doesn't mean that nothing is solid, at least in a provisional sense, but that nothing in this world may be regarded as real in the sense that it has independent existence and is not subject to any influence. At any one time, the phenomena that we sense afford only a brief glimpse of this dense, frenetic, impenetrable thicket of change. There is no actual substance upon which to base our lives. In fact, we make matters worse with our own involvement. We often project many of our own conceptions, meanings, and wishes upon the shifting screen of the universe, taking both the object and our own projections as totally real. A mountain is "beautiful." An earthquake is "an utter disaster." When it comes to relationships, we entangle ourselves in layers of love and desire and need. Yet in this interplay between our minds and the objects, there is no true reality. We only have a constantly changing world overlaid with a very thick web of emotions and thoughts. The Taoists say that we can't depend on anything. Just as Han Zhongli suffered defeat and Lu Dongbin saw that a worldly life was nearly futile, the Taoists felt that there were no phenomena capable of being the basis for life or philosophy. They said life was but a dream, without any inherent or lasting tangibility.

The Taoists call this emptiness. There are no phenomena that are solid, real, eternal, absolute, nonrelative, and nonchanging. The ongoing thicket of phenomena is dependent upon a myriad of factors that are tied into our own subjective projections. Even our interior worlds of thoughts and feelings are like this. They are part of the thicket, reacting and changing according to the interactions with the outer world and our own consciousness. There is nothing that is immutable and objective, so nothing is "real." This is why Han Zhongli calls the world of phenomena empty. He means that it is empty of any inherent reality.

That is why the Taoists seek liberation from the world. They too are infected with the habit of looking at everything as if it were real. Lu Dongbin himself acted upon his sensual desires and his mischievous feelings. He manipulated the five elements with his sorcery and could accomplish things on heaven and earth, but he had not freed himself from the world of phenomena itself. He was acting as if it were the ultimate reality when he was merely engaging in the transitory interplay of yin and yang.

Lu Dongbin also failed to see his own ultimate emptiness. Perhaps it's even harder for an immortal. They can frolic for all eternity, with no lasting consequences for their mistakes. But he failed to look within himself and see that none of his feelings, perceptions, or impulses, nor his consciousness, could be a true basis for a self: they too were constantly changing and engaged in an ongoing dialogue with the outer world. Within ourselves, there is no abiding, absolute self. There are only phenomena. This is the second definition of emptiness. We ourselves are empty, for there is no absolute self.

It's ironic that the preoccupation of youth is to "find oneself" and establish an "identity." Han Zhongli is asserting that there is no self to find, because nothing absolute is abiding inside ourselves or anywhere else in the universe. If you still do not believe the assertion that there is no absolute self, the Taoists invite you to contemplate it yourself.

Do You Exist?

The question of whether you have an absolute self is one of the most fundamental and profound questions in Taoism. The masters ask their students this question repeatedly, and the students spend many years in meditation in the quest for their answer.

When confronted with the question, people initially show themselves in their physical form as evidence that they do indeed exist. "I am here in body," they assert. "You can touch me, I can touch you. This is my absolute self."

But the body is not sufficient evidence to a Taoist. The body, they assert, changes. It ages; it is subject to disease and accident; and it can be destroyed through even rather casual means. It is quite a fragile vehicle when one thinks about it. True, the body is a physical object. But what animates it is not quite clear. Science has been able to determine the exact chemical components of a human body and has been able to catalogue numerous types of electrical impulses and chemical reactions and the use of oxygen. But in spite of these insights, no one with a bag of chemicals and water and air can make a living human being. We cannot use the physical body alone to show our tangibility, for there is clearly something besides the physical that accounts for our personality, our thinking, ourselves.

Have you seen a dead person? The body is there. It exists. But the person isn't there anymore. In fact, the face doesn't even quite look the same as the one you felt was so familiar to you. The body changes, withers, dies, yet it does not account for the other things that mark us as human.

Of course, there is more to a human being than a body. We can all think. In fact, it is our minds that are the true humans. "I think, therefore I am," we assert. But this answer does not satisfy the masters. They ask us to explain the mind. That is not simple, we might protest. But they insist, and so we begin to catalogue the different aspects of the mind:

Memory	Emotion
Perception	Intuition
Reasoning	Habit
Intelligence	Consciousness
Creativity	Subconscious

The master asks about the ego. Don't we all have a sense of self, something that becomes outraged when we are mistreated? Something that is the vehicle for all our ambitions and our hopes? Don't we have desire, ambitions for ourselves, goals? Aren't we always checking ourselves in the mirror? Aren't we conscious of the way we appear to others?

More importantly, when we meditate, there is a voice that carries on a constant internal dialogue, a voice we are always trying to still while we contemplate. This is the true ego, says the master. This is what keeps us in existence. We exist because we are always telling ourselves that we exist. We are constantly busy with the practice of noting how the world is and then defining ourselves in relation to that constantly shifting perception. Well, all right. We are happy. We exist because our minds maintain our existence. That must be the answer. For once, the master cooperated and helped us solve one of those aggravating spiritual riddles.

But naturally, the master doesn't leave well enough alone and begins to probe further. What if, just for the sake of inquiry, our minds stopped their constant assertions that we exist?

All right, all right. Maybe if we stopped thinking about it—I mean really stopped thinking about it—we might not exist anymore. Maybe we'd just fade away. If our minds, on a subconscious level, forgot to tell our hearts to beat and our lungs to breathe, we'd die very quickly. But the master clearly means something beyond such a literal interpretation. The master is saying that if we truly stopped believing in our own existence we would indeed not be here.

We feel justified in our confusion. After all, we have spent many years as Scholar Warriors on precisely the opposite side of this question. We have never had to confront any hint that our sense of self was wrong. We have been encouraged to defend ourselves, to cultivate ourselves, to define ourselves, to strive vigorously to achieve our goals. Now we are on the other side of this question, and we are to consider that it was all for nothing?

That is right, the master answers. For we had to do all those things in order to clear away all those aspects of our personalities and our socialization. Only by living as a Scholar Warrior could these elements be discharged. If we tried right away to confront the idea of whether we existed or not, we would never succeed, because we would lack the insight gained from our struggles in life. After having traveled the world over, after having tried all the things that society puts forth as "real" and "important," after having spent a lifetime seeking our own personal success and realizing the essentially ephemeral nature of such success, only now can we simply ask whether we exist.

We resort to religion. After all, the master is devout. Maybe we can catch our elder in a contradiction. It will be a first in spiritual history! Student traps teacher! According to what we have been taught in our religious theories, a human being consists of three sheaths: the body, the mind, and the soul. Of course, the body cannot exist without the mind, and the mind's primary function may well be to continuously assert our existence, and if we were to stop that assertion, we might not be real anymore, but what about the soul? Surely, then, *it* must be the source of our true existence.

The sages mention the "immortal soul." We are told that our souls have existed since the very creation of the universe, that they cannot be destroyed even though the body and mind are destroyed, that they will exist forever. We are challenged, however, to show our souls, or at least to confirm that they exist.

What about the light, the illumination that we experience in meditation? Isn't that proof that there is a soul? But we must be careful to point out that this isn't a soul in the sense of an individual identity, a thing that is "ours," or a thing that is the "true self." Those who experience that inner light aren't experiencing something individual but something universal. That light has no features. It has nothing that can be construed as belonging to us, nor can we be construed as belonging to it. When we experience the light of meditation, we're experiencing a universal oneness, an eternity that's part of the enormity of the universe. That greatness can't be claimed as our own. Therefore, even the ultimate level of consciousness that we achieve can't be confirmation that we exist as independent beings. Quite the opposite, it's the experiential confirmation that we're just a facet of all other things and that we're merely a minor distinction in the continuum of Tao.

The masters assert that we do not, in fact, exist. More precisely, we cannot even quantify where we begin and end. We cannot define ourselves as individuals, because we are always in flux. We do not know exactly where the self begins and where it ends. It can be thinking of the next meal, or it can be toying with the nature of the outer edges of an infinite universe. It might have existed as some indefinable soul since the beginning of time, or we might have made the whole thing up a minute ago. If we succeed in stopping our conversation with ourselves during meditation, we experience a curious absorption in which ordinary modes of consciousness do not function; there is no rational way for us to describe it to ourselves, let alone others. We do not, admittedly, exist in either quantifiable or qualifiable ways; one cannot really define something infinite.

The masters teach that our own sense of self-existence is really a way of thought that we use to keep ourselves functioning on an everyday level, but that such a mode of thinking is not sufficient for ultimate realization. When they say that we don't exist, they are trying to get us to abandon the mind that constantly asserts its reality, and instead encouraging us to use direct experience. If we do, then we see that our sense of ourselves, our sense that we are separate individuals, is a mental construct that has become habitual. In spite of our long and exhaustive inquiry, we have never breached the limits of the categories that Han Zhongli defined as characterizing all phenomena: physical form, feeling, perception, impulse, and consciousness. Nothing about ourselves may be used as an absolute self. All phenomena are empty, and we ourselves are empty. By dissolving our attachment to body, mind, and spirit, we dissolve the veils that divide us from the Tao. It is because we see the five forms of phenomena as having objective reality apart from Tao that we cannot see Tao itself. Understanding that phenomena are empty takes us beyond that barrier.

EMPTINESS IS ALL

空是即色

But the Taoists are very careful at this point. There is a danger that we might see phenomena as somehow separate from emptiness. This is not the case. It is our own identification with phenomena that is the problem. Emptiness is not the opposite of the known universe. If we could actually remove all things in existence, we would not find emptiness. That would make existence and emptiness opposites. Then emptiness would be one half of a duality with existence, and according to the Taoists, emptiness would not then be absolute. For if it is defined as part of a duality, it is thereby quantifiable.

Instead, the Taoists assert that a true state of emptiness, in an absolute set, may not contain any dualities at all. The moment duality enters into emptiness, emptiness is no longer absolute. All the myriad workings of yin and yang are summed up by the term *tai ji*, or "the supreme ultimate." It is everything in existence, from matter to thought. Emptiness is called *wu ji*, or "limitlessness." Only in emptiness is there a total absence of definition and distinction. Yin and yang are totally unified and therefore cease to operate. According to the rules of yin and yang, you cannot have either yin or yang without the other. They define each other. When you remove one, you automatically remove the other. They are a true pair. But in emptiness, there are no distinctions. As long as you can reduce something, you have not arrived at the ultimate truth. Everything in this world is here as a result of something else, whether that be the circumstances that caused it, or the opposite that defines it (like black and white or night and day). The Taoists say that being and nonbeing cannot be a true duality.

They are not truly yin and yang, for as long as there is the relativity of yin and yang, there cannot be absolute truth. Being and nonbeing then, are inseparable. For there to be a true state of emptiness, there can be no limits. As long as there are yin and yang, there are distinctions and thus limits or boundaries.

This startling view is akin to a logic formula: A is B, and A is not B. B is A, and B is not A. Right from the start, Han Zhongli permits no discussions in logic. The Tao is to be grasped through mystical, not rational, means. Being and nonbeing are one and the same. Thus, Han Zhongli first asserted that being is tantamount to nonbeing. That is to say, not only is there emptiness behind the screen of our minds and worldly phenomena, but that emptiness is actually the phenomena themselves. Thus, there is no ultimate reality to search for. The ultimate reality is nothingness.

Emptiness, we might think, is complete negation, a denial of all that we have come to consider reality. But Han Zhongli identifies phenomena with emptiness and emptiness with phenomena. He denies duality, or as Lao Tzu asserted, "What is the difference between a yes and a no?" It is a more specific way of identifying the oneness of the world. Only when you are one are you absolutely one with the Tao. Only when you overcome your sense of individual identity can you truly and unequivocally enter into the Tao. Then you are the Tao, and Tao is you. But you cannot find any trace of yourself. You will no longer have any cognizance of yourself. You will have no individual thoughts; you will have no life or death; you will not exist. You are one with infinity, and infinity cannot limit itself by thinking like a human being ever again.

That may well be what Lao Tzu meant when he said, "Those who know do not speak; those who speak do not know." How can those who have entered the Tao speak any longer? They no longer exist as individuals. Entering into the Tao in the ultimate sense, then, means the complete realization of the illusion of the self.

If one truly understands that tai ji is wu ji and that wu ji is tai ji, then there is no heaven or hell, no holy and unholy, no worshiper and no god. True understanding of emptiness signifies the transcendence of duality. We cannot call the realization of emptiness heaven. For if there were a heaven, there would have to be a hell, and the wisdom of Han Zhongli is that there is a transcendence of duality. Perhaps that is what the sages mean when they say that the soul can never be defiled: there is no soul; there is no defilement. Holiness is only a definition. It is only something that we mention in our talks, and thus it is not any ultimate state. It is still a relative state, still something in the realm of yin and yang. If one attains to emptiness, there can be nothing holy and nothing unholy, for one ceases to make distinctions.

There could neither be god nor worshiper either, for in emptiness, all things are one, and one is emptiness. Do the gods exist? Yes, answer the masters. But they believe in their own existence, just as humans do. So except for having more powers than people, they may well be no more realized than the rest of us. Look at Lu Dongbin. He strongly believed in his own reality, so indulged in all sorts of actions. If he had understood emptiness, he would have realized his essential oneness with emptiness, and that he himself was empty.

Is there an ultimate god above all others?

The answer: God exists as long as you believe in yourself.

If there is no self, there is no god. There cannot be. There is only oneness. Just as there cannot be oneness plus me, there cannot be oneness plus god. There can only be One.

Therefore, if one succeeds in overcoming the view that the self is separate from the oneness of the universe, then one is god; god is you; you are the world; and you have no more individuality, no goals, no ambition, no thoughts. You are actually gone. You no longer exist as a separate individual, but you are one with everything. You are One.

One who has attained emptiness has no fear of death. Why? Because such a one realizes that there is no self to die. This notion therefore negates afterlife, reincarnation, and karma. There is no self to suffer these things. The sage has no vulnerable spots.

Thus, Han Zhongli, by asserting that there was neither sacredness nor defilement, further extended the idea of transcending duality and transcending all definitions. In emptiness, there were no forms, no perceptions, no feelings, no impulses, no consciousness. Thus, there was no path; there was no attainment; and there was no nonattainment. Emptiness could only be realized by a paradoxical state of nonrealization by eliminating any dualism between thoughts and objects, eliminating all distinctions of the mind, and eliminating the ultimate distinctions of yin and yang—reality and nonreality could not be regarded as a true dichotomy. Realizing emptiness truly meant the absence of all distinctions. Only then could one realize the Tao.

In the end, there is no body to be purified. There is no need for cleanliness, because there is no distinction between clean and unclean. There is no mind to grapple with issues and philosophy, so what use is there for words? There are no goals to strive for, so why should one strive at all? There is no soul to be saved, so why fear damnation? All is emptiness, and to emptiness, all things return.

The understanding of emptiness is a stage of Taoism even higher than that represented by the South Goose Beach Taoist. Contrasting his poem with that of his elder, Danger Evader, will give the best summation of the differences.

> Like a raft adrift on the ocean
> It does not matter where I float or stop.
> Reaching the Tao is a matter of continuous motion.
> True nature is born from profound splendor.

In a sense, this poem is a line-by-line repudiation of the less-accomplished Taoist. When Danger Evader says that he is like a raft adrift in the ocean, he automatically establishes his difference from the South Goose Beach Taoist. Where the latter is still concerned with matters of likes and dislikes by saying that court robes no longer attract him and that he loves white clouds and emerald mountaintops instead, Danger Evader merely states that he is adrift on the ocean of Tao. He has no preferences, for it does not matter where he floats or stops. He trusts himself wholly to the Tao, and there are no distinctions to be made. One place is no different from another, so why make a fuss? In addition, by using the image of a floating raft, he is also saying that the ocean supports him without fail.

He goes on to say, "Reaching the Tao is a matter of continuous motion." In this sense, he has shown that he has gone even beyond the practices of renunciation and meditation. He does not need to isolate himself on a mountaintop; he does not need to disdain the world below him. He has gone beyond the need for isolation, realization, and illumination. All that matters is continuous motion as he follows wherever the Tao takes him. The world is the same for him as it is for us: he eats, he sleeps, he moves. But he ceases to project his feelings upon the world, even while he himself is in it. He has erased the duality between himself and the world, and though he may act, it is always at the beck and call of the Tao.

The result, then, is that his true nature is born. This is not something gained from effort; it is not something that is a blessing from heaven; but, rather, it is something that happens spontaneously from his being afloat on the ocean of Tao. The profound splendor that gives birth can be none other than the source. This source is emptiness. True nature is born from emptiness. Danger Evader shows himself to be far beyond the dreams of a Scholar Warrior and far beyond the ascetic. He is one with all things. He is one with Tao. He is emptiness itself. His words are the final hint about following the Tao in everyday life. Once you realize their full impact, you too will be like a raft afloat on the Tao.

The Tao is difficult to fathom. That is why the sages called it xuan, "the dark mystery beyond all mysteries." It is here with us every day, yet it is difficult to sense. It is within us, like a bright candle smothered inside a steel lantern, but we see only darkness. It moves constantly, yet we fail to detect its flow. It is emptiness, but we dwell only in the world of appearances. The Tao is truly great, beyond all descriptions, beyond all conceptions, and beyond all names. It is a mystery, but there is no awakening to life without it. Those who enter into the Tao become one with eternity. Those who enter into the Tao dissolve into Tao itself.

ANNOTATED BIBLIOGRAPHY

The primary source for the contents of this book was my study directly with my Taoist master. Though there are published references to the Scholar Warrior and Taoism, the body of knowledge in the English language is not comprehensive. This lack is the result of secretiveness on the part of experts, false information disseminated by the mediocre, improper translation, and simple mistakes by various scholars throughout the years. The body of available works is therefore hardly complete, but this bibliography will give some of the titles that I believe would be most helpful to those who would like to explore further.

FIRST READINGS

For those who have not read very much about Taoism, I recommend three books. They should give a good foundation, not establish too many odd notions and assumptions that will have to be unlearned later, and provide an understanding of Taoism that is not merely academic.

Feng, Gia-fu, and Jane English. *Lao Tsu: Tao Te Ching*. New York: Vintage Books, 1972.

 A separate section in this bibliography deals with the *Tao Te Ching*, but a first-time reader in Taoism has to read at least one translation of this important book. Bear in mind, however, that it is but one of a vast corpus of Taoist holy books, the majority of which have never been seen by the English-speaking world, let alone translated.

Ware, James T., trans. *Alchemy, Medicine, and Religion in the China of A.D. 320: "The Nei P'ien of Ko Hung."* Cambridge: MIT Press, 1966. In spite of the rather formidable title, and the translator's open use of Christian equivalents for Taoist concepts, this is an excellent book. It conveys much of the idiosyncratic personality of the Taoist; takes a critical approach to the tradition of immortality; presents a clear analysis of the interrelationship of ethics, physical practice, physical understanding; and discusses the taking of elixirs. The Ko Hung of the title was a famous alchemist and Taoist and is still revered as the patron saint of alchemical and internal practices.

Welch, Holmes. *Taoism: The Parting of the Way.* Boston: Beacon Press, 1957. Revised 1966. This is one of the best scholarly overviews of the entire development of Taoism. It gives a sense of the historical problems and indicates how many different types of spiritual traditions coexist under the umbrella of Taoism.

SCHOLAR WARRIOR

Chinese Martial Arts. Beijing: Zhaohua, 1982. A history of martial arts, with photographs.

Deng, Ming-dao. *Gateway to a Vast World.* San Francisco: Harper & Row, 1989.

———. *Seven Bamboo Tablets of the Cloudy Satchel.* San Francisco: Harper & Row, 1987.

———. *The Wandering Taoist.* San Francisco: Harper & Row, 1983.
These three books form a biographical trilogy about the life of my master, Kwan Saihung, and how he was raised in the tradition of the Scholar Warrior.

Griffith, Samuel B., trans. *Sun Tzu: The Art of War.* London: Oxford University Press, 1963. In its discussion of Chinese theories of warfare and strategy, this book shows warriors' intellectual approach to their activities.

Legge, James. *The Sacred Books of China: The Texts of Confucianism.* London: Oxford University Press, 1885. See especially "The Conduct of the Scholar" and "The Meaning of the Ceremony of Archery."

Lo, Kuan-chung. *Romance of the Three Kingdoms.* Translated by C. H. Brewitt-Taylor. 2 vols. Rutland, VT: Charles E. Tuttle, 1959. An account of the time of the Three Kingdoms. Look especially for such people as Zhuge Liang, the Taoist master of strategy; Guan Gong, the general who would later become the god of war, and Hua Tuo, the surgeon and herbalist.

Ma, Y. W., and Joseph S. M. Lau, eds. *Traditional Chinese Stories: Themes and Variations.* New York: Columbia University Press, 1978. Although this is a literary anthology, it does suggest the depth of the Scholar Warrior tradition in Chinese culture. See especially two subsections: "The Knight-Errant" and "The Superhuman Maiden." There are other stories pertaining to Taoists and Scholar Warriors throughout the rest of the book.

Morrison, Hedda. *A Photographer in Old Peking.* Hong Kong: Oxford University Press, 1985. See the photographs of martial arts in daily life and of Baiyun Guan (here identified as Pai Yun Kuan).

————. *Travels of a Photographer in China, 1933–1946.* Hong Kong: Oxford University Press, 1987. A book of invaluable photographs documenting life prior to the revolution. See especially the section on Huashan, including two Taoist priests posing in a dueling formation.

Shih, Nai-an. *Water Margin.* Translated by J. H. Jackson. Shanghai: The Commercial Press, 1937. Translated into many different versions, including Pearl Buck's *All Men Are Brothers*, this book tells the tale of 108 "outlaws." Among them are many Scholar Warriors, Taoists, and exiles from imperial service. Nearly all these figures have assumed archetypal proportions in Chinese culture, and some of the weapons styles in martial arts reputedly have been passed down from these men and women.

Sports and Games in Ancient China. China Spotlight Series. Beijing: New World Press, 1986. An excellent book for establishing the variety of sports and martial arts in China, as well as their connection to such arts as qigong, daoyin, archery. It also deals with the place of sports, martial arts, and therapeutic exercise in society.

Waley, Arthur D. *The Poetry and Career of Li Po.* London: George Allen & Unwin, 1950. This work provides a background to the Tang dynasty; discusses the connections between Taoism, poetry, and Li Po; and mentions Li Po's involvement with the sword.

Wing, R. L. *The Art of Strategy: A New Translation of Sun Tzu's Classic "The Art of War."* New York: Doubleday/Dolphin. This book is easy to read, and it is fascinating to see Taoist concepts applied to warfare. See especially the various contexts for the word *tao*. Indeed, Sun Tzu states that Tao is the first condition of any strategy.

Wu, Zuguang, Huang Zuolin, Mei Shaowu. *Peking Opera and Mei Lanfang: A Guide to China's Traditional Theatre and the Art of Its Great Master.* Beijing: New World Press, 1981. A study of the effect of the Scholarly and Military division on theater and its reflection of cultural realities.

TAOISM

Blofeld, John. *Taoism: The Road to Immortality.* Boulder, CO: Shambhala, 1978.

————. *Taoist Mystery and Magic.* Boulder, CO: Shambhala, 1982.

Burkhardt, V. R. *Chinese Creeds and Customs.* Hong Kong: South China Morning Post, 1982.

Creel, Herrlee G. *What Is Taoism?* Chicago: University of Chicago Press, 1970.

DeWoskin, Kenneth J., trans. *Doctors, Diviners, and Magicians of Ancient China: Biographies of Fang-shih.* New York: Columbia University Press, 1983. *Fang-shih*, or "prescription masters," were people who tried to find the formula for the elixir of immortality. This book also includes a biography of Hua Tuo and has many references to various Taoist arts, such as divination, cosmology, and feng shui.

Giradot, N. J. *Myth and Meaning in Early Taoism.* Berkeley: University of California Press, 1983.

Kaltenmark, Max. *Lao Tzu and Taoism.* Translated by Roger Greaves. Stanford, CA: Stanford University Press, 1969. An overview of Lao Tzu, his teaching, the concept of the holy man, Chuang Tzu, and Taoist religion.

Maspero, Henri. *Taoism and Chinese Religion*. Translated by Frank A. Kierman, Jr. Amherst: University of Massachusetts Press, 1981. An enormous work about Taoism with a great deal of interesting information about Taosim as a religion.

Palmer, Martin, ed. *T'ung Shu: The Ancient Chinese Almanac*. Boston: Shambhala, 1986.

Saso, Michael. *Taoism and the Rite of Cosmic Renewal*. Pullman: Washington State University Press, 1972.

———. *The Teachings of Taoist Master Chuang*. New Haven, CT: Yale University Press, 1978.

Welch, Holmes, and Anna Seidel. *Facets of Taoism: Essays in Chinese Religion*. New Haven, CT: Yale University Press, 1979.

Wu, K. C. *The Chinese Heritage*. New York: Crown Publishers, 1982. The origins of Chinese civilization and early forms of Taoism that predate Lao Tzu.

HISTORICAL CONTEXTS

Coye, Molly Joel, and Jon Livingston, eds. *China Yesterday and Today*. 2d ed, revised. New York: Bantam, 1979.

DeBary, W. T. , ed. *Sources of Chinese Tradition*. New York: Columbia University Press. 1963.

Han, Suyin. *The Morning Deluge: Mao Tsetung and the Chinese Revolution, 1893–1954*. Boston: Little, Brown, 1972.

Needham, Joseph. *Science and Civilization in China*. 6 vols. Cambridge: Cambridge University Press, 1954–1988.

The Opium War. Beijing: Foreign Languages Press, 1976.

Seagrave, Sterling. *The Soong Dynasty*. New York: Harper & Row, 1985. See "Boxer Rebellion," "Green Gang," and "Secret Societies" for these aspects of the martial world.

Smith, D. Howard. *Chinese Religions*. London: Weidenfeld and Nicolson, 1968.

Spence, Jonathan D. *The Gate of Heavenly Peace: The Chinese and Their Revolution, 1895–1980*. New York: Viking, 1981. General history, secret societies.

The Taiping Revolution. Beijing: Foreign Languages Press, 1976.

The Yi Ho Tuan Movement of 1900. Beijing: Foreign Languages Press, 1976.

Waley, Arthur, trans. *The Analects of Confucius*. London: George Allen & Unwin, 1938.

TAO TE CHING

Blakney, R. R. *The Way of Life: Lao Tzu*. New York: Mentor Books, 1955.

Chen, Ellen M. *The Tao Te Ching: A New Translation with Commentary*. New York: Paragon, 1989. Not only are Ms. Chen's comments cogent and agreeable, but she defines individual words and concepts so that the content of each poem is easier to grasp.

Henricks, Robert G., trans. *Lao-Tzu: Te-Tao Ching: A New Translation Based on the Recently Discovered Ma-Wang-Tui Texts*. New York: Ballantine, 1989. This translation is based on recently unearthed texts reportedly predating versions that other translations are based on. (The earliest known paintings of daoyin came from the same excavations.) Note that the title is transposed—*Te-Tao Ching* instead of *Tao Te Ching*—to correspond with the way it reads on these findings.

Legge, James. *The Sacred Books of China: "The Texts of Taoism; The Tao Teh King and Writings of Kwang Tze."* London: Oxford University Press, 1927.

Waley, Arthur, trans. *The Way and Its Power.* London: George Allen & Unwin, 1943.

Wei, Henry. *The Guiding Light of Lao Tzu.* Wheaton, IL: Theosophical Publishing House, 1982. A good translation that does not concentrate on the *Tao Te Ching* as an exclusively philosophical work.

Wing, R. L. *The Tao of Power.* New York: Doubleday, 1986. This work has several advantages: it is bilingual, highlights some Chinese words and explains their meanings, includes meaningful art reproductions, and features cogent commentaries. The translation weights the meaning toward practical leadership and business concerns; traditionalists might find that objectionable.

CHUANG TZU

Feng, Gia-fu, and Jane English. *Chuang-Tsu: Inner Chapters.* New York: Vintage Books, 1974. Chuang Tzu is generally regarded as having expanded on Lao Tzu's ideas. See also James Legge's book, listed under *Tao Te Ching.*

Waley, Arthur. *Three Ways of Thought in Ancient China.* Garden City, NY: Doubleday, 1956. This book compares Chuang Tzu's to other Chinese schools of thought.

Watson, Burton. *The Complete Works of Chuang Tzu.* New York: Columbia University Press, 1968.

I CHING

The *I Ching* is a valuable book not merely for its use in divination but because it can give insight into so many aspects of Taoist cosmology, ethics, government, leadership, and so on. It has been used for divination at every level of Chinese life, from the imperial house down to the uneducated peasants who consulted wandering fortune-tellers. Generals have used it in war; scholars have used it to study the ways of the ancients.

It is best to consult the *I Ching* sparingly, and with an experienced person to help you interpret the answers. Because the book seems mute, it is too easy to impose one's wishful thinking on the responses. In addition, dependence on the *I Ching* can be a big problem, especially for those inclined to be superstitious or indecisive. It is far better to absorb the spirit and thought of the *I Ching* without allowing it to become your crutch in life.

Kwok, Man Ho, Martin Palmer, and Joanne O'Brien. *The Fortune Teller's I Ching.* New York: Ballantine, 1986. A good translation from the point of view of contemporary use of the *I Ching* as an oracle.

Wei, Henry. *The Authentic I Ching.* North Hollywood, CA: Newcastle Publishing, 1987.

Wilhelm, Richard, trans. *The I Ching or Book of Changes.* 3d ed. Translated by Cary F. Baynes. Princeton, NJ: Princeton University Press, 1967. Wilhelm's book has remained a classic. Although there are problems with its translation (not the least of which are the problems inherent in reading a translation of a translation), it has been quite influential. It should probably be seen as a book in its own right. The future will undoubtedly bring us better translations and greater scholarship, but this volume will remain a sentimental favorite for many people.

Wing, R. L. *The Illustrated I Ching*. Garden City, NY: Doubleday, Dolphin Books, 1982. The interesting features of this work are its definitions of key terms, good selection of art, and fresh translation.

MEDICINE

Beijing College of Traditional Chinese Medicine and other schools. *Essentials of Chinese Acupuncture*. Beijing: Foreign Languages Press, 1980. A textbook of the theories of Chinese acupuncture and a thorough exposure of the twelve major meridians and their junction points. Note, however, that its version of the Eight Meridians differs from those mentioned in Taoist texts.

Hsu, Hong-yen, Chen Yuh-pan, et al. *Oriental Materia Medica: A Concise Guide*. Long Beach, CA: Oriental Healing Arts Institute, 1986. A detailed reference work on herbal medicines based on Li Shih-chen's *Bencao*, it shows herb names in both Chinese and English.

Kaptchuk, Ted J. *The Web That Has No Weaver*. New York: Congdon & Weed, 1983. An excellent, very readable introduction to the theories of Chinese medicine.

Keys, John D. *Chinese Herbs: Their Botany, Chemistry, and Pharmacodynamics*. Rutland, VT: Charles E. Tuttle, 1976.

Li, Shih-chen. *Chinese Medicinal Herbs*. Translated by F. Porter Smith and G. A. Stuart. San Francisco: Georgetown Press, 1973. Li Shih-chen is known as the father of Chinese herbal medicine, and his documentation of herbs in 1578 was such a landmark work that it continues to be used to this day. This edition is not as comprehensive as *Oriental Materia Medica*, but it does have some background information not available in other translations of Li Shih-chen's crucial work.

Maciocia, Giovanni. *Tongue Diagnosis in Chinese Medicine*. Seattle: Eastland Press. 1987. Consult this work for an in-depth discussion of the body types and how to determine your own more accurately through tongue diagnosis.

Reid, Daniel P. *Chinese Herbal Medicine*. Boston: Shambhala, 1987. An attractive introduction to Chinese medicine with many color photographs and recipes.

Revolutionary Health Committee of Hunan Province, The. *A Barefoot Doctor's Manual, Revised and Enlarged Edition*. Seattle: Cloudburst Press, 1977. One of the great uses of this work is in its extensive herb section. Many Chinese herbs are known by a variety of abbreviated names, local names, and synonyms, which makes the learning of herbs terribly difficult for a beginner. This book lists a respectable group of equivalent names along with the major designation for each herb.

Teeguarden, Ron. *Chinese Tonic Herbs*. Tokyo: Japan Publications, 1985. This book is good for its in-depth treatments of tonic herbs. It also contains formulas, but you should experiment with these under guidance, or at least with some circumspection.

Veith, Ilza. *Huang Ti Nei Ching Su Wen: The Yellow Emperor's Classic of Internal Medicine*. Berkeley: University of California Press, 1966. A translation of part of the ancient classic that is the theoretical basis of most Chinese medicine to this day.

Wallnofer, Heinrich, and Anna von Rottauscher. *Chinese Folk Medicine and Acupuncture.* New York: Bell Publishing, 1955.

QIGONG, INTERNAL PRACTICES, AND MEDITATION

Berk, William R., ed. *Chinese Healing Arts: Internal Kung-Fu.* Originally translated by John Dudgeon. Burbank: Unique Publications, 1986. Interesting woodcuts and instructions for a variety of qigong, including Hua Tuo's Five Animals, baduanjin, and a discussion of Bodhidharma's exercises.

Chang, Stephen T. *The Book of Internal Exercises.* San Francisco: Strawberry Hill, 1978.

Chang, Weizhen. *14-Series Sinew Transforming Exercises.* Translated by Hong Yunxi. Beijing: Foreign Languages Press, 1988. Instructions on the Marrow Washing exercises similar to the set in this book.

Chia, Mantak. *Awakening Healing Energy Through the Tao.* New York: Aurora Press, 1982. A different approach to the Microcosmic Orbit.

Eisenberg, David. *Encounters with Qi: Exploring Chinese Medicine.* New York: Norton, 1985. A contemporary account of a doctor's experience with herbology, acupuncture, and qigong in the People's Republic of China.

Huang, Jane. *The Primordial Breath.* Vol. 1. Torrance: Original Books, 1987. A translation of various Taoist texts regarding the breath.

Jou, Tsung Hwa. *The Tao of Meditation: Way to Enlightenment.* Piscataway, NJ: Tai Chi Foundation, 1983. See the account of the Eight Meridians, Microcosmic Orbit, and Taoist esoteric anatomy, as well as the way these are combined with philosophy.

Liu, Da. *Taoist Health Exercise Book.* New York: Links, 1974.

Lu, K'uan Yu. *Taoist Yoga: Alchemy and Immortality.* York Beach, ME: Samuel Weiser, 1973. A fairly opaque work, but it does discuss the Eight Meridians, Microcosmic Orbit, and Taoist esoteric anatomy.

Sivin, Nathan. *Chinese Alchemy: Preliminary Studies.* Cambridge: Harvard University Press, 1968.

Wilhelm, Richard. *The Secret of the Golden Flower.* Translated by Cary F. Baynes. New York: Harcourt, Brace & World, 1962. It is impossible to actually practice anything out of this book (the key technique is omitted), but it is interesting for its indication of how elaborately Taoist meditations are usually taught.

The Wonders of Qigong: A Chinese Exercise for Fitness, Health, and Longevity. Los Angeles: Wayfarer, 1985.

Wu, K. K. *Therapeutic Breathing Exercise.* Hong Kong: Hai Feng, 1984.

Zhao, Dahong. *The Chinese Exercise Book: From Ancient and Modern China—Exercises for Well-Being and the Treatment of Illnesses.* Point Roberts, Washington: Hatley & Marks, 1984.

FENG SHUI

Lip, Evelyn. *Chinese Geomancy.* Singapore: Times Books International, 1974. Useful especially for urban feng shui.

Rossbach, Sarah. *Feng Shui: The Chinese Art of Placement.* New York: Dutton, 1983. A good discussion of urban and interior feng shui.

Skinner, Stephen. *The Living Earth Manual of Feng Shui*. London: Routledge & Kegan Paul, 1982. Good especially for its discussion of the feng shui style of looking at land forms.

POETRY

Alley, Rewi. *Bai Juyi: 200 Selected Poems*. Beijing: New World Press, 1983. Bai Juyi is widely admired for the Taoist content of his poetry. See "On Dreaming He Had Become an Immortal" and "A Broken Sword."

Cooper, Arthur. *Li Po and Tu Fu*. New York: Viking Penguin, 1973.

Hawkes, David, trans. *A Little Primer of Tu Fu*. Oxford: Oxford University Press, 1967. A bilingual book that helps the reader to understand the poetry of a man much admired by the Taoists.

Liu, Wu-chi, and Irving Yucheng Lo. *Sunflower Splendor: Three Thousand Years of Chinese Poetry*. Bloomington: Indiana University Press, 1975. With the biographical sketches in the back of the book, one can easily identify those poets most allied with the traditions of the Scholar Warrior and with Taoism—a good introduction to Chinese poetry.

Schafer, Edward H. *Mirages on the Sea of Time*. Berkeley: University of California Press, 1985. The Taoist poetry of Ts'ao T'ang, and an overview of much of the fantastic and even romantic background of Taoism.

Watson, Burton. *Su Tung-Po: Selections from a Sung Dynasty Poet*. New York: Columbia University Press, 1965. A classsic translation that discusses many of the Taoist influences on Su Dongpo's work.

Xu, Yuan Zhong, trans. *Su Dong-Po: A New Translation*. Hong Kong: Commercial Press, 1982.

TAOISM AND ART

Chiang, Yee. *Chinese Calligraphy: An Introduction to Its Aesthetic and Technique*. 3d ed. Cambridge: Harvard University Press, 1973.

Cohn, William. *Chinese Painting*. New York: Hacker Art Books, 1978.

Lee, Sherman E. *A History of Far Eastern Art*. 4th ed. New York: Harry N. Abrams, 1982.

Legeza, Laszlo. *Tao Magic: The Chinese Art of the Occult*. New York: Pantheon, 1975.

Sze, Mai-mai. *The Way of Chinese Painting*. New York: Vintage Books, 1959.

TAOISM AND SEXUALITY

Chang, Jolan. *The Tao of Love and Sex*. New York: Dutton, 1977.

Ishihara, Akira, and Howard S. Levy. *The Tao of Sex*. Yokohama: Shibundo, 1968.

MARTIAL ARTS

China Sports Editorial Board. *Wushu Among Chinese Moslems*. Beijing: China Sports Magazine, 1984. A discussion of Islamic-style martial arts, the two styles of *tantui* and *Chazuan*, and biographies of contemporary masters.

Jou, Tsung Hwa. *The Tao of Tai Chi: Way of Rejuvenation*. Piscataway, NJ: Tai Chi Foundation, 1981.

New Approach: Chinese Kung Fu Training Methods. 3 vols. Hong Kong: Commercial Press, 1984.

Smith, Robert W. *Chinese Boxing: Masters and Methods.* Tokyo: Kodansha, 1974. Nearly everyone who explores Chinese martial arts picks up Robert Smith's books. He is an entertaining writer, and he has studied with many martial artists, primarily on Taiwan. His views seem to have been accepted as gospel by an entire generation, but we should remember that his are only one man's experiences. They are valid, but you should explore personally as well.

———. *Hsing I.* Tokyo: Kodansha, 1974. See especially his "Advice from the Masters."

———. *Pa Kua: Chinese Boxing for Fitness and Self-Defense.* Tokyo: Kodansha, 1967. Good information about the history of baguazhang.

———. *Secrets of Shaolin Temple Boxing.* Rutland: Charles E. Tuttle, 1964. This book gives history, discusses Bodhidharma and Shaolin, and has woodcuts of the earliest known version of Yijinqing, the companion exercise to the Marrow Washing Classic.

Staples, Michael, and Anthony Chan. *Wu Shu of China.* San Francisco: Willow, 1976.

Wushu! New York: Simon & Schuster, 1981. Qigong, daoyin, tai chi, and other martial arts.

Yang Style Taijiquan. Compiled by Morning Glory Press. Hong Kong: Hai Feng Publishing; Beijing: Morning Glory Press, 1988. Orthodox tai chi chuan featuring Yang Chengfu's son. Included is a discussion of the relation between mind and body in martial arts.

Yeung, Sau Chong. *Practical Use of Tai Chi Chuan: Its Applications and Variations.* Boston: Tai Chi Company, 1977. Actual photographs of Yang Chengfu are included.

Yiu, Kwong. *The Research into Techniques and Reasoning of Tai Chi Chuan.* Hong Kong: Yiu Kwong Herbalist, 1978. Orthodox Yang style as practiced in Hong Kong today.

OTHER CULTURES

Covell, Jon, and Yamada Sobin. *Zen at Daitoku-ji.* Tokyo: Kodansha, 1974. Toward the end of this beautiful book, there is a curious account of a "Taoist" priest at this Zen temple.

Hari Das. *Ashtanga Yoga Primer.* Santa Cruz: Sri Rama/Hanuman, 1981.

———. *Fire Without Fuel: The Aphorisms of Baba Hari Das.* Santa Cruz: Sri Rama, 1986.

———. *Silence Speaks: From the Chalkboard of Baba Hari Das.* Santa Cruz: Sri Rama, 1977.

Herrigel, Eugen. *Zen in the Art of Archery.* New York: Vintage, 1971.

Iyengar, B. K. S. *Light on Pranayama: The Yogic Art of Breathing.* New York: Crossroad, 1981. Pranayama is the yogic equivalent of qigong.

———. *Light on Yoga.* New York: Shocken Books, 1977. Compare the yogic system with the Scholar Warrior tradition.

Kammer, Reinhard. *Zen and Confucius in the Art of Swordsmanship: The Tengu-ge'jutsu-ron of Chozan Shissai.* Translated by Betty J. Fitzgerald. London: Routledge & Kegan Paul, 1978.

Kuvalayanada, Swami. *Pranayama.* India: Kaivalyandhama, Lonavla, 1966.

Leggett, Trevor. *Zen and the Ways.* Boston: Shambhala, 1978.

Lopez, Donald S., Jr. *The Heart Sutra Explained: Indian and Tibetan Commentaries.* Albany: State University of New York Press, 1988.

Lysebeth, Andre Van. *Pranayama.* London: Unwin Hyman, 1979.

Musashi, Miyamoto. *A Book of Five Rings.* Translated by Victor Harris. Woodstock: Overlook Press, 1974. Aside from being an author and master samurai, Musashi was a master painter whose works are still in private and museum collections today.

Norbu, Namkhai. *The Crystal and the Way of Light: Sutra, Tantra, and Dzogchen.* New York: Routledge & Kegan Paul, 1986. Dzogchen is the aspect of Tibetan Buddhism that is most like Taoism.

Suzuki, D. T. *Zen and Japanese Culture.* Princeton, NJ: Princeton University Press, 1970. An excellent and handsome book containing information about Zen's relationship to Taoism, Bodhidharma, swordsmanship, and numerous other subjects.

INDEX

Cravings, food, 24
Creation and destruction, 321–22
Creativity, 54, 186, 187, 293
Crown point, 264, 267, 277, 278–79
Crystals, 49
Cultural Revolution, 17

Daimei meridian, 93, 95
Dairy products, 26, 30
Da mai (barley), 166, *167*
Damp state of the body, 25, 26, 27
Danger Evader, 7, 331–32
Dang gui (herb), 139, *140*, *151*, 152
Dang shen (herb), 132, *133*, 134, *135*
Dan shen (herb), 141, *142*
Dantians, 91–92, *92*, 96, 97, 99, 101, 102, 107;
        and *daoyin*, 255, 256, 257, 260, 281, 283;
        and meditation, 299, 300, 302, *302*
Dao ren, 196
Daoyin, 46, 48, 252–55
Daoyin exercises and meditations, 256–84; Belt
        Meridian, 270–71; Bringing Energy to the
        Palms, 268–70; Building Qi in the Kidneys,
        257–58; Deep Breathing, 259–61, 284;
        Developing the Gate of Jing, 258–59; Lower
        Gate Yin Training, 281; Microcosmic
        Orbit, 265–67, 284; Nourishing the
        Dantian, 256–57; Opening the Central
        Meridian, 261–62, 284; Opening the Front
        Gate, 280–81; Opening the Microcosmic
        Orbit, 262–65, 284; Opening the Upper
        Gate, 278–79; Sending Energy to All Four
        Limbs, 283–84; Sending Energy to the
        Legs, 275–77, 284; Sending Qi to the Kid-
        neys, 272–75; Standing Meditation, 271–72
Da zao (herb), 134, *135*
De dao (to realize the Tao), 315
Death, 18, 19, 192, 205–6, 230
Dehydration, 160
Depression, 141, 143, 149
Diabetes, 134
Diarrhea, 130, 163
Diet, 6, 18, 113; cultivating *Jing,* 24–30; and
        sexual energy, 33
Digestion, 41, 141, 166
Discipline, 18–19, 209, 225, 232–35
Disease, immunity to, 41
Diuretic herbs, 139
Divination, 177, 186

Dizziness, 146
Dong chong xia cao (herb), 137, *138*
Dong Haichuan, 90
Doubts, resolving, 224–49
Dreaming, 141
Drugs, 21, 22, 35, 208, 232, 246
Dry state of the body, 25, 26, 27
Duality, 181–82, 190, 210, 328–32
Duck, 137
Dumei meridian, 93, 95, 96, *96*, 99; and daoyin
        exercise, 262, 263, 266, 279, 281
Du zhong (herb), 120, *122*, *125*, *126*, *151*, 152
Dysentery, 163

Eating, over or under, 28
Education, 53–55, 309
Egg recipes, 143, *144*, 158
Ego, 207, 209, 325
Egotism, 219–21, 230, 232, 253, 309, 312
Eight Brocades Qigong, 320
Eight Immortals, 317–19
Eight Meridians. *See* Meridians
Eight Trigrams Palm, 90, 91
Electricity, and *qi,* 112, 241, 243
Elements, 321
Embroidered silk, Qing Dynasty, *318*
Emotions, 35–36
Emptiness (*wu ji*), 182–84, 185, 188, 192,
        200, 210, 247, 252, 314, 316, 320–23,
        328–32
Energy, cycling and recycling, 262
Energy flow and circulation. *See* Meridians; *Qi*
Enlightenment, 313, 315
Enuresis, 130
E shu (herb), *151*, 152
Ethics, 51–53, 54
Exercise, 6; lack of, 18; and sex, 34; thera-
        peutic, 12
Exercise sets. *See Daoyin;* Marrow Washing
        Classic; Northern Star *Qigong; Qigong*
Eyesight. *See* Vision

Fan (returning), 188, 315
Fasting, 28
Feet, bound, 231
Feng shui, 49–50
Fevers, 173
Fish, 29
Fish bladder, 166, *168*

Fist sets, 44
Five Animal Frolics, 39
Flaws, in oneself and others, 225, 228, 229–32
Flower teas, 169–73, *171*
Foods, 24–30; cravings, 24; fresh, in season, 28; fried, 25; salty, 25, 26; spicy, 25, 28. *See also specific names*
Forbidden City, 15
Foxnut, 127
Frog, 153, *154*
Fruit, 30

Gan zhe (sugar cane), 160, *162*
Gaohuang point, 95, *96*, 99
Gas. *See* Wind
Gate of Life. *See Mingmen*
Gems, 49
Genitals, 102, 119
Geomancy, 49–50
Ginger, 163, 166
Ginseng, 28, 114, 132, 137
Goals, 207–9
God(s), 177, 179, 180, 183, 288, 314, 330
Gou teng (herb), 143, *145*, 146
Grains, 26, 29–30
Green tea, 169, *170*
Guan (to contemplate), 285, 286
Guan Gong, 11
Guns, 14, 15–16, 232
Gu zhi (herb), *151*, 153

Hai long (herb), 122, *123*
Hai ma (herb), 122, *123*
Hand posture in meditation, 290, *291*
Han Zhongli, 309, *318*, 319–24, 327, 329, 330
Harmonizing the Qi, 98–99
Headaches, 137, 146, 149–53, 279
Health, 2, 6; assessment of, 20–21
Heart, 95; meridian, 139, 141, 163, 173; recipes for building, 139, 141, 163, 166, 173
Heaven, 179, 183, 184, 205, 329
Heavenly Well point, 281
Hei dou (black bean), 155
Hell, 179, 329
Herbal recipes, 119–73; aiding meditation, 153; building blood, 139–43; building brain and nervous system, 146–53; building kidneys and *jing*, 119–26; building liver, 143–46; building *qi,* 126–34; expelling and purify-

ing, 160; for lungs, 134–37; for recovery after illness, 155–59; teas, 169–73; porridges, 163–69
Herbal teas, 169–73, *172*
Herb(s), 29, 114–72, 206; baths, 41; broths, 41; cautions about, 117; and energy flow, 37; medicine, 12, 25, 27; preparation of, 117–18; preparation vessels, *119;* sedative, 139; and sexual energy, 33; stores, 116–17; tonification, 115; tranquilizing, 141. *See also specific names*
He shou wu (herb), 124, *125*, 126
Hinduism, 320
Honeysuckle tea, 169, *171*
Hong Kong, 176
Hong zao (herb), *131*, 132, 146, *148*, 149, 155, 167
Hot state of the body, 25, 27, 127, 130, 137, 139, 146
Hsieh Shih ch'en, 8
Huai shan (herb), 134, *135*, 158, *159*
Huang jing (herb), 158, *159*
Hua Tuo, 12, 39
Hu gu (herb), *151*, 152
Huiyin point, 95, *96*
Hun dun (chaos), 183
Huo Yuanjia, 16–17
Hygiene. *See* Cleanliness

I Ching (Book of Changes), 90, 91, 177, 191, 195
Illness, 18, 22, 30, 90, 91; herbs for recovery after, 155–58
Immune system, 23, 26, 42, 113, 132, 298
Impotence, 122, 137, 158
Indian arts, 39
Individuality, 310, 311, 330
Information, 241–44
Insomnia, 141, 149
Intellect, cultivating. *See Shen*
Intellectualization, 312
Intestine, 130
Iron Guanyin tea, 169
Iron Palm, 231
Islam, 179
Isolation, 225, 237–38, 305–16

Jade Emperor, 180, *180*
Jade nectar, 39, 261, 300

Jing (essence), 3, 22, 24–34, 91; and *daoyin,* 255; dead, 33; and diet, 24–30; herbal recipes for, 119–26; and sexual conservation, 30–34

Jing Qi Shen, 22

Jin Guang (golden light), 298

Jin yin hua (honeysuckle tea), 169, *171*

Joints, skeletal, 57

Journal, daily, 209

Juan Hsiu in A Landscape (Ch'en Hung-shou), *115*

Jue xue (give up learning), 186–87, 190, 246

Ju hua (chrysanthemum tea), 169, *171*

Jujube, 122, 132, 134, 141, 149, 166

Junction points, 95–96, *96,* 267, 277, 313

Kao Ch'i-p'ei, *Three Laughing Friends, 174*

Karma, 330

Kidneys, 91; and *daoyin,* 255, 257, 258, 272–75, 281; herbal recipes for building, 119–26, 130, 134, 137, 141, 143, 146, 152, 153, 155, 158, 163, 166; meridian, 120, 122, 126, 127, 153, 166

Kidneys, pork, 120–22

Killing, 52, 235

Knees, 158

Knowledge, 225–27

Ku shen (valley spirit), 182

Kwan Saihung, 1, 2

Lacquer: chrysanthemum cups, *16;* dish, *13*

Lamb, in herbal recipes, 124, 139, 166

Laogong point, 95, *96,* 99, *100,* 101

Lao Tzu, 11, 177, 180, *180,* 192–93, 196, 246, 316, 320, 329

Lao Tzu On a Water Buffalo, 178

Laziness, 220, 234

Learning, 198; continuous, 225–27; giving up, 186–87, 190, 246

Legs, 163; sending energy to, 275–77

Leukorrhea, 127, 149, 166

Lieh zi (herb), *165*

Life: balance in, 5–6, 18, 51; impermanence of, 191–93; stages of, 200–206

Life after death, 177–79, 205–6, 330

Light, inner, 327, 332

Lily (*bai he*), 163, *165,* 166

Ling yang jiao (antelope horn), *145,* 146

Li Po, 12

Liquor. *See* Alcohol

Liu Pei, 11

Liver: building recipes, 124, 126, 134, 141, 143–46, 155, 158, 166; meridian, 120, 122, 126, 139, 143, 146, 152

Liver, pork or beef, recipes using, 143, *144*

Loneliness, 239–40

Long jing (tea), 169, *170*

Long yan rou (herb), 141, *142*

Lost Track school of martial art, 233

Lotus seed meal, 163

Lu Dongbin, *ii,* 243, 308, *318,* 319–20, 323–24

Lungs, 95, 126, 153, 158; herbal recipes for, 134–38, 146; meridian, 130, 132, 134, 153, 163, 166, 169

Lu Yu, 169

Machines, 199, 240–44

Macrocosmic Orbit, 255, 275

Malnutrition, 22, 25

Manchus, 14

Mandalas, 44, 48

Mantras, 39, 47

Marriage, 239

Marrow Washing Classic, 40, 46, 48, 56–89; Ape Descending the Mountain, 86; beginning movement, 58–61; Breath Regulation, 89; Butterfly, 72–73; Cat Looking at the Moon, 79–81; Cloud Hands, 64; Clutching Eagle, 73–74; Crane Standing on One Leg, 88; Dog Wagging Tail, 68–69; Elbow Pushing in Goose Stance, 82; Extend the Waist to View the Moon, 76; Fisherman Rowing the Boat, 62; Fisherman Rowing the Boat, Wrist Twist, 63; General Taking off His Boots, 82–84; Hit the Tree in Horse Stance, 64–66; Monkey King Walking on Clouds, 87; Monkey Lifts the Cauldron, 84–85; Raising the Flag in Goose Stance, 81; Scholar Opening the Scroll, 69; Squatting and Lifting, 66–68; Swallow Returning to Nest, 77–78; Swimming Snake, 70–72; Young Lad Worshipping Buddha, 74–76

Martial arts, 12–14, 40, 44–45, 203, 231, 232; schools of, 44; women in, 12–13, 14, 15

Massage, 37, 41

Masters, 204, 208, 211–23, 238 306, 326, 327; false or bad, 212; faults of, 216–17; finding, 245; meditating with, 288; qualities of, 214–16; selecting, 212–14; western counterparts of, 213

Masturbation, 33

Materialism, 18, 218, 248, 309–10

Meat, 24, 25, 26, 29; blanching, 124; organ, 29, 120, 122; red, 26, 29. *See also specific names*

Medicine, western, 21, 22–23, 42, 155

Meditating Taoist, stoneware altarpiece, *295*

Meditation, 2, 39, 44, 47–48, 92, 199, 205, 206, 210, 252, 254, 284, 285–98, 311, 312; balancing following, 300–304, *300–304*; cautions about, 299; concentration, 294–96; Golden Light Meditation, 298–99, *299*; and herbs, 169; motivation for, 286–87; posture, 288–92, *289*, *291*; relaxation and imagination, 292–93; standing, 104, 271–72, 275; types of, 47–48, 286; varied experience of, 296–98. *See also daoyin*

Men, stages of life, 201

Meng (dream), 223

Menstruation: and building blood, 139, 141; disorders, 149; and *qigong*, 113

Mental: energy, 23, 92; health, 20, 21, 42; illness, 22

Meridians, eight, 36–37, 38, 44, 46, 57, *94*, *96*, *96*, 313; bridging, 255; in *daoyin*, 252, 254, 255; junction points along, 95, 96, *96*, 267, 277, 313. *See also specific names*

Metabolism, 24, 25, 57, 160

Mi (rice), 153

Microcosmic Orbit, 265–67, 276; opening, 262–65

Mind: and absolute self, 325, 326; calming, 146. *See Shen*

Ming (brightness, clarity), 314

Mingmen (Gate of Life), 34, 267, 270

Mingmen point, 95, *96*, 267, 277

Mint tea (*bo he*), 172, 173

Mi zao (herb), 122, *123*, 124

Monasteries, 13–14

Morality, 219

Mucus, 26

Mu Guiying, *12*

Muscle Change, 40

Muscles, 57; herbal recipes for, 124, 146, 158

Music, 186

Nature, 187, 241; harmony with vs. domination of, 177, 184, 186; worshippers, 177

Neijing (medical classic), 200

Nervous system, 23; herbal recipes for, 146–53

Neutral state of the body, 25, 27

Nightmares, 141

Niu xi (herb), 120, *121*, 122

Niyuan point, 95, *96*, 99, 279

Nocturnal emission, 127, 134

Nonaction. *See Wu wei*

Noncontention, 187–88, 195

Nonviolence, 225, 235–37

Northern Star Qigong, 46, 48, 90–113; cautions for, 97; guidlines for, 112–13; practice of, 97–98

Northern Star Qigong exercises, 98–113; Accumulating Treasures into the Vase, 99–100; Clear All Meridians, 111; Draw in the Rainbow and Radiate Its Colors, 101–2; Draw the Bow to Shoot the Eagle, 104–5; Eagle Flying in the High Heavens, 100–101; Enter the Crown and Wash the Marrow, 103; Harmonizing the Qi, 98–99; Hold the Breath and Warm the Body, 102; It's Wise to Look Back, 107; A Stable Stance At the Water's Edge, 108; Swaying the Head and Wagging the Tail, 108; Travel Ten Thousand Miles to Hold Up the Sky, 104; Turning Heaven and Earth, 105–7; White Crane Spreads Wings, 109

Nuo mi (rice), 163

Nutrition, poor, 22, 25

Obsession, 231–32

Old age, 202, 205–6, 239–40

Oneness, 330, 332

Oolong tea, 169, *170*

Opposites. *See Yin and yang*

Organs, 57, 91, 116

Original Being, 180, *180*

Ovaries, 102

Pain control, 149, 152, 158

Parents, 202–4, 212–14

Philosophy of Tao, 4–7, 176–210

Phlegm, 137, 160, 166
Pictographs, 3
Pimples, 160
Plantain seed tea, 160, *161*
Pollution, 23
Porridges, 163–69
Posture, 57
Poultry, 29, 130, 137
Pranayama, 39
Pranjnaparamitra, 320
Pregnancy, 239
Protein, 24, 25
Pu (simplicity), 197, 245
Pulmonary weakness, 126

Qi (breath, vitality), 3, 22–23, 35–50, 91; circulating, 36–37, 254, 255; and cleanliness, 35–36; and *daoyin,* 272–75; and electricity, 112, 241, 243; herbal recipes for building, 126–37; origin of, 321; zhong qi, 126, 134. *See also Qigong*
Qianlong, Emperor, 15; calligraphy of, *14*
Qian shi (foxnut), 127, *128, 129,* 130
Qigong (cultivating breath), 23, 37, 38–50, 254; calisthenics, *44, 46;* colors and mandalas, 44, 48; concentration exercises, 44, 46–47; general guidelines for, 112–13; martial arts, 44–45; Northern Star, 46, 48, 90–113; sounds, 47; stones, 44, 49; visualization, 44, 47; weapons practice, 44, 45–46; weather and location, 49
Qihai point, 97
Qing dynasty, 13, 14–15, 17
Qin jiu (herb), *151,* 152
Qin shi Huang, 38
Qi zi (herb), *125,* 126, 134, *135,* 146, *148,* 149, 158, *159,* 166, *167*

Rabbit, 132–33
Rashes, 160
Rationalization, 312
Realization, 311–14, 327, 329
Realized One, 6
Recipes. *See* Herbal recipes
Red tea, 169
Reincarnation, 177–79, 205, 330
Relationships, 225, 228, 238–40
Religion, 19, 179–80, 190, 205, 218, 287–88, 314, 326

Renmei meridian, 93, 95, 96, *96;* and daoyin exercise, 262, 265, 267, 275, 277, 281
Rheumatism, 26, 152
Rice, 132, *133;* porridges, 163–69
Romance of the Three Kingdoms, 11
Ru dao (entering the Tao), 310

Saliva. *See* Jade nectar
Salivation, 153
Salt, 25, 26
San Bao (Three Treasures), 21
San qi (balancing), 300
Scallions, 143, *144*
Scholar Warrior, history of, 10–19
Sea dragon, 122
Sea horse, 122
Seasons, 201; and stages of life, 202–6, 210
Sedative herbs, 139
Self, existence of, 324–28. *See also* Emptiness
Selfishness, 220
Self-mutilation, 35
Semen, 30–31
Service, 205
Sex (sexual conservation), 30–34; abstinence, 30–31, 34; and dead jing, 33; excessive, 22, 33–34; and exercise, 34; frequency, 32–33; organs, and herbs, 152, 166; and qigong, 113; rebuilding energy after, 33; sexual alchemy, 31; in winter, 33
Sexes, attraction between and training, 306
Shamans, 177
Shang dynasty, 11
Shang shan (ascending mountain), 306
Shaolin Temple, 13, 15
Shellfish, 29
Shen (spirit, mind), 22, 23, 50–55, 91, 92; cultivating intellect, 53–55; cultivating mind, 50–53
Sheng di (herb), 139, *140,* 141
Shenque point, 95, *96*
Shou (longevity), 312
Shou di (herb), 146, *147, 151,* 152
Shou zao ren (herb), 141, *142*
Shui (water), 198
Simplicity, 225, 244–47, 316
Sino-Japanese War, 16
Six Arts, 11
Six Sounds qigong, 47

Designed and illustrated by
Side By Side Studios
San Francisco, California

Photography by
Michael Falconer
San Francisco, California

Typesetting by
Asco Trade Typesetting Limited
Hong Kong

Display and text typeset in Sabon

Printing and binding by
R. R. Donnelley & Sons
Harrisonburg, Virginia